Cross country?

On a scooter?

That's right—New York to California on a motor scooter. By the author of *A Fine and Private Place*.

"Immensely enjoyable!"
—*Stanford University Daily*

"The only way to see the country . . . superbly entertaining."
—*Chicago Tribune*

"A young man's book . . . an original and sustained performance."
—*San Francisco Chronicle*

"Tremendous appeal—especially to the college generation."
—*Publishers' Weekly*

And *Time* magazine calls it "an enchanted journey to 'the kind of country you dream of running away to when you are very young and innocently hungry, before you learn that all that land is owned by somebody.'"

*I
See
By
My
Outfit*

Peter S. Beagle

BALLANTINE BOOKS • NEW YORK

ACKNOWLEDGMENTS
The following publishers have kindly granted permission
for the inclusion of copyrighted material owned by them,
as follows:

Oxford University Press, Inc. for lines from *The Lady's
Not for Burning* by Christopher Fry.

Sausalito Music Corporation for title and for lines
quoted from "Laredo" by Nick Reynolds, Bob Shane, and
John Stewart. Copyright © 1962 by Sausalito Music Corporation.

Studio Music Company for lines from "Kansas City
Blues" Copyright arrangement 1960 by Studio Music Co.

Wyncote Music Publishing Company, Inc. and Kalman
Music, Inc. for lines from "Twenty Miles" by Mann and
Lowe.

Library of Congress Catalog Card Number: 64-21796

SBN 345-02359-5-095

This edition published by arrangement with
The Viking Press, Inc.

First Printing: February, 1966
Second Printing: September, 1971

Illustrations by Nicholas Krenitsky

Cover art by Sal Barracca
Printed in the United States of America

BALLANTINE BOOKS, INC.
101 Fifth Avenue, New York, N.Y. 10003
An Intext Publisher

To the people in the house—
For Phil
For Tom
For the children: Vicki, Kalisa, and Danny
And for Enid, with all my love

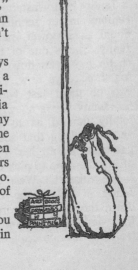

At seven o'clock on a cold April morning we are sitting in Phil's kitchen drinking coffee. There is a wind up, jerking at hanging laundry like an Indian wrestler and meowing around the corners of the building. The sky is gray as a dirty handkerchief. I say, "It'll clear up. It always does. April mornings are very deceptive."

"What they are mostly is cold," Phil says. "You and your goddamn Aprils. I keep telling you, it doesn't get warm in New York till May."

"When I was a boy it was always warm in April. I remember it as a friendly and delicate month." Visions of bright sidewalks, forsythia growing golden in the park, my father in his undershirt, and the war—whatever it had really been —comfortably past. "The winters have gotten colder since then, too. Melting polar icecaps. Return of the glaciers. Fallout."

"You don't remember April. You were indoors reading a book in

7

April, same as every other month. I was outdoors freezing, and your mother was asking me to get you out of the house. That's the way it's always been. I don't suppose you'd consider waiting another week or two."

He does not expect an answer. I say, "I called Enid last night." Enid lives in Menlo Park, California, and is the real reason we are up at seven on a cold morning, staring dully at a hallway full of our suitcases and duffel bags.

"Which does she want, Pete or a Petesicle? It's brutal out there." He puts his cup in the sink and stands with his back to me for a moment, looking out of the window. Sigunick. Scrawny, bearded, tense, miserable, gifted, mean, crooked enough to veer into the fourth dimension. My buddy, my confused mentor. We have been friends since we were three or four: in a free-for-all, most of which seemed to be happening on and over me, I bit the first butt that swam into my ken, and it turned out to have him attached to it. Our relationship has not altered significantly since that moment. "Come on, then," he says. "Let's get the hooha over with."

Jenny is downstairs waiting at the curb. Jenny is a Heinkel motor scooter, the best on the market, functional as a flower, named after Bertolt Brecht's Pirate Jenny. She is one of the matched pair, but Phil's Couchette has been down at a repair shop on 65th Street for three days now, getting new rings. We bought the two of them last winter; Couchette was secondhand, but Jenny was a showroom model of the year before, so totally unused as to have cobwebs in her carburetor and something that seemed to be cooky crumbs in her gas tank. I start her, Phil climbs on behind, and we set off for the shop to pick up Couchette.

We take the West Side Highway. Hoping to break Jenny in before the trip, I have driven her up and down the highway scores of times this past winter, with the wind off the river making her as stable and controllable to ride as a marble, although she is a heavy machine. Today the wind is not that bad, but the water is sluggishly choppy, and Phil mutters, "I'm cold. The blood is freezing into crystals in my veins. I feel like a Coke."

"It's not that cold," I say brightly. "I think it's warmed up some already." But it is cold, as I knew it would be on the day we left. We have been cold and wet together too often really to believe in warmth any more.

Another part of the hooha involved leaving Jenny parked on 98th Street and West End Avenue and picking up Brave Margot, who has been parked there long enough to collect a ticket. Margot is a Lambretta, smaller than Jenny and powered by a two-cycle engine, whereas Jenny's is a four-cycle, like a car's engine. I have spent the last few days frantically trying to sell her, and have finally decided to take whatever the dealer who is working on Couchette will give me. We hop off Jenny, hop on Margot. . . . "Like the Pony Express," I say to Phil as we start down West End again.

"Best damn scooter we ever had," he says, for Couchette has cost him a lot of time and money in the four months he's owned her. And I agree wistfully as we jounce along the cobblestones. I have owned Margot since September of 1960, when I went out to California for the first time and found out that nobody walks there except dogs and escaped criminals. She has taken me over ten thousand miles, alone and with Phil, in California, in Michigan and points east, and over a lot of New England last summer when we shared a shack in Cheshire, Massachusetts. Whatever we know about scooters we learned from Margot: how to clean mufflers, decarbonize pistons, install rings, adjust brakes and clutches, and, most important of all, how to start her when she wouldn't go, and start her again when she stalled immediately after. You take out the spark plug, wave it around, look grave, scrape carefully at it with your special spark-plug file, blow on it, and put it back in. This satisfies her that something is being done, and she usually starts. It works with most scooters.

Couchette is ready at the dealer's, or at least as ready as he can make her. The dealer's name is Max, and he looks like Peter Lorre. He is delighted to hear that we are finally leaving; we have been in and out of his shop with our scooters all winter, and he really knows very little about working on Heinkels. They are still as rare as kangaroos in this country, and he thinks it would be nice if they were considered undesirable aliens. He pays me $125 for Margot—fair enough, considering that I had nowhere else to sell her—and one of his assistants wheels her into line with a row of other used Lambrettas. She is the only one of them who has a sack strapped to her legshield. It is blue and white and very ragged, because I crammed a lot of things into that sack.

Max has claimed to be something of a connoisseur of painting, and Phil has brought about thirty drawings and gouaches down to the shop this last time. Max looks them over, taking his time in an oddly nervous way—like Peter Lorre forced to prove he really is an Anglican bishop—and finally buys one for ten dollars. "Well, it's been a good winter after all," Phil says.

At noon we are back at Phil's house, drinking coffee. We dawdle a little (in this apartment that Phil hates, the word is not "linger"), looking at the unfinished paintings in his room, sorting out sketchpads, drawing pens, and spare parts for the scooters. "No more Paladin," Phil says thoughtfully, looking at the battered TV set. "No more *Maverick* reruns. No more Road pictures on the Late Show." We have identified frighteningly easily with Hope and Crosby and carry their stock dialogue in our heads, much as the Greek minstrels carried epic poetry.

"No more double solitaire." I pick up the keen. "No more steal-the-bundle. No more Tropicana orange juice and ginger snaps."

"Boy, do we have roots," Phil says wryly. He walks

to the window and opens it. Directly across the street a piledriver has been at work since 6 a.m., which is about the hour Prometheus's vulture used to report for duty. Phil has been waking up to it every morning since we came back from Cheshire last fall. "No more of that," he says, and it is hard to tell whether he is speaking of the pile-driver; or of the nearby subway that rumbles ceaselessly through the heads of all New Yorkers; or of the three teen-age girls, with skulls like ice-cream sundaes, who pause to gawk at Jenny and Couchette; or of *Gunsmoke,* which follows Paladin and is always watched through inertia. "Let's go," he says.

Loading Jenny is no real problem for me, for the Heinkels are designed to carry a lot of luggage, and I can strap a suitcase, a tent, and an Army shovel on the rear luggage-carrier, and a sleeping bag on the front one, and have room left in my scooter sack for a litter of kittens, if they are stacked properly. But Phil's duffel bag is swollen with art books and supplies, and when it is at last strapped on his luggage-carrier it extends so far forward that he can lean back against it while he drives. Couchette looks like an ant staggering under the weight of an enormous crumb of cake; it affects her balance and makes putting her up on the kickstand a two-man job. People stare and giggle as they pass us, but they always do. They have excellent cause.

Suddenly it has become the last time for everything. It is the last time we set off anywhere from Phil's house, the last time we circle the block and cross the Concourse (can there really be a last time for the Concourse?), the last time we stop for this irritatingly long traffic light, the last time we drive along the Expressway toward the river, whose scent, mixed with the smells of gas and rubber and stone, is blown to us through the cold arches. I do not know if this makes me feel anything. My nose is stopped up already, anyway, and I can't really smell the river very well.

During the winter evenings when Phil and I used to

talk ourselves into a kind of trance planning the un-important details of the trip, I insisted that we should turn our heads as we crossed the river and look back at the city—briefly, of course, so as not to run into the Rahway bus. But the traffic is heavy on the George Washington Bridge, and we have enough trouble keeping track of each other. When we reach the Jersey side, Phil catches my eye and flutters his fingers slowly and mournfully at me; this is our supreme gesture, and indi-cates bewilderment, acceptance, and dread all at once. I wave back and mouth the words, "We left, we really left." Phil puts his fingers in his mouth and begins to chew on them.

We drive less than a hundred miles this first day, but we cross into Pennsylvania, which satisfies us both and makes us feel that we are covering the greatest amount of ground with the least amount of effort. Our journey has been plotted on an AAA Triptik, requested with the idea of keeping us away from turnpikes and toll roads; and we have spent a lot of time this past winter following red arrows and blue lines from one strip map to the next, telling ourselves the trip over and over, until it almost seems that we traveled that blue road long ago, to the happy ending and whatever after.

In the late afternoon the sun comes out long enough to go down, and it begins to get lonesomely cold. We stop for coffee in East Stroudsburg and consider. We have planned to camp out as much of the way as possible, but there is something sad and frightening to both of us in watching the day waitresses at the Dairy Queen going home. We would marry them right now, just to have a place to go. Other people have their own scary times of day and get married then.

There is a tiny state park half a mile down the road, and we decide to spend the night there. A couple of cars are parked at the entrance, but the only people we see are an old couple traveling in one of those trailers that fit onto a pickup body. They have built a fire near the trailer and stare up without expression as we wander by. Phil mutters, "God, I wish we had one of those."

"We're too young," I answer. "We haven't suffered enough. How can we be artists if we don't suffer? Suffering is good for you. Get suffering today. This is NBC."

"Does it count like suffering if you make me sick all the time? What are we waiting for? Let's put up the damn tent here; there's a sort of natural windbreak, whatever that is. Let's put up the tent and start suffering."

There are two kinds of tent stakes on the market, wooden and aluminum. We have both. The aluminum ones bend if driven into anything harder than new snow with anything harder than daisies, and the wooden stakes rip the already weakened grommets into lacework. We prop the poles upright with rocks, tie the main ropes to a couple of saplings, punch holes in the tent fabric itself to do for the grommets, and then discover that the flap faces directly into the wind. The tent billows and flaps like a butterfly net in a monsoon. We take it down and turn it around.

"This is insane," I say. "Let's cut the damn thing in half and make ponchos."

Phil unrolls his sleeping bag and drags it inside. "It's not so bad," he says. "Keeps the wind off, at least. Pity we don't have a groundcloth. Well, get the beans out. All that work's made me hungry."

We lie on our sleeping bags and scoop alternate forkfuls out of a can of beans. They would taste better hot, but we are both a little afraid of our brand-new stove. It really is warmer in the tent, and we are pleased with ourselves and almost comfortable. I say, "God, I thought we'd never leave."

"I still don't believe we have. I won't for quite a while. If I really believed we're doing what we're doing, I'd cry."

"If we ever started that, we'd never stop. Jollity is the keynote. Terrified jollity. Dance for the enemy."

"What town are we in?"

"East Stroudsburg, Pennsylvania. If we toss any during the night, we'll be out of it."

"East Stroudsburg, Pennsylvania," he says. "That's silly."

It is quite dark now. We take off our shoes and scramble into the sleeping bags. I kick over a tent pole, and we prop it up again in silence. Phil sticks his head out through the tent flap and says, "Boy, give a look the sky." There is no moon, but the stars seem very close and strangely yellow-white. The old couple have let their fire burn to embers and gone into their trailer, where a light still shines. We can hear the rattle of the stream that races through the campground and vanishes under the road.

"It's like *The Lord of the Rings*," I say. *The Lord of the Rings* is a fantastic odyssey written by J. R. R. Tolkien, and it forms part of our private Gospels, along with *The Once and Future King,* the songs of Georges Brassens, the world of Pogo, and a few other strangenesses. "The beginning of the journey," I say, "the first night on the road to Mordor. This could be Bree, I guess, the edge of the wild country. What could Ann Arbor be?" We are detouring to Ann Arbor to visit friends.

"Rivendell, where the elves live," Phil says happily, "if I remember what Kisa looks like."

I fall asleep almost instantly, and when I wake up I am colder than I have ever been in my life. I burrow frantically back into my sleeping bag, shoving my hands between my thighs and curling into a fetal position, but there is no stray warmth to be found, and I can't breathe that way, anyway. There is not as much wind as there was, but what there is is inside the tent now, gentle and relentless. The ground is completely unyielding; lying on it is like being beaten, no matter how I turn. I have been using my jacket for a pillow, but now I drag it into the bag with me and try resting my head on my arms. Interesting sensation. Very much like sleeping on a pool table with your head in a corner pocket. I put the jacket back.

It is pitch dark (what time is it? how long did I sleep? when did we go to bed? does it have to be snowing for you to get frostbite?), but I can make out Phil's shape against the opposite wall of the tent. His back is to me, and he does not move. Well, I'm glad the little bastard's getting some sleep. Somebody should. God damn him. Better men are awake and freezing. My side of the tent flaps against me, and I become quite certain that the whole thing is coming down. There is a moment of real claustrophobic panic—the smell of the earth is choking me, the ceiling's coming down and I can't breathe—when all that prevents me from screaming and bursting through the top of the tent is the fact that I really can't move. Through it all the stream boils and thunders nearby, and after a while I get it confused with the sound of the wind and my own breathing. A rooster crows a long way off, but there is not even a hint of false dawn in the sky. I wrap my arms around myself and whimper.

Then the sun is shining. It's that sudden a thing. It isn't a bit warmer, but the sun is shining. Phil is awake. He says, "I'll get up if you will."

"You're out of your mind. It's freezing out there."

"It's freezing in here." This seems to sum up something or other admirably, and we begin to laugh hysterically as we stagger to our feet. We wobble in circles, making vague gestures toward rolling up the sleeping bags and taking down the tent. An empty bean can falls out of my sleeping bag, and we invent a kind of stiff-legged soccer designed to make the other bend down to retrieve it. We are delighted to find ourselves alive, and afraid to take our hands out of our pockets.

There is frost on the seats of both scooters, but they start up very well, which is a great relief. The morning is very bright, and the fact that the sun gives us no heat is almost unimportant. Once Phil points to our shadows, rippling along the road a little way before us. The shadows of the scooters blur into each other, but our own are quite distinct, even to the cut of our beards, the way we hold our heads and shoulders, and—to us, at least—the different ways we look at the road and at the world around us. When we rode together on Margot, we cast a shadow like something out of a medieval bestiary; that was the Fuzzy Shadow, and we said that it fell across faces and hearts from Pittsburgh to Martha's Vineyard. It didn't really, of course, but cops always stopped us.

We turn in at the first diner we come to. The air inside is warm and damp and greasy, and we huddle into it, drawing it around our shoulders. We see ourselves in the mirror behind the counter and begin laughing again—red-faced, crack-skinned, puff-eyed, our beards looking as though we had been trying to shed them by rubbing against trees, and our hair as stiff and shaggy as hemp. We drink a lot of black coffee and wash it down with a lot of watery scrambled eggs. The toast is yesterday's and could be used to build shipping crates. We smear it with gluey jelly and ask for more.

"That was the coldest night I ever spent in my life," Phil says. He has a cold. "Also the longest. I wish I needed an alibi for a murder. I can account for every goddamn minute of last night. I should only be so clear about a few other nights."

"I thought you were asleep. I lay awake hating you."

"I thought *you* were, and you didn't hate like I hated." The helpless flutter of the fingers and the tired giggle. We talk all the time, usually lying—for fun or from fear—but whatever emotions we share come out in a kind of shorthand. It saves a lot of commas.

When the waitress brings us more coffee she asks very politely, "Excuse me, but are you boys beatniks?" We're used to the question: since we grew our beards it has been put to us, silently or noisily, by nearly everyone we meet, from three-year-old children who have seen us on television to old people who make sad jokes about

16

the House of David. But this is a nice lady, and she really does want to know. We go into Routine B, the Cuddly, Lovable Wanderers bit: wash our faces and take us home with you; we play with balls of yarn, sing little songs, eat all your food, and leave you pregnant. Just passing through, ma'am. It works appallingly well, considering our general grubbiness, on anything short of Meter Maids and the wisest waitresses.

"No, it's not usually this cold in April," she says when we ask her. "It gets pretty cold till around May, especially at night"—Phil hates me—"but it doesn't usually get this cold. We've had a bad winter in the mountains."

That's a pity, ma'am. When do we get out of the mountains?

"Oh, I guess around Warren," she says, and so Warren becomes the first in a long series of magic names and numbers. Once we reach this town it'll get warmer and the land will start leveling off; once we cross this river into this state there'll be less wind because the mountains will break it up; once we hit this highway we'll really make time. Anyway, we'll get coffee.

We did not make it to Warren this second day, not by seventy miles. The sun has not set when we stop in a little town called Roulette and look for a motel. There is no question of camping out tonight. Phil's gimpy hip—he has been plagued by it as long as I have known him—is hurting him badly, and I am beginning to have trouble picking things up. We find a room; the manager turns on the heater for us, and we lie across the bed for a long time, feeling our blood moving like applesauce in our veins.

Before we go to bed, Phil takes out his sketchpad and stands inside the door to do a pen-and-ink sketch of the bare hills across the road. He has been wanting to stop and draw all day, but the cold has made it completely impossible. The sketch is spare and wintry; nothing but the Apocalypse will warm those hills. He says, "It

17

figures. A cross-country trip on motor scooters, cooking out and sleeping under the stars, and all my sketches will be done from motel windows. Story of all my paintings. The great world, as seen by a claustrophobic goldfish."

"We're doing something wrong," I murmur. "Other people don't camp out like this. They know all sorts of ways to keep warm. Woodsy lore."

"Woodsy lore, like wait until June. I'll give you woodsy lore, boy. Beagle, we're going to freeze before Sandusky, we keep this up. Fat white brother, you have led your Indian buddy up the garden path into the Alps. I am not an Alp Indian."

We play an old game that might be called "The Lone Ranger and Tonto at Home." I answer, "Vile but equal companion, you didn't have to come with me. You could just as easy have stayed home and spied on your relatives for future reference. There are certain things a man has to do alone."

"There are indeed, but you can't do them. No, you need me, old *kemo-sabe*. You're thirty-nine years old, you know. That's getting up there for a man wants to go running around in a mask, shooting guns out of people's hands, especially a man likes his mashed potatoes the way you do. It's a little late to start putting on your own disguises."

"I could if I had to. Don't forget the time I garbed the old self as a Blackfoot warrior. You're a Blackfoot, or something pretty near it, and you couldn't tell it was me."

"All Indians look alike to me," he says. "What do you think about laying over a couple of days, just to let the spring catch up with us? This isn't exactly what we had in mind."

"I know. But I can't, Phil, not even a day. Maybe later, you know, when I really believe we're going to California. Unless you feel really lousy." He shrugs; he makes his "forget it" sound. "It'll get better once we're out of the

18

mountains, little friend. It'll get warmer and warmer the farther west we go."

"We're going north," he says.

"Yes, but west too. Northwest."

"But mostly north."

Before we get into bed the room has become so warm that I turn off the heater. This is a mistake. We are both up at three in the morning, trying to turn it back on. Phil does not speak to me until long after breakfast, possibly because he can't. His lips are quite blue.

After breakfast we walk to a general store near the motel and ask the owner if he stocks any long woolen underwear. "You gents came about two weeks too early for the warm weather," he informs us, introducing a refrain we will chase all the way to the Grand Canyon. He sells us Thermal undershirts, Thermal longjohns, Thermal socks, and Thermal gloves. "Great stuff for keeping your body heat in." It seems useless to explain to him that we produce nothing but body cold.

The Thermals keep us almost warm, warm enough for Phil to stop and draw if he jumps around a little from time to time. We make it all the way to Warren in a single hop and discover, stopping at a diner for coffee, that Couchette's speedometer cable has broken. This is a shadow, rather than an aggravation; we have no illusions about our fates if the Heinkels really break down on the road. It would be easier to find spare parts for a flying carpet than to get Jenny and Couchette serviced between New York and San Francisco. And yet, motorcycle and scooter people look after each other in a curious way. The waiter in the diner is a motorcycle person, and he suggests a motorcycle repair shop in Union City. The man in Union City can't make up a cable for a Heinkel, but he knows a place in Erie and the place in Erie improvises one. The cable will break again, but somehow the incident feels like a good omen.

At Erie we pick up Interstate 90, one of those sleek divided highways that say by their very appearance:

Pedestrians, Bicycles, and Motor-Driven Cycles, Off.
Ordinarily we avoid these as much as possible, but
both of us want to make time now. An odd mutual
guilt forms between us when we either gain too much
time or lose it. Phil knows that I have seen Enid once
in the last eighteen months and that I couldn't have
waited the two weeks more to leave, and I know that
the trip is worthless to Phil if he cannot draw; at the
rate he's been able to work so far, he might better have
stayed in New York with the pile-driver and the subways.
But this particular afternoon the vague guilt is his, and
we roar along the faceless highway all the way to North
Madison, Ohio, where we make camp.

Before we go to bed that night I find a pay phone and
call Alex Rodriguez in Ann Arbor to tell him that we will
arrive in time for supper tomorrow, thus giving Kisa
plenty of time to prepare chicken curry. Mooching off
a cook of Kisa's quality is something beyond mooching
and requires consideration. We sleep surprisingly well
this second night in the open, waking only long enough
to realize how uncomfortable we are. In the morning I
have a cold too.

The day begins bright and pleasant—very much like
spring—and we take our time along the road to Cleveland. The flat farming country of Ohio is a relief after
the Poconos, but not as pretty, lacking the rich purples
and violets of the mountains. If you look long enough at
even the barest landscape, however, you can see the
damnedest colors: russets, silver-grays, pinks in every
tree trunk, sudden single blades of grass that look almost
white. The grass is thin and hesitant; now and then we
pass a patch of deep, bright green, which is almost
always a golf course.

Phil stops to sketch an apple orchard, and I sit on
Jenny and look around. On both sides of the road are
hundreds of little apple trees, as alike in their basic
shape of a twisted *V* as though God were Japanese, and
yet capable of small, surprising individualities. The tall

trees beyond the orchard are all bare, but if you look very closely there is a kind of fuzzy greenness on them, so light as to disappear again if you stare too long. Back along the road a small pony is cropping grass; he looks rather like a hyena and moves like something billowing lazily in the wind. Some kind of soundtruck passes slowly, gargling absolutely incomprehensible phrases of that metallic language that frustrated employers are forever silently screaming at Charlie Chaplin. There are car tracks swirling through the black earth of the orchard, and there are crows calling, and there is the apple-turpentine smell of Phil's fixative as he sprays his drawing.

I had forgotten through the long winter how good it is to be driving a scooter on a warm day. You become painfully aware of how much there is in the world to be smelled, tasted, listened to, looked at, touched, and comprehended before you die—a lifetime in every blink of the eye—and you find yourself twisting the throttle until she surges under you like a river, wanting to get to it all, all at once. You begin to fear death on the prettiest days.

The sky begins to grow dark and overcast as we come down the highway to Cleveland. Arches, bridges, meaningless towers and spirals spring up around us as swiftly as a tropical jungle but totally colorless under the city's private sky. I have never seen a city that looked as iron as Cleveland, and it frightens me a little, as though the freeway were spinning us straight into the jaws of a great machine. "It's like going to Mordor," I yell at Phil, although in the book Mordor is the last country, the end of the terrible journey. He shakes his head and calls back, "Not Mordor," I can barely hear him above the roar of the highway and the rumbling of the cranes on the waterfront below. "Not Mordor, Syracuse!" I remember that Phil was married once and lived there. I remember it like a dream, the way I remember most things.

We pass through Sandusky, which pleases me for a

silly reason: my roommate during my freshman year at college had a pet phrase he used to employ whenever a boy in our dormitory got a girl pregnant. (This happened with remarkable regularity that year. My adviser said it came in predictable cycles, like the seventeen-year locust.) "Well," Ben would say gravely, "we all got to go by way of Sandusky sometime."

Lake Erie is a presence on our right almost all the way between Cleveland and Toledo, shoreless as the ocean in the heavy mist, with only one boat in sight. We get lost in Toledo, so hopelessly bewildered that the only clear image of the city I take away with me is that every street in town is named for Mad Anthony Wayne, which is absurd. A driver finally tells us to follow him to the highway, but just as it comes in sight Jenny makes a noise as if her entrails were tearing loose and dragging along the ground, and cuts out completely. Phil roars away up the road without looking back, and I let Jenny roll to a stop at a gas station.

The silence of an engine that has just cut out under you is one of the most chilling quietnesses I know. Drive a scooter for even a little while, and she becomes strangely yourself, yourself grown swift and powerful and untiring. In turn, you feel what she feels—a quirk in the wind, a difference in the road surface, the rise or fall of the land—and her sounds become like the noises of your own body, her vulnerability becomes your own. Jenny's engine has not fallen out, but with that discovery my understanding of the four-cycle motor comes to a dead stop. I try my old remedy for most of Margot's ailments, fussing with the spark plug, and discover that the little metal cap that fits over it has come completely off, and that the plug itself is within a thread or two of wriggling completely loose. It is the work of a moment for skilled fingers and steely wrists to tighten the damn thing, jam the cap back on, and put the tools away, just as Phil comes back down the street, looking for me. I start Jenny up as he approaches, and the engine turns over without a miss.

"What happened?" he asks. I give him a nod and a terse professional shrug. "Ignition trouble. High-tension lead. Wasn't getting any juice from the mag. Fixed her."

On the highway, for the first time since we left New York, there is no headwind against us. I discover this by stepping out to pass a slow-moving truck and glancing down at the speedometer in time to see the needle slide past sixty and hold at sixty-five. Margot never went much over fifty for very long, and we haven't been able to coax the Heinkels to do over fifty-five. As I stare at the speedometer Phil comes alongside and passes, yelling, "Seventy! Seventy!" like a Sabine woman trying to keep score. We race at speeds between sixty and seventy for about ten miles before we slow down to drive abreast and stare at each other. "We've been babying them," I say weakly, and Phil nods. Seventy miles per hour isn't much for a motorcycle, but it fills our minds with wonderful estimates of time gained and long pauses for drawings—perhaps even watercolors. The wind will resume the day we leave Ann Arbor, and the scooters will never go that fast again until California, but our speed makes for a triumphal drive to the Rodriguezes', even though we do get lost for an hour in Ypsilanti.

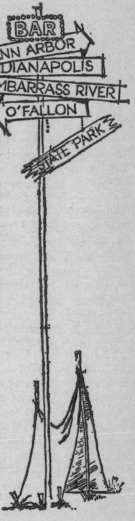

Alex and Kisa Rodriguez, besides being our friends, are our touchstone, our pet marriage, our reassurance against a number of night's black agents. We are both envious enough persons to covet Kisa, if Alex weren't Alex, which kills that right there, even for us. It is very nice to know that they exist, especially now. We still haven't figured out how our stove works, and we are very hungry. Kisa has made the chicken curry.

In the evening we sit in the tiny apartment that Kisa has made beautiful, and talk. Alex has managed to borrow a couple of guitars for us, and we play for them; we have never had the chance before. We have evolved, in playing together since we were nine or ten, two performing styles, separate and yet related. One is based on seduction—seduction of camp audiences, crowds at a party, girls in the crowds —and it's quite often fun, but it has no love in it and only occasional humor. The other is for ourselves, and we cannot always command it, especially if we've been doing too much of the other. It is for sharing with friends from whom we want nothing, and to whom we have little to give except a kind of music that we love and a style that is ourselves. We play Brassens, Léo Ferré, Aristide Bruant, ballads, blues, improvisations, ridiculous games, finger exercises. We forget that we have an audience, and that, for us, is Nirvana.

Late in the evening odd clankings, toots, and flutings begin to sound in the apartment down the hall. "Lindsay's having a Happening," Alex says. I remember the phrase from deadpan reviews in *The New York Times*—something to do with John Cage and gadgets that destroy themselves. "You have to see this," Alex says, and we follow him into a room full of very young people. The room smells of matches and sweaters. It might be any party I have been to in the last three years, except for the machine in the middle of the floor, and the four men squatting around it. The machine reminds me at once of the Harrow in Kafka's "In the Penal Colony," and of the projector in the Hayden Planetarium. The room itself is shaped like a huge boiler, extremely high-ceilinged, quite wide, but almost cylindrical. There are mirrors everywhere and burlap and bamboo tacked all around the room; against the far wall there is a kind of scaffolding made of pipe leading up to a grimy skylight. The music we heard is coming from a couple of hidden speakers. Very skirling stuff, no question about it. Muzak for bats. Phil closes his eyes.

One of the men by the machine pulls a couple of switches, and the thing begins to revolve, very slowly at first. Patterns of color begin to slide around the room and over the ceiling: circles of white light, thick stipples of yellow, great strawberry weals, like hives. One lovely, remote blue that really shouldn't be whirling like this. The movement of the whole thing is clockwise and rather soothing. I don't usually like home movies, but this is very nice and undemanding. Then somebody touches another switch and gets a second set of colors wheeling in the opposite direction, faster now, crossing and re-crossing, blending where they touch, sweeping across the floor and lighting up strings of blank white faces like dud firecrackers. "Radio City used to do something like this," I whisper to Phil.

"Yeah, I remember. It was their big Christmas program." The colors suddenly give way to black-and-white patterns that seem to be based on both biological and molecular structures. We are strafed by atomic diagrams; an X ray of a rib cage stoops at us from the skylight; teeth and toes and fingerbones fall around us like snow. Now and then there is a meaningful dab of suffering flesh: a pair of lean, hard hands, more or less matched, or a woman's mouth yawning sorrowfully. Certain shots recur quite often; these are leitmotifs, I tell Phil. I begin to explain about leitmotifs to him. He tries to bite me, but I am too agile for him, although we are both very cramped from sitting on the floor.

The Happening is going full blast now, I guess. The room feels very noisy, although the only sound is the whir of the machine and the electronic music, which is becoming more and more urgent and elemental in its own way. Its own way sounds something like a couple of pterodactyls committing adultery. Nobody speaks, except for a girl behind me who keeps whispering to the boy beside her, "You have to be high to get the full impact. High on something, I don't care, pot, bennies, methedrine, cough syrup even. *Then* it'll talk to you, *then* you'll get the impact. Next time . . ." No other voices. I glance around the room at the faces that flicker on and off as the lights touch them, the college faces that I have come to know so well since I got out of college. I see puzzlement and boredom and amusement—all equally guarded—and even, once, a face all but coming apart with fear; but the expression I see the most and recognize with the greatest ease is the face of the person

26

who is really trying to work up an emotion, trying to make himself see something beyond mirror after mirror and hear something beyond the sound of his own voice. Nobody speaks, nobody asks a question, nobody laughs, nobody gets up to leave, nobody does anything but shift his body on the hard floor and look around at his neighbors, as I am doing.

Now and then the two wheels of light, spinning against each other like grindstones, merge at the dark skylight and then fall away, leaving it blank for a moment: cobwebbed and dingy, offering nothing, all the emptier for the flashing and slipping, the tooting and honking and whining going on everywhere around it. Wondrously relieving to the aching eye and the sullen mind, but it happens as rarely as it should, which is too rarely. One by one, Phil and Alex and Kisa and I walk quietly out of the room. The last thing I see, looking back, is the machine in the middle of the floor and the four men around it, each turning or pulling or twiddling his own something. The machine is the one dancing.

Back in the Rodriguezes' apartment, Alex begins to make coffee. He says, "Lindsay has a fellowship for the Happenings."

"That doesn't surprise me," Phil answers. He does not speak about the Happenings again. I say, "The name intrigues me. As though things only happened to these people—what is it?—every Friday night. Experience by appointment only."

"Things happen to them," Kisa says thoughtfully. "Things keep happening to them, things drop on them. They want something to happen besides all the things that keep happening." She and Alex go to bed, and we unroll our sleeping bags on the living-room floor. The music is still sounding from the enchanted room down the hall when I fall asleep.

We spend the next day in Ann Arbor, resting, reading, eating, walking around, taking the Rodriguezes riding on Jenny and Couchette. Somewhere during the day, alone for a while, I buy a notebook and sit down on a bench at one corner of the U. M. campus. The idea is to record my impressions of the trip so far, like a proper professional, but all I feel like writing about is another journey, the one Phil and I made on Margot from here to New York, just about a year ago. We went over the Alleghenies that time, a route I knew well enough from the four years I traveled back and forth between New York and Pittsburgh. But it was different on Margot. We were like children being carried swiftly through Christmas morning, too young to do anything but stare and wonder and try to hold on to things, and, perhaps, to cry for not being able to speak. Now and then one of us would say to the other, *Smell,* and the other would answer, *I been.* That was a good trip. It was the first time Phil ever rode on a scooter, the first time we ever traveled a long way together, the first time the highway cops ever radioed descriptions of us on to the cops in the next town, the first time that an entire town seemed to be looking after us as we bounced down the main street and over the old bridge at the end of town. I put down my notebook and watch the girls walking across the campus—some already wearing their spring dresses, some still shapeless in duffel coats like cocoons—and think about that first journey.

We dawdle over saying good-by to the Rodriguezes the next morning, staying until it is time for Alex to teach his first class, and then walking to the campus with them. The morning is cold, and Alex and Kisa seem the only warmth between here and California. We do not know when we will see them again, and as we drive out of Ann Arbor we begin to realize how long a way there is to go. Kisa has packed what was left of the chicken curry for us, but we have forgotten to take it; discovering this, somewhere around Bryan, Ohio, makes us as absurdly sorrowful as though we had lost a magic charm that was protecting not us but them.

The people of Indiana seem almost alarmingly friendly and polite, although our private samplings are limited to such places as gas stations, diners, state parks, and occasional motels. There is a curious advantage in encountering people as we do: at first there is nothing there but the trade, the profession, labor and parts, minimum rates, how much do you want to spend? There is no reason to affect humanity, no need to put on the various masks worn before families, friends, superiors— nothing but the need for money and a real reluctance to deal with people who have no money, as though it might be catching. But we talk, we ask directions, we use the men's room, we fuss with the scooters or we have another cup of coffee, we tell about the trip, about the roads and the weather back East, about Jenny and Couchette, about our beards—and more often than not a waitress slips us an extra portion of vegetables, a mechanic gives us free run of his tools, a cop suggests a place to camp where the cops won't bother us; and somehow we set off again with the feeling that we are making the journey in many more names than our own.

Sitting by the roadside the next morning, watching Phil work, I am chilly and content. We have had a good breakfast, made forty quick miles, and have enough day left to be liberal about taking breaks. Phil is doing a gouache of two old red barns, so far off that the darkness in their doorways looks deep blue. The trees around them are snarly and spidery; they look like nerve ganglia, like veins in eyes streaked with red and yellow. The air is mild today, not at all raw. I think it's starting to get warm.

It begins to rain. Phil puts his materials away and we don what we call our rubber *bubbe* suits. They are two-piece rainsuits made of cheap vinyl, uncomely enough for a junior high school graduation, and surprisingly good protection against cold as well as rain. The legs go *sish-sish* against each other when we walk. With the pointed hoods on, we look like mad grandmothers, fierce-eyed, hairy little old ladies roaring along on red motor scooters, pointing at each other and laughing with monkey mouths. The rain is falling heavily now, like snow.

Within five miles it stops being funny. There is a wind up, and it smashes the rain at us almost horizontally. We cannot see through our windscreens at all, and when we peer around them the rain blinds us; we are driving entirely by the white line and the feel of the road. There is no place to stop until we reach a diner a few miles from Indianapolis, where we sit in our *bubble* suits and drink coffee and watch the rain come down. The drops bounce off the highway like marbles.

"Might as well find a hotel in Indianapolis," Phil says. "Dry off and take it easy. I wouldn't mind poking around a big city for a bit."

I am suddenly angry, childishly so; to spite the rain and the wind I am sure that I could drive all that day and night. "God damn it, we haven't made sixty miles today. I don't want to poke around in Indianapolis. I want to make some goddamn time."

"I know you do," Phil answers quietly. "That's what's going to foul up this whole trip, you aren't careful." We stare at each other for what seems a long time, each one hearing the other's argument in his head, understanding it, and wishing he didn't. I say, "I know I'm pushing. What can I tell you?" That last is a much-used phrase between us, and it is never really a question.

"What, indeed?" Phil points outside where the rain is drilling down as fiercely as ever. "See what it's like when we get there, anyway."

Couchette falls over into a puddle as Phil is pushing her off the stand, dragging him with her. She is not damaged, but her rear wheel has landed in a puddle and the brake is soaked and deadly. Phil tries to use it once and is almost jolted through the windscreen. That about settles it. We limp very slowly into Indianapolis, trying to avoid stopping for red lights. The rain is beginning to let up.

We have long since learned to pass up hotels endorsed by anybody from the AAA to the *Hobo News*. The first rule of cheap lodging in a strange town is *Cherchez les brownstones*. The one we find gives us a single with a double bed for five dollars. It's the sort of room to which you might bring someone else's wife, but it's warm and it gives us a place to spread out our drenched clothes and sleeping bags. Most of Phil's art supplies, wrapped in plastic sheets, have stayed dry, and his books are about the only dry things in his duffel bag. We change our clothes and go out into Indianapolis. It has just about stopped raining—not entirely, but almost. It's going to be a pretty day.

We spend it browsing through pawnshops in search of old guitars, which is what we always do in strange cities. We know so many towns by the same few streets, the same undersea windows filled with dead men's real bones. Very few good Spanish guitars ever turn up in pawnshops; what we find are cracker-thin jazz guitars, colored like lollipops, and sheaves of the kind of machine-made guitars that must go directly from the factory to the hockshops, for no one can ever have played these. The real collectors have always been there ahead of us, and most dealers know about guitars now, anyway. I don't know what we'll do the day we find a guitar we know we have to have. We never have any money, and we are terrible businessmen. Lowell, Lawrence, Albany, Poughkeepsie, Peekskill, Saratoga, Pittsfield, Adams, Lee, Flint, Kinsman—it will happen one day in just such a stupid town as a man meets his love in.

The next morning turns out warm and beautiful, the kind of day you try to take into yourself. We drive easily, sometimes abreast to talk, sometimes half a mile apart, keeping an eye on each other in our mirrors. We stop often for Phil to draw. The trees look thicker now, and the earth is yellow-brown and seems inviting and summery through the trees. We've been seeing some lovely violet flowers for the past couple of days, but neither of us knows what they are. They grow on trees and catch the eye as surely as snowflakes would. Phil does his best sketch so far after we cross into Illinois: a drawing of a cement bridge over a slow-moving river. The movement of the bridge is light and alive, and the sketch has the feeling of the afternoon, leaning against a tree, looking down at the river and dropping bits of wood into it, trying to make out the faces of three young girls walking through a gully near the river, and having actually taken off our Thermal undershirts.

When Phil has finished the sketch we remain where we are, looking at the river. I say, "Today's my birthday. What did you buy me last night, sneaking so tippy-toe out so I shouldn't notice your sacrifice?"

"I sold my beautiful hair to the toothbrush people and bought you a hernia operation. When's my birthday?"

"July twenty-second. How come you never remember?"

"I don't know. I don't like birthdays much. You're birthday-happy enough for the two of us. You remember everybody's birthday."

"I like birthdays. They catch you at the strangest times, in the weirdest places, and then you remember where you were a year ago, and the year before that. Imagine spending your birthday in Greenup, Illinois, on the Embarrass River. I'll like remembering that."

He stares at me and shakes his head slowly. "Where are we? What the hell town?"

"Greenup, Illinois. Actually, we're between Greenup and Jewett. Closer to Jewett."

"What river?"

"The Embarrass River. Look at the Triptik."

"The Embarrass River." Phil begins to laugh very quietly. "The Embarrass River in Illinois. Now what in God's name are we doing here? You live on Gunhill Road, and I live on Selwyn Avenue. What the hell are we doing here?"

I shrug and laugh with him, but it is a little different, because I know where we're going. "What the hell are we doing anywhere?" Stock question, stock answer.

We always stop driving before sunset, partly in order to set up camp while it is still light, but partly, I think, because the hour before dark is a strangely lonely time to be driving something as small and open as a scooter as far away as we are. The thin orange light is going away so swiftly, and yet our own lights seem so feeble against the thickening air. Coldness begins to bloom inside both of us like a night flower, and each feels as alone as though the other were not there, and more deeply homeless than being a long way from home should make him. Tonight we camp on a picnic ground in Altamont, Illinois, within sight of a diner where Phil orders supper for us while I call Enid to tell her that we are somewhat farther west than we are.

"Weirdest thing happened while you were calling," Phil says when I come back to the table. "A couple of guys and a girl sat down at the counter and started talking motorcycles. So I asked them if they knew where I could pick up a cable for Couchette"—her speedometer went again just before we stopped for the night—"and it turns out one of the guys runs a cycle place in Vandalia and he can make me up a cable, so we got to be there tomorrow at ten o'clock. Where's Vandalia?"

"Up the road, maybe twenty miles." As naturally as if it were happening in a dream, the diner turns into a bowling alley—the rear wall is actually a pleated partition—and everyone gets up to bowl. Phil and I watch for a while and then go out to the picnic grounds. We are suddenly very tired.

Putting up the tent, we become the two aging comic-strip campaigners again. "Help with the poles, white man," Phil commands. "Do not lean too heavy on my woodsy lore, account I am a Sac and also a Fox, and we do not sleep in tents, reckoning them white man's magic

33

like harmonicas and water pistols. Also, pound the pegs with the rock, not my foot. I ain't loose. Pound the pegs."

"I have great faith in you, old blackamoor," I reply in the creamiest bass I can pump up. "In such matters as tracking, scouting, spying in bars, and getting hit over the head and captured, you are absolutely without equal. A great pity you aren't quite human, but you're a good old fellow nevertheless, you old *kemo-sabe,* you. Pat, Pat."

"Don't pat me," Phil says through his teeth, looking more and more like a sour, scrawny Indian. "You're skooshing my feather, my one lousy feather. Why don't you buy me a new loincloth, you like me so much? Seventeen years listening to you tell me how I'm white, clean white inside, and not one new loincloth from the day I found you bleeding and left for dead on the prairie. I ain't white, clean white inside that goddamn loincloth, let me tell you. Bet Gene Autry wouldn't make me go seventeen years without a new loincloth, boy."

"Breechclout, old chap, and don't tax my liberalism too far. I've lost a lot of clients traveling with a sidekick who keeps his hair in a bun, you know. You want to be Gene Autry's *kemo-sabe,* feel free. Just remember, two hundred and twenty pounds, and it sings 'Frosty the Snowman.' "

Phil punches a new hole in the tent for a peg, muttering, "Seventeen years on the trail, not a break, not a Christmas, not a two weeks off in July even, nothing but riding the range saving white people from their relatives. Bleeding and left for dead on the prairie, and I had to bite your toe to see were you ripe or not. Ho-ho, nosy me. Serves me right. What are we talking about?"

"I have no idea." We crawl into our sleeping bags in Altamont, Illinois, near enough to the highway so that the lights of passing trucks throw tree shadows into the tent, near enough to the diner to hear a susurrus of voices murmuring through our dreams all night. Before we fall asleep I discover in one of the shadows the

reason for all the games we play, and even for the Albert
Alligator-Gregory Ratoff voices in which we play them;
but both of us are asleep by the time I can find the right
words, and when we wake all I can remember clearly
is the phrase, "We wish they were true." I know there
was more to it than that.

It is after ten when we reach Vandalia and find the
street at the edge of town where the motorcycle shop
is located, but it makes no difference. The shop is closed
and no one is around. "It's Sunday," I say. "I lost track."

"We wait," Phil says, and we squat on the doorstep
of the motorcycle shop. I have never been in such a
totally silent town; it is not the humming silence of most
small-town Sunday mornings but the silence that must
come to a plague-ridden city. The only people we see
are small boys who ride past us on bicycles with bits
of cardboard and metal jammed into the front spokes
to make the chirring sound of a baby motorcycle. Each
one twists his neck nearly out of joint to stare at us, and
two of them just miss driving straight into the same
picket fence. They move their mouths at us, but I can
hear nothing, and I am certain that if their bikes
crashed and fell they would make no more noise than
the falling of dust through sunlight.

The motorcycle dealer shows up at last. He is a lean
man in the early thirties, wiry, muscular, losing his
hair. A thin mouth and pale eyes, like a lion's, with a
lion's way of being absent from his own eyes when he
talks about anything but motorcycles. We talk to him
while he is jury-rigging a cable for Couchette, but we
never really make contact. Our lovable fuzziness means
nothing to him, beyond provoking a sluggish suspicion
that his eyes never quite lose. The trip interests him a
little, but the slow pace puts it completely into another
world. He mentions having recently driven his black
Harley to Florida for a meet, a thousand miles in two
days. When I remark that most of the bikes I've seen in
the Middle West have been Harley-Davidsons, but

that Hondas seem to have taken over both coasts, his pale eyes gleam with real fury and he looks directly at us for the first time. "Those goddamn stinking Japs!" He is so angry he forgets about the propane torch burning in his hand and almost ruins the cable. "Stinking Jap bastards, put a thing out so goddamn cheap a white man can't compete, they don't give a shit if they run you out of business, take your job. Boy, I hate them bastards, run you right out of business, them Czech bastards . . ." Neither of us corrects him. We are too occupied with looking silently sympathetic without actually compromising our principles.

The road between Vandalia and Saint Louis is fast but not especially attractive, even on a pretty day. Illinois in general seems less attractive than Indiana—flatter, drier-earthed, less richly colored. Still, it is good to be driving anywhere today, breathing and singing, for the first time as quiet inside myself, as receptive, as though I weren't going anywhere. Everything I see interests me, and if I don't stop and dismount to look at every pattern of branches against the sky and down every dirt road, still, some part of me stays behind each time. I see a house by the highway, and I put myself into it in the seconds it takes me to go by—difficult, because very few houses, seen as you pass, seem big enough for people to live in—and not all of me catches up with me before I am out of sight. A car passes Jenny and takes a fragment of me wherever it is bound. I wonder if many people above the age of five are this caught up in what they see around them, this aware every day and every night for all their lives. I don't think there's enough of me to keep it up for very long, unless you can grow yourself again from a single morsel, like a starfish; but today I would scatter myself along the road like a handful of seeds, if I could, as far as I could.

We spend the night in a state park in O'Fallon, about twenty-five miles west of Saint Louis. The park is run by a friendly man named Jack Williams, who is glad of company this early in the camping season and spends the hour before sunset sitting on a hillside with us, doing most of the talking—a really remarkable feat, considering the kind of dust storm we can raise. It is pleasant to sprawl out in the grass, watching the sky turn pink and green, and listen to Jack Williams talking easily. He points out several oddly twisted and broken trees and says, "A hurricane did that, two years back. Crumpled those trees just as easy as mashing potatoes. There wasn't a thing I could do about it."

He sounds sad and a little guilty, as though even now he privately believes there must have been something he could have done to save the trees. Phil says, "We just missed a twister around Indianapolis." A newspaper had predicted that a Kansas hurricane would pass over the city the evening we were there, but it didn't. I chant, "We just caught the fringes of it." We have silently decided that the rainstorm we ran into that day was a fringe. The story will become true in time.

"Oh, they're wicked things," Jack Williams says. "We get small ones every couple of years, and there was one real big one come along seven years ago, the year they opened this park. Tore the whole house right off one fella, like a little wind takes off your hat, you know. Left him and his whole family huddling round the piano, hanging on to keep from taking off themselves. That's about the only things hurricanes won't take and blow somewheres else, pianos. I had a big brood mare once, solid, heavy, determined old girl, and she disappeared in one of those hurricanes, vanished right out of a pasture with a six-foot bob-wire fence around it. You know, she turned up two days later and two more bob-wire fences away, eating grass, calm as could be. No, I tell you, the only thing safe in a hurricane is a piano. Only thing *I* know of."

Phil wakes me early the next morning because the

sky is full of purplish-gray clouds and it smells like rain. But it has cleared by the time we are on the highway again, and by ten o'clock the temperature must be in the eighties. It is the first really hot day of the trip, and with the heat comes a new problem: if we stop for coffee or a drawing after a thirty- or forty-mile hop, the odds are good that Jenny and Couchette will either not start at all or else simply wobble along the road, sputtering, backfiring flatulently, and refusing to go into the higher gears. Rested for fifteen or twenty minutes, they start off smoothly enough, but for all the rest of the trip overheating will be our most nagging problem. We have a hazy notion that scooters as well designed as the Heinkels shouldn't overheat quite this easily, but it takes us a long time to discover that Max the Art Collector has sold us spark plugs that are much too hot for our engines and that only a minor miracle has kept us from burning our pistons into slag. We trade them in for popsicles in Oakland.

We have a short, savage argument over Phil's idea of starting out early, resting during the hottest part of the day, and driving later than we usually do. It was bound to happen. In the course of the dispute we both say Just don't take it out on me, man, several times, until at last I shrug and plump down right there by the roadside, and Phil crosses the highway to do several heavy sketches of straggly trees and bushes. I lie on my back and explain things to Phil in my head. There is a breeze coming out of the west, very pleasant on such a dry, angry day.

Within an hour the breeze has grown into a bitter, abrasive gale; within two, the temperature has dropped thirty degrees. We do not really appreciate the force of the wind until we realize that we cannot put the scooters into top gear going downhill. We would get off the road, but the only places to stop are gas stations, and with their signs flapping like laundry and even their gas pumps trembling, they seem as impermanent as tumbleweeds. Remember what Jack Williams said about houses and brood mares and pianos. There is nowhere to stop until Columbia, twenty-five miles ahead. If it's still there. This wind could blow it right off the Triptik.

The moment we turn off the highway, the wind lets us go. We can look back and see the dust whipping low along the road, the way the cutting, powdery snow comes sidewinding to meet you on a winter night, but for us the wind has ceased almost completely, except for the small breeze with which it began. We drive on into Columbia. It is a pretty town, about half the size of Ann Arbor. We make a package of Phil's art books here and send them ahead to Enid. That's a strange feeling—not at all like writing to her, not even like sending her flowers for her birthday. We park the scooters in front of a bar and go inside to decide about driving any farther today.

"College town," says Phil before we go in.

"University of Missouri. How'd you know?"

He points to the name of the bar, spelled out over the door in staggered ebony letters: THE DARKSIDE. "Don't be silly," he says.

It is a good-sized place, with a small bandstand scrunched into a far corner. According to the signs on the walls between the bullfight posters, The Darkside has a jazz group three nights a week and folk music on Friday nights. There are only four people in the bar— two boys in their early twenties, a girl, and a bartender who looks about twenty—and they all look and talk astonishingly like characters in a certain type of college novel or movie. I have my troubles distinguishing fiction from reality anyway, and these people are doing nothing to make life any easier for me. One of the boys is obviously The Hero. He is good-looking, crew-cut, tall and rangy (I was never quite sure what *rangy* meant, but he's it), and has surely been The Hero all his life, from the absolute assurance with which he speaks his lines. The second boy is The Hero's Best Buddy, stocky, with a quizzical pug face and his hair brushed forward. The young bartender is practicing hard to be an Old Bartender. It's a fine, durable part—I wouldn't want any better social security than that part—but his face is soft and seamless, almost too pretty for the role. He may make it, though, for he knows the lines well, but he really ought to stop looking so interested in The Hero's Girl. I feel like telling him.

The Hero's Girl. She is probably no older than the bartender, not that it makes any difference. She has fine blond hair, worn shoulder-length, and she wears a red blouse, blue jeans, and sneakers. Her legs are long and beautifully made. Her body is beautifully made too, out of some kind of good plastic, polystyrene. It looks unused. I am quite certain that there are still bits of flash clinging to the hollow at the base of her throat, between her breasts, in her navel. Her face is clear, flawless, poreless, the face of the Barbie Doll. She knows more than we do. It was built in.

"The older I get," Phil mutters in my ear, "the harder it gets to tell are the store dummies getting more like people or the other way around."

We order beer and watch The Hero romp with his Girl. He picks her up and sits her on the bar, takes her down again and places her on the juke box, lifts her down once more and waves her over his head, looking like a child with an unused Roman candle on July 5. The Girl squeals, struggles stiffly, smiles and gestures apologetically to the Bartender while The Hero flops her. "Put me down, you big lug," she says. Now and then he hugs her from behind, or clasps his hands over her breasts, more with the air of checking to make sure they're still there than out of any delight to his palms. The Girl leans back against him, nibbles his neck, and moves away. She is never still for long, one way or another.

The Hero's Best Buddy leans against the bar and looks on, keeping up a drizzle of best-buddy jokes: amused, tolerant, charmingly cynical, pretending to be jealous. I watch him with great interest, as an actor would watch his understudy, noting refinements, ad libs, bits of business that indicate a different approach at work, for this was always my most natural role. This boy is pretty good. He is talking books with the Bartender—a very nice scene-stealing bit if the Bartender can play back to him. "And it suddenly hit me," the Best Buddy says, " 'Fuck' is really a beautiful word. I never thought about it before."

The Bartender nods silently. You know it and I know it, man. The Best Buddy catches The Hero's eye and grins, spreading his hands like a conjuror. "Think about it," he says to The Hero. "It really is. 'Fuck' is a beautiful word." There is a delighted, somehow wistful daring in his voice that makes something go *click* in my head about Henry Miller. The Best Buddy has not been talking directly to The Girl, but she shakes her hair and smiles and says, "Why, sure!" This is the expensive model, guaranteed unshockable. Totally insulated.

They talk about their friends. The Best Buddy does most of the talking, and some of his stories are like little poems. The one about crazy Nancy, who was in bed with a man and got out of bed to go to the bathroom, cut her wrists open with a broken toothglass, and then went back into bed to her man. "He had the light out, and he reached over for her, and he felt something wet. . . ." They laugh, but it is not at all vulgar, unfeeling laughter. It is very well modulated and sounds older than they.

We drive to Kansas City the next
day, crossing the Missouri River
twice. I don't understand that
river. Both of us are glad to be
leaving the state: if Illinois was
pale and dry, the Missouri landscape seems almost bleached of
color, bled out somehow. The farms
along the road look lifeless, as if
they had no foothold in the land.
We pass through Kansas City,
Missouri, without ever seeing it,
except for a quick glimpse of the
riverfront from the highway.

Coming into the other Kansas
City, we pick up a motorcycle escort—three teenagers on Hondas.
They drive alongside of us, curious
and quite courteous, all the way
into town, leaning close to ask the
usual questions about Jenny and
Couchette. The boy riding abreast
of me is dark-haired and heavy-set,
with dandruffy sideburns. When
Phil and I see a promising side
street to park on, the three kids
turn in with us and stop when we

42

do. It is about four o'clock, and the street is sunny and quiet, once the five engines are still.

We chat with the motorcycle kids for a while, standing hipsprung with our hands in our pockets, enlarging on our travels, gradually sliding into Routine B-1, which is somewhat more masculine and less cuddly than the basic approach. It is practiced more generally on men than on women and seems to work best when delivered in our "scooter drawl." This is, I think, our own idea of all-purpose American speech: somewhat Southern, somewhat Western, part hip, part hillbilly, hoping for a vaguely Midwestern effect, and not very New England at all. "Jus' ramblin' roun' lookin' at things. Buy guitars and sell 'em—play 'em if we're really hurtin' for money. Stay someplace if we like it, move on if we don't. Camp out a lot, cook out, jus' take things easy and wander along." The effect of about fifteen yards of that is more soporific than seductive, but its main purpose, which we have almost ceased to recognize, is to allay the mistrust our eyes and voices have been causing since we were children.

"Wouldn't know where the hockshops are, would you?" Phil asks the motorcycle boys. The dark-haired one points silently over our shoulders. We have parked in front of Harry's Loan Office, and the windows are strung with so many guitars that the instruments look like toys, like decorations, like candies. We laugh our *woops, hur-hur-hur* laugh and go inside.

Harry's is a very big place, as big as a Woolworth's but more spacious. Except for the three cashiers' windows at the back of the store, it might as easily be a sporting-goods store as a pawnshop. A gray-haired, monochromatic sort of man comes forward to meet us. "Hello, boys. What can I do for you?"

"Well, we're just looking for old guitars, mostly," Phil answers—or is it me? In how many shops have we opened like that? in what towns? who remembers? The gray-haired man smiles. "By all means. Look at them, take

them down, play with them, fondle them, love them . . ."
He leads us over to a rack of guitars, calling a boy to
bring in the ones in the window, and leaves us with
them. There are never many people in the store at once
—at any given moment the help out-numbers the
clientele—but there are always a few coming and going,
mostly old Negroes and young Mexicans. The Negroes
have faces like graves, but the faces of the Mexicans,
even the children, are wrenched and broken with bitterness. The children seem to scramble along sideways,
like crabs.

Several of the guitars are older than the sort we
usually find, but none of them are especially attractive.
There is one very old Gibson, much smaller than
average and shaped almost like a nineteenth-century
"lady's guitar"; stroked, it has a sound like an old zither,
distant and jangling. It needs new strings and more
repairs than we would know how to give it. I am almost
relieved when we put it back in the rack and turn toward the door—one day more, and the costly darling
not met! I do want to find her, perhaps even to stumble
onto the little pocket of Martins and Gibsons Phil day-
dreams about, but not right away. *When? I don't know.
Not just yet.*

A pleasant-faced girl and a jowly man with shrewd
eyes are standing at the door, looking out at Jenny and
Couchette. We are the only people in the store who
could possibly be the owners, and they also begin to ask
questions, the man about the scooters, but the girl
about the journey. Both of us are silently reluctant to go
out into the late-afternoon sun again and start looking
for a campsite. We are tired and strangely dispirited,
for no understood reason.

"Boy, that's a great way to travel," the girl says ex-
citedly. "You don't know how I envy you. I used to camp
out all the time when I was going to school. I'd get in
my little plane, and I'd sneak off somewhere and just
camp out when it got dark, sleep under the wing. I

44

loved it." Neither of us really takes in that mention of an airplane, but it is nice to be able actually to talk to a girl without too much offhand preening going on. Likable girl—with her short curly blond hair, thin pink cheeks, and wide mouth, she looks amazingly like a young prostitute named Monique who was my first friend-to-talk-to in Paris. She was a likable girl too, almost as new to the city as I was, but slightly less bewildered.

The jowly man points to the New York license plates on our scooters. "You boys from the city?" he asks. His accent is almost New York but not quite, maybe Jersey. "Where you from, Brooklyn? Bronx. Jewish? Jewish. And you're going to Los Angeles, San Francisco, on those things? San Francisco. A couple of Yiddisher boys from New York going to San Francisco on a couple of motorcycles. God *damn!*" He has been speaking quietly, but that last word almost shivers the windows. He turns around and begins to bellow for the other clerks. "Charley! Charley, you animal, come over here! Jerry, you want to see what real men look like, come here, come on! Abel, you mean, miserable old man, come out of that cage and meet some free people!" It is joyous roaring, magnificent roaring, the Hallelujah Chorus of roaring, and it scares the living hell out of us, especially when every head in the store, cashier and customer, turns to discover who these brave, free people may be. But the girl smiles reassuringly at us and says, "Leon, Leon, stop yelling. You can't eat them." It is some kind of a private joke between them, for he stops yelling and starts to laugh.

The other cashiers do come over one by one, Charley, Jerry, and Mr. Abel. Charley is in his forties, balding and nervous, with a gambler's black mustache. Jerry is the boy who brought the guitars in for us, a tall friendly-looking kid of eighteen or so. Mr. Abel is a thin old man, quite old, with clear, papery skin in which the lines seem to be drawn with a big black pencil, as though he were a young actor trying clumsily to make himself look old. Walking appears to be very painful to him.

45

Leon walks around and around us and the others, stops to say "God damn, two Yiddisher boys from the Bronx," and walks around us again. "Two Yiddisher boys from New York going cross-country on those things. That's what I keep telling you, Jerry, that's what men are supposed to do. That's what I'd do if I wasn't such a fat, scared slob. Boy, it takes a New York Jew to do something like that." He considers the matter and then adds, "Maybe a West Coast Jew too. I know some tough Jews on the Coast." He thinks it over once more and says, obviously making a determined effort to be fair, "Maybe Chicago too."

Through all this Phil and I stare at each other with wonder and horror. Nothing frightens us more than to be taken seriously, and about the time Leon says, "Damn, that takes real guts," the growing need to set this particular man straight, even though we go on lying to the rest of the world, overrides Phil's consideration for useful old Routine B-1.

"The word is not 'guts,'" he protests earnestly. "The word is 'stupid.'"

"Maybe 'crazy,'" I suggest, "if you want to be kind." It is, after all, a perfectly good routine.

"That's all right," Leon says seriously, "that's all right now. You got to be crazy to be a man these days. Listen, I know. I used to do things like that myself, after I got out of the Army. I was pretty crazy." The girl nods vigorously but does not speak.

Phil and I have not played guitars since we left Ann Arbor, and all we really hope for from this welcome is a chance to sit down and play for a while. The request is received with delight by Leon and the other clerks. "Help yourselves, help yourselves," they chorus, shooing us affectionately back toward the guitar rack, while Leon shouts, "Jerry, get the guitars out of the window again and let the gentlemen choose their weapons." Charley pats my shoulder and whispers, "If you break a string or something, don't worry, it's on the house."

I pick up an old jazz guitar which has a fair tone and will do as well as any for rhythm accompaniment. Phil finds a rather characterless Martin. We tune to each other and begin to play—"Crawdad" first, which is a mistake. "Crawdad" is a song to be played when relaxing at the end of a long, productive day, and we are both too tense and excited to have any fun with it. We play some Brassens, which the girl likes, but which makes the men respectfully restless, even enthusiastic Leon. Phil and I react very strongly to the moods of our audiences and often fall into a broad, sloppy style to hold their attention. This is beginning to happen when, for no reason, I remember one of my mother's favorite songs, "Der Rebbe Elimelech," which is a kind of Yiddish "Old King Cole." I start singing it, muffling the words when I am not sure of them, which is often. Phil picks it up very quickly, although we have never played it together, lacing the rich minor-key melody with sharp, tart runs, making the Martin sound almost like a balalaika. By the last chorus, it is dancing between our guitars like *der rebbe* himself, and no one in the sudden crowd around us is more amazed and delighted than we are.

Except possibly Mr. Abel. He leans against a counter full of blackjacks, wagging his head, shuffling his feet, his smile stained with physical pain. Once he nudges the beaming Leon and whispers, "You understand the Jewish?"

Leon does not turn his head. "Some. I forgot a lot."

"I understand Jewish," says Mr. Abel. When we end "Der Rebbe Elimelech" he asks immediately, "Please, you could play some more Jewish?" His voice is high and hoarse, with an oddly carrying quality.

Phil looks inquiringly at me. "You got any more? I didn't know you had any." Me neither, and although I would love to play some more Jewish songs for Mr. Abel, I can't think of a single one. My mother sings snatches of a pretty song called "Margaritkes," but it's a long song and I know only bits of it. Then, just as an experiment, I

47

begin to play the introduction to a French lullaby called
"Tire l'Aiguille." Phil laughs aloud at the first bar and
picks up his harmony. It is one of the first songs we ever
played together and, French lyric or no, it has an unmis-
takably Yiddish melody, schmaltzy and sad, and una-
shamed of either quality, all the way to a chorus that
goes:

> Lai, lai, lai, lai,
> Tire, tire l'aiguille, ma fille . . .

I have always wondered about the origins of that song.
The Arabs have a parody of it, which adds to my suspicion.

I wonder no longer after one look at Mr. Abel. He does
not actually begin to dance before God, with his eyes
on the ground and his hands behind his back, putting his
feet one after the other and giving little jumps, like a child
playing hopscotch, but I think he would if his body would
let him. Closing his eyes, he chants the Yiddish words,
often losing the melody but never in doubt of finding it
again. He waves his hands as gently and rhythmically as
if he were conducting the movement of grass in the wind.
The other clerks look on, amused and a little puzzled;
Phil and I play "Tire l'Aiguille" with complete seriousness
(we are almost always mocking it, at least a little), and
Mr. Abel sings and dances to himself.

"Hoo, you could smell the chicken fat bubbling," Leon
says when we finish the song. The gray-haired man is
looking at us now, and he waves Charley and the girl
back into the cages, but he does not come over to us,
either to listen or to break it up. Mr. Abel's eyes open
slowly and close again when Phil begins "Tumbalalaika,"
which both of us and, surprisingly, Leon knows. But in
the middle of the song Mr. Abel turns abruptly and
moves heavily out of the pawnshop, without speaking or
looking back. Phil and I are surprised and oddly hurt.
"Tumbalalaika" trails off and ends before the end with
Mr. Abel gone. We begin to play the blues.

Phil plays good blues, although an adolescence spent trying to sound like Josh White will mark any man. I play the blues only well enough for the ears of people who have never had them. We are more relaxed now, and together we surprise ourselves a couple of times. The pawnshop people are enjoying us, anyway; they hurry away at the beckon of the gray-haired man, but they always come back. Two Negro men stop on their way out of the store to listen to us. Their faces are polite and attentive; they seem to be waiting for something to happen. They leave quietly after a little while.

Charley waits for us to finish before he asks shyly, "Do you boys know 'She was only a pawnbroker's daughter, but oh, how she could hock'?" It is a gift, not a request, and we meet it with the proper helpless grins and groans. I offer him the one about the jockey's daughter in return. Leon has vanished somewhere, and we are debating striking up "The Ball at Killynoor" to fetch him back when Mr. Abel returns, carrying two containers of coffee and bags full of doughnuts and, of all things, *Hamantaschen*, the three-cornered Purim pastries. "I think they would be hungry, so much traveling," he says to everyone and no one. We have an awkward time of it trying to eat, drink, and play High Holiday music for Mr. Abel all at once, but we do the best we can.

Mr. Abel's CARE package is hardly out of the way when Leon reappears with another shipment. "Eat, eat, my friends," he thunders. "Seeing the world and playing guitars is hungry work." Leon knows about hungry work. He talks about food the way other men talk about women —not all other men, either, but the great sensualists who enjoy women with their whole beings. When Leon talks about encounters with wonderful meals, it comes out like Casanova reminiscing, counting noses or whatever Casanova counted. Leon remembers cities by their restaurants, years by what he could afford to eat ("The ground-beef year wasn't so bad if you used your imagination, but those first couple of years after I got married—boy, two poultry years in a row!"), streets by outlandish food stores, birthdays and other celebrations by sheer tonnage acquired, girls by how they fed him. A nice noisy man who has been places and eaten things.

He shows us a snapshot of his six-year-old son; the picture is actually a photograph of an oil painting done from photographs. Even in the rosy blandness of the photo, three times removed from its living subject, the boy looks handsome and sweet-natured. "He's mentally retarded," Leon says. "Not a lot, not like some of the other kids you see. He can do a lot of things."

Everyone talks to us this afternoon. One of the things that has struck both of us deeply on this trip, in spite of —or perhaps because of—the fleeting contacts we have made, is how badly people want to talk to someone. They cannot make anyone hear them unless they scream, but they seldom really scream. Instead, they put letters in bottles and throw them into the sea of strangers, and the letters always seem to say, "Save me, save me."

Jerry is going into the Navy, but he doesn't really want to. Charley's wife sounds like a mean woman. Mr. Hagar's son (Mr. Hagar is a Negro, an old friend of Mr. Abel's, and often drops in to the pawnshop to visit with him) is a musician touring with a jazz group and writes letters from Denmark and Holland to his mother, but never to his father. We sit and listen and finger the guitars now and then, and feel unbelievably foolish and insensitive, understanding nothing and smiling as though we did.

We talk longest with Leon, because he is the head clerk and more or less his own master in the pawnshop, and with the girl, because she is the gray-haired man's daughter, Harry's daughter, the pawnbroker's daughter. We never do learn the name. That story about the plane was quite true. She used to go to the University of New Mexico—she graduated last year—and she always flew back and forth between Albuquerque and Kansas City in her own Piper Cub. "I know how you must feel about

50

those scooters of yours," she says. "I was crazy about that plane. Sometimes I'd just want to get away from the whole world and I couldn't, because I had a test or something, or I had to write a paper. I'd go out to the airport and I'd sit with my plane for a while and just look at her. It helped a lot, you'd be surprised."

"Do you still have the plane?" I ask. She shakes her head, smiling crookedly. "No, I had to sell her. The upkeep on a plane is just tremendous, the gas and the oil and the taxes and airport fees and everything. It just got to be too much."

"*Zoom,*" Leon growls softly, stunt-flying his hands. "*Zoom, zoom,* her old man just loved all that zooming." The girl frowns at him, and he shrugs and grounds his hands. "You ought to go with them," he says. "You ought to get up on one of those scooters and go to California with them."

"A comfortable ride and all the roast-beef hash you can eat," Phil offers, and the girl laughs. "Don't tempt me." She says that very often. She lives at home now and works part time for her father, whose one desire appears to be to see her married as soon as possible to someone as safe as possible. "No beards," she says, smiling at us. "No scooters. Just conform and live like everybody else. My mother's teaching me to play mah-jongg. She says I'll need it."

"The thin edge of the wedge," I say foolishly. The girl sighs and looks down at her hands. She has good long fingers, but she bites her nails. "The trouble is," she says, "that you fight and fight *against* playing mah-jongg, *against* going to this party, *against* joining this club or that club, *against* staying home tonight because somebody's coming over, against all the conformity and everything, and after a while you start getting tired. Fighting against things all the time, it just wears you out and you never get anywhere."

"Hold out!" we cry to her, waving ourselves at her like banners. "Don't let them get you, don't let them make you do things you don't want to do, hold out, hold out, holdoutholdoutholdoutholdoutholdout."

She reassures us. "Oh yes, I will, I will, but sometimes I don't know what I'm doing it for. I can't even grow a beard."

Seeing us talking to his daughter so long, the gray-haired man comes over to us at last. He is pleasant and polite and never suggests that we may be taking up too much of his help's time to no purpose. When he learns that we have decided to sleep in a hotel tonight—Phil's hip is acting up again—he thinks for a moment, waves aside Leon's suggestion of a cheap brownstone, and then calls to Charley in the cage, "Charley, you think you could let these boys sleep at your place one night?"

Charley, it turns out, actually owns a small hotel near the river. Behind the barred window his round face is a brawl of emotions. He says hesitantly, "Well, I wouldn't mind, Harry, but I honestly don't think it's safe. I mean, it's in sort of a rough neighborhood and there's a lot of rough customers living there all the time. I'd worry about them if they went to the hotel, Harry, I really would. I don't go there much myself, except when I have to."

Throughout the lazy, easy afternoon faces have been going in and out of the store, fierce, hurt, helpless faces that must surely belong in another story, faces that cut like sharks' fins through the kindness and friendship that Phil and I have been feeling around us. I stare at them now, wondering if any of them live in Charley's hotel in the rough neighborhood. Charley the absentee landlord. The *Post* would expose him if he lived in New York. I say, "Well, we'll try this place Leon mentioned. It sounds pretty inexpensive."

Charley is relieved and apologetic. "It's not the money," he tells us earnestly. "You could sleep there for nothing, the money doesn't matter. But there's a new manager there now, and he just doesn't bother to keep order. When the other fellow was running the place it was different, it was a nice safe place, I wouldn't have worried a minute about sending you there. But this new man, I guess he just doesn't care. I'm always talking to him about it, writing him letters. He doesn't care."

Phil and I leave the store, promising to come back after we find a hotel. But we have hardly gotten halfway up the block, barely begun to explain to each other how silly and amazing life is, when Leon comes running up behind us and shoves a five-dollar bill into Phil's hand. "The old man's daughter," he says with a curiously abashed grin. "She said to give you this. Said she didn't want to do it in the store with everybody there." He reminds us again to come back before the store closes, and lumbers off down the street, a fat round-shouldered man who seems smaller going away than he really is.

"This is insane," Phil says slowly. "This is absolutely insane. She felt sorry for us. Think that over. The boss's daughter felt sorry for us." He rubs the bill between his fingers as if he were at market, testing it for ripeness.

"Well, why not? We're pretty pitiable objects, you come right down to it. I think between us we're at least a ten-dollar pitiable. Incidentally, maybe you better let me hold that, being the treasurer and all."

"Touch that money and count your fingers," he says absently. "The thing is, damn it, we weren't playing pitiable. We didn't talk poormouth, we didn't make wistful little jokes about beans and beans, we didn't even go into Routine B. We didn't want a thing from her, and she gave us five dollars. Jesus, Beagle, maybe we really are pitiable little wanderers. Maybe it's all real." It bothers him for a couple of blocks.

The hotel gives us a good room for $3.50, leaving us $1.50 of pure largess for some sort of meal. We amble back toward Harry's Loan Office, singing what we remember of the "Kansas City Blues."

Goin' to Kansas City, sorry but I can't take you.
Goin' to Kansas City, sorry but I can't take you.

53

Ain't a thing in Kansas City
that a gal like you could do.

Whenever we look at each other we burst out laughing and have to start over.

Jerry is already beginning to turn the lights out in the pawnshop when we get back. We try to thank the girl for the money without actually saying the word, and she accepts our edited gratitude with graciousness. "That's all right," she says. "I know what it's like, traveling without money. It's an awful feeling sometimes." Charley has been waiting around to make sure we found a room, and he sighs with real relief when we tell him we have. "You wouldn't have liked that hotel," he says. "All sorts of people—it's gotten so you about have to speak a couple of languages just to get by."

"We speak a couple of languages," Phil answers. Charley smiles tightly and shakes his head. "You don't speak their language, believe me." He shakes hands with us, says, "Charley Schuster," and goes home.

Mr. Abel is standing in front of a mirror, putting on a collar and tie. It seems strange to think of Mr. Abel wearing such a thing as a tie. He catches sight of us in the mirror, smiles his slow, aching smile, and says, "Remember, you find what you look for," picking up the thread of a conversation we had been having with him earlier until Harry called him away. "You find just what you look for," he tells us. "Listen, I know. I had once a friend, a rabbi, Conservative, and this rabbi, he went to Paris, so a month, two months, I don't see him. Then one day he comes back and he comes by my house, and he says to me, 'Abel, the things I saw in Paris you wouldn't believe, I couldn't tell you. Terrible, filthy, so filthy I couldn't tell you, I would be ashamed. I would be ashamed to tell you the way those people live in Paris.' And do you know how I answered him?" He does not pause, not even when his collar stud slips from his fingers and clicks on the floor. Harry bends down to pick it up.

Mr. Abel goes on. "I say, 'Listen to me, Rabbi, listen. I'm an older man than you are, I want to tell you something. You find always what you look for, always. You want to see, I don't know, bad people, bad women, thieves, drinking, murder, filthy, you would see all of that you want. It is in your head what you want to see, bad women, gambling, you took it to Paris with you. But for me, if I would go to Paris, do you know what I would see?"

The girl giggles. Harry is muttering, "Abel, here, Abel, you dropped your tie thing, your stud." He is curiously shy with the old man, and it suddenly occurs to me that they must be related.

Mr. Abel does not even turn his head. " 'I would see books and great paintings, I would go to museums, I would go somewhere I could hear great music. That is what *I* would do in Paris, that is what *I* would see, because that is what I want to see. The other things, the bad women, you could see them if you want to, but myself, I don't want to see them, so for me they are not there. I don't see them. You take it all with you, what you want to see. I would see good people, great paintings.' " The collar stud pushes against his closed fingers like a moth against a lighted window.

"Abel," Harry says, "how about we continue the debate outside?" Embarrassed but determined, he pries the mist-colored fingers open one by one, drops the collar stud into the palm, and pats the fingers around it again. He helps Mr. Abel put his coat on and is about to shepherd everyone out of the door when he asks suddenly, "Could you boys use a couple of caps?" We blink at him, and he produces two fungus-like objects, one brown with tiny black spots, the other as fuzzily yellow as a gaslamp. "I have no idea how we got them," he says. "I wish you'd take them." We cram them jauntily onto our heads and look at each other with an awe greater than our incipient hysteria. We look like two villains from the frontispiece of a Tom Swift book. "Schmucks with earlaps," I say softly. Phil nods. "We finally made it."

Outside, it is beginning to get dark, and the air feels like autumn somehow. Mr. Abel shakes hands with both of us and says, *"Sei gesund."* He adds something else in Yiddish that neither of us catches, but we chuckle and nod and say, *"Sei gesund."* A young woman comes by in a car to pick him up; he bends his body into the front seat, and they are gone.

"Come with me, comrades," Leon directs us. We bid overhasty good-bys to Harry and his daughter and follow Leon a block down the street, where he ushers us grandly into a small delicatessen. "These are the Yiddisher boys I told you about," he says to the proprietor and his wife, who are the only people there. "I want you to stuff them like turkeys, because they have a long way to go and they don't eat enough. Tell me how much they ate tomorrow, and don't take their money, not if they beg you. They're travelers and musicians."

When we try to thank him, which is done by saying, "Jesus, Leon, we couldn't," he thumps our shoulders, sits us down at a table, and tells us, "Listen, I'm the one ought to be making this trip, not you. Any man'd turn down a free meal deserves to be thirty-nine years old, clerking in a hock-shop calls itself a loan office." He shakes hands with us, tells us a quick dirty joke for the road, and leaves, turning around once on the sidewalk to wave.

We dine tonight on pastrami sandwiches, potato salad, and Royal Crown Cola, all of which the owner's wife keeps replenishing before we are nearly through with the previous plenishment. They sit with us while we eat, as one does with guests, seeming more inquisitive about our parents' reactions to the trip than about the thing itself. Did they object to it? Would we have gone if they had objected? Did we let them know where we were all the time? Would we be going back to New York to see them? They themselves have two sons in the service and a daughter who will be graduating from college in June. The daughter is brilliant and beautiful and remarkably mature for her age. The eldest son has decided that he will go to college when he gets out of the Army. These two are the safe children; safe for now, at least, drifting between waterfall and waterfall. But the younger son— he is neither beautifully nor officially brilliant nor noticeably mature, and he is not safe at all, and so neither are they.

"He joined the Army between lunch and supper," the mother says. "Made up his mind to it and *bang*—there he was, in the Army. He said he wanted to be with his brother, but they haven't even seen each other since he went in. He's sorry about it now." There is no triumph in her voice.

"If he was here right now," the father says, "you couldn't keep him from going to California with you. He'd just get himself a little scooter and go, and you couldn't stop him, you'd have to kill him to make him stay home. We wouldn't hear a thing from him till we got a postcard from—where are you going, San Francisco? He'd like that. He'd be crazy to go to San Francisco."

We reassure them for our supper. The boy will be all right. He's aimless, so many people are, really, he needs to find something he likes to do. That's the key to it— you wouldn't want him to spend his whole life doing something he hated, just so you'd know where he was. We're not much older than he is, we know what it's like. Kids snap out of things like that very suddenly; they seem to settle down overnight. My own brother . . . And then the mother says something very surprising for a mother, surprising especially to two hungry experts in painless honesty. "I don't know if I want that, he should settle down just like that, the way he joined the Army. How do I know what he should do?"

They refuse flatly when we try to pay them, and I think that it has very little to do with Leon's admonition. "You do something good for somebody, it comes back to you," the mother says. "If my son was doing something like you're doing, I'd be hoping all the time somebody he never heard of would give him a meal. Maybe now you'll do something for somebody, and one day they'll remember and do something for my son. It goes around like that. You have to do things for people."

The father gives us a piece of advice before we leave. "Sometime when you're in a strange town like this, and you don't know anybody, you don't have any money, what you should do is to go to the rabbi. You say, 'Rabbi, look, we're two Jewish boys trying to get to California, we've got nothing to eat and no place to sleep, what should we do?' The rabbi would take care of you. I'm telling you, that's the way to do it. Rabbis take care of their own people."

I have a sudden marvelous vision of the two of us presenting our displaced selves and our Orthodox beards on the front lawn of some young crew-cut, assimilated, adjusted, Fromm-reading Reform rabbi. But I think also of the Russia where my parents were born, and of the New York where they grew up, where the rabbis did take care of their people as well as they could, because there was no one else at all to do it. We thank the father and promise to take the idea under consideration; which we do, for that is not an idea to crumple up and throw away. When we say good-by to them, the mother gives us two bags to take along for tomorrow—apples and cupcakes. "You can eat them now if you want to," she says.

It is quite dark now, and the streets of this part of Kansas City are not well lighted, but we could find our way in a blackout by the foxfire glow of our caps. Two girls passing us giggle like scraping knives, and one looks back to call, "Now *there's* two real hepcats!" We look at each other without expression, neither wanting to speak first. Phil says slowly, "My God, have you listened to all the things people have been saying to us today?" He counts them off on his fingers. "Kindness, freedom, manhood, how to take the broad view—I wouldn't believe the things people say if I read them in a book. Damn, what an incredible world. I want to go home."

"It's like something a friend of mine said about Western songs. He was from a little town in East Texas, and he grew up listening to I guess almost nothing but these mournful, sentimental songs. Love. Death. God. Honor. Dogs. Mother. Children. All the clichés, every one of them. He said you wouldn't believe how many people in this country lived their lives by those songs, and he wasn't laughing at them either. What should people live their lives by?"

"What's in it for me?" Phil says. "Serves you right. Nothing for nothing. Credit makes enemies, let's stay friends. Something I can do to help? and don't ask me. That's too bad, I know just how you feel. I'd help you but the boss wouldn't like it. You left out a whole mess of clichés, boy, you want to write songs people live their miserable lives by."

"What nice people. God *damn!*"

"Yeah. Gets so you can't rely on anybody."

In front of the darkened pawnshop the girl, the pawn-broker's daughter whose name we never learned, stands by herself. She looks, in the dim light of our caps, even more the way I remember Monique, wandering and wait-ing around the Place de l'Opéra in just this kind of light. We invite her to a movie and, when she turns out not to be free, offer to take her wherever she wants to go. But she laughs and thanks us and shakes her head, no. "Some-one's picking me up in a car," she tells us. "I'm going to a bridge party."

We look at her with so much disapproval—quite real and arrogant, for all its playfulness—that she has to say, "Well, I couldn't get out of it, and it's not like mah-jongg."

I think we both feel like apologizing, but instead we say, "Don't forget, don't let them get you. Hold out."

"Oh, I will," she answers. "I'm no conformist, don't worry about me." Standing in her father's doorway, smil-ing hesitantly in the half-light, she tells us a secret. "I still sneak off to the airport sometimes and fly. I rent a plane. Nobody knows. Have a lovely trip," she says. "Boy, I wish I were going with you."

"The offer's still open," Phil says. Is he joking? Is it real? Hard to tell with us. Sometimes I think we'd like to take everybody who wants to run away along with us on Jenny and Couchette. Sometimes I know we wouldn't. We'd have had a nice quiet Ark.

"Don't tempt me," she says, laughing sadly, and we don't any more. We drive the scooters to the hotel through the early-quiet streets and unload them in the parking lot. There is a red Honda parked near the entrance—rare to see more two-wheeled vehicles than ours in a hotel's lot —but we give it no special thought going upstairs. We are both very tired. The trip is beginning to catch up with us now.

In the hotel room Phil sits down in a chair, holding a glass of water in his hand and staring straight ahead. I sprawl on the bed and begin to read the Triptik. There is a knock on the door. Phil opens it, and one of the motorcycle boys enters. The dark sideburned kid who rode next to me. He lives in this hotel; it's his Honda out in the lot, and he recognized our scooters. Standing up, he's no bigger than we are, but you could play baseball with his bones and live all winter off a slab of face steak. His name is Earl.

"Thought you guys might like to come for a ride," he says. I am hesitant, thinking he means on the scooters, but he has a car too. His face is tough enough to suggest that he might want to spend a pleasant evening like this kicking over fire hydrants, but all Earl wants to do is to get some hamburgers and maybe ride around town a little. Phil and I shrug Sure, why not, at each other; obviously the day has no intention of letting go of us yet. Thanks, Earl. Couple of hamburgers'd sit real well about now. Routine B-1 again, automatic as a refrigerator cutting in. And after we'd spent all afternoon remembering how to be New York Jewish.

Earl owns a bright red Corvette—where the hell does he get the money, a kid his age, living in a cheap hotel? That bright red motorcycle isn't off a box of corn-flakes, either. Earl, it turns out, is a railroad brakeman on the Missouri side. Kansas City is still one of the country's largest railroad centers, and a brakeman can make a lot of money if he watches where he puts his toes. Besides, Earl doesn't spend very much of the money he makes. There isn't much he wants. He eats, he pays his rent, he buys clothes when he needs them, he goes to movies sometimes. He sends some of the money home—home is a very small town in northern Kansas—to be put aside for his younger sister's education. He owns a good rifle and a couple of traps, a phonograph and a lot of records, mostly Latin American dance music with some rock-and-roll, and he owns the red Honda and the red Corvette. The car is not quite paid for yet, but it will be. He has lived in this hotel since he first came to Kansas City two years ago, when he was eighteen.

We learn all this in the course of a quarter hour's driving around this town that gets surprisingly dark at night. Earl drives the Corvette very much as if it were a motor-cycle, pointing it in and out of traffic like a darning needle, stopping for lights at the last possible moment, throwing her into low gear on downgrades with a suddenness to make her sigh hoarsely, accelerating so fast as to cover the block between green light and red light entirely in first gear. Phil and I are so tired and limp that we feel oddly calm; in an auto accident, what could happen to a couple of drenched postage stamps? Earl is talking about hunting, about being up very early in the morning to inspect a trapline. "Best smell in the world comes off a field of alfalfa right about dawn," he says. "Man, love that smell. *Look* out, you jackass!"—this last to a truck looming above the Corvette like a thunderhead over a ladybird. "Best smell in the world," Earl says.

We stop at a drive-in to buy hamburgers and eat them

in the car. Earl is curious about both our trades, but especially about Phil's painting, because his sister also draws, and he is very proud of his sister. "I didn't know you could make a real living from that kind of stuff," he says. "I thought it was just for fun, like a hobby." Phil grins and says, "Don't let it bother you."

Unlike most of the people we have met on the way, Earl has never wanted to visit New York. He is afraid of the city and does not pretend not to be. "They give you dope," he says. "A lot of guys told me how they make you take dope and drugs and everything." He is very earnest; in his incongruously soft and polite voice he says, "I tell you guys, if somebody ever came up to me in the street and tried to make me take that dope, I'd kill him. Boy, I'd just kill him." We explain to him that nobody forces you to take dope, not in the way he means, that the choice is very nearly yours alone. Earl is puzzled—how could anyone develop the craving of his own free will? *why?*—but he is not dogmatic, and he always listens to the answers to questions. "I always thought they made you take it," he says and laughs.

A little later he asks with great hesitancy, "I don't mean to be nosy, but I'd sure like to know—do you guys believe in God?" The question comes completely out of nowhere, but not really. You can play the lean-souled drifter in casual search of the truth for only so long before someone calls you on it.

There is a long silence, quite a long one. The last time I told a comparative stranger that I didn't believe in God he pushed me off the sidewalk for being a Jew. Earl seems a perfectly nice guy, but people do the strangest things, and it's his car. I do not want to offend Earl. Phil, presumably off his own working experience as a chicken atheist, does not want to offend Earl. And Earl, who is surely not one to ask such questions of hamburger acquaintances, obviously does not want to offend us. It is a very long silence.

"Well," I begin at last, "um. Well. Well, not in or-
ganized religion. I mean, we never were church people."

Phil leads a wavering flank maneuver. "You take the
Bible," he suggests. "Now there's a lot of great poetry in
the Bible, wonderful language. But too many people take
it as absolute truth, you know, the word of God, there
it is. Now, *that* I don't believe."

In and away, rear covered, diversion completely suc-
cessful. "No, I don't believe that either," Earl agrees.
"The way I feel about the Bible, I think it's like a book
of instructions, how to live, like a code. You read it long
enough, and it'll tell you how to live right. And all the
stories in it, they're to help you read it right. You're not
supposed to take them for real, they're like examples. I
been thinking about it a lot." He looks from one to the
other of us genuinely eager for our opinions in a way few
of our college professors ever were.

We react very much as if we were in college. "Sure,"
Phil says. "Hell, you can't get much better advice than
the Golden Rule." I exhibit my acquaintance with the
Christian part of the Bible by relating the story of the
woman taken in adultery. " 'He that is without sin among
you, let him cast the first stone.' Boy, that's the way to tell
those hypocritical bastards. Oh, yeah, you can learn a
lot from the Bible, Earl, never doubt it." Phil and I are
catching fire from each other. We'll convert Earl yet.

So we drive amiably and aimlessly through the silent,
empty streets of Kansas City, Kansas, talking, pretending
to watch for pawnshops, listening to the car radio. We
point out Harry's Loan Office to Earl and relate our
afternoon's adventure, trying not to make it seem as if this
kind of welcome attends us everywhere the wind takes us.
Earl listens carefully, nods, grins, agrees, yes, those were
good people, that was a good way to treat strangers.
"You got to watch those people, though," he warns us
jovially. "They're Jews; they'll take every nickel you've
got if you ain't watching them every minute. I know those
guys."

Woops. Go back three spaces. People always say the wrong thing if you let them. "Earl," we begin firmly. "Look, Earl."

Earl is unruffled to find that we are Jewish, and completely unembarrassed at being clearly, if somewhat cautiously, rebuked. He does not even bother to say, "No offense," which is his emergency phrase if he feels that he has said something wrong, whether he understands his sin or not. It never crosses his mind that he may have given offense; we must know that he meant no harm; as well apologize for saying, "Hot enough for you?" "Sure, they're fine," he says cheerfully, "they're okay. You just got to watch them. I know."

He drives us near the riverfront, and we see the lights of Kansas City, Missouri, shining across the water. We can almost see the Triptik's dotted state line stuttering down the middle of the river: on our side the dark water is almost invisible by contrast with the Missouri side, which glows as though schools of jeweled fish were milling near the shore. The Kansas City across the river is about four times the size of this one, Earl tells us. "It's too big for me," he says. "I wouldn't live there if you gave me a million. This place is too big too, but you get used to it. I used to get so lonely, the time I first got here, I just felt like nobody all the time." He has friends now, and possessions, and places that know him when he walks in. "I like it okay now," he says, "but I wouldn't want to live nowhere bigger than this."

"Why should you?" Phil asks. "No city's any better than this. Stay here. Drive your motorcycle."

"Well, I don't figure to stay here forever," Earl says. "Someday I'll go home." We are silent, and he must feel that we are mocking him in our minds, for he adds after a while, "I never had much desire to go traveling. In foreign lands."

We say good-by to Earl back at the hotel, for he will be gone to work hours before we wake. "Wish you guys could stay around a couple of days," he says. "I got a friend who plays the electric guitar."

Can't, Earl. Time to be rambling. Old road just a-callin' . . . "Well, take care of yourselves," he says. "Hope I see you again." His handshake is as dry and rough as bark, and as light.

Phil and I lie awake in bed for a while, talking about the day. "People have the damnedest splits in them," Phil says. "Everybody we met today. The old man, talking about seeing what you want to see, and how you look for the good things and don't look at the bad, and all the time saving and damning, good or bad, this or that. Nice Charley, making a little money out of a rough neighborhood, writing letters to a manager who just doesn't care. He really did want to help. You know he'd have let us stay in that hotel of his if we hadn't found a place. Harry's daughter, wishing conformity had another name. Nobody lying to us, everybody saying good things and believing them, and all the little arrangements going on in the head. I hate having to figure people."

"We do the same things, all of them, all the time. The arrangements take care of themselves. Like old Earl. Earl'll forget we're Jewish by lunchtime tomorrow, if he ever really believed it. Let me tell you about Pirandello."

"I'll hit you if you do. Don't ment me at this time of night."

A little later he says softly, "You want to hear the funny part?" I grumble a drowsy assent, being already a long way off. "Just suppose we hadn't been Jewish. Hooboy. No coffee, no confidences, no five dollars, no free meal, no philosophies of life, no little insights into humanity. They probably wouldn't even cash a traveler's check. We got ourselves adopted, all right, but we're damn lucky we knew the password. One of the very few we do know. I got half a mind to go back there and play them Christmas carols till hell won't have it."

Out of a half-sleep in which my dream is happening in the same world as the gray neon sign outside our window,

I ask him a very important question. He says irritably, "What? Are you awake?"

I am now, more or less, and it takes me a minute to remember what I asked him in the dream. "Oh. Yes. Phil, do you think, in the 'Kansas City Blues,' which Kansas City is it, here or there?"

"I don't know," he answers. "Whichever side we ain't on. Jesus God." I fall asleep.

DINER

SALINA

OAKLEY

LAUNDROMAT

LIMON

The next day is mean and cold and miserable from its inception, a perfectly useless day for anything except suicide by sleeping pills, a day that came out of the oven too soon. Late in the afternoon we pass through Fort Riley, which is strangely reminiscent of college living quarters as I remember them. But the image begins to turn menacing in a quiet, dusty way, as irresistibly as the face of a friend becomes a demon's face in a dream turning nightmare: here is a rifle range; over there, as carelessly double-parked as a scooter, is a small tank; on that distant field they are running at a tackling dummy, but the sunlight winks off lean metal. Trudging young men turn to watch us come racketing through, and they all have the same face, a bone face with no adolescent give to it. They all look at us in the same way as we sail foolishly by.

It is surely going to rain soon; the sky is sagging with plum-colored clouds. Phil wails a despairing question that I cannot hear but understand. "Salina!" I yell back at him, remembering the name of the next town. "We'll stop at Salina." He nods, and I hunch down behind Jenny's wind-screen, reaching back now and then to warm one numb hand or the other against her side.

Salina is surrounded by railroad tracks, like dry moats; we must bump over eight or ten sets of them to reach the center of town, and it really does feel like sneaking past fortifications. It is a dry, silent town, a little frightening in the way a particular small town, identical with so many others, can be frightening on a certain afternoon. The peo-ple we ask for directions smile and smile and back away. We find a cheap single room at a hotel the color of our aching ears, leave the scooters there, and go out into the main street to seek supper. Phil says, "Jesus, it's a small town. I guess everybody lives at the hotel."

"The Triptik says it's the biggest town between Topeka and Colorado Springs. Population's over forty thousand."

"Old Triptik lies worse than you do. I ain't seen enough people on the street to play double solitaire."

"No, the Triptik never lies. I think I see their error, though." I know the map very nearly by heart from study-ing it at night, wishing us a few pages nearer to the fold-out map of San Francisco, and I quote: " 'Four miles east of the city is Indian Burial Pit, which has yielded the skel-etal remains of a hundred and forty-six Indians and in-numerable artifacts.' Well, you see what happened. They got the population and the skeletal Indians completely turned around. I bet that's one hell of a burial pit, espe-cially with all those artifacts."

"Show more respect, white man, or raise my salary. One or the other."

A patrol car comes sliding up the street toward us, and a uniformed arm waves us to a stop. But we have already stopped, almost without thinking about it. We know about patrol cars. This is the first time we have been stopped since we left New York, but we have been expecting it for a long time.

There are two of them, as there always are, one young, one nearing middle age. The older one stays in the car; the young one, who was driving, gets out and walks slowly over to us. He looks just a touch embarrassed in his first steps, almost as though he had been pushed from behind, but he gets over it. "Afternoon," he says. "You boys aren't from around here."

No. We're just passing through, officer. Going to California.

"California, mm? Hitchhiking?" The eyes inspect us carefully, slowly enough to make sure that we realize how carefully we are being inspected. God, how they must practice; on each other, perhaps. No, sir. We have a couple of scooters.

"Going to California on scooters?" Why, he almost likes the idea. "That's quite a trip." The older cop moves closer to the window, drumming his fingertips against the side of the car. "Mm. You got any identification?"

Big, meaty hands that other one has. Real cop hands, thick, slap your head around backward and not feel a thing. Driver's licenses do?

They will do very well, and he knows it, but he makes a small production out of checking them, as though they might be obscene. That's all right, all cops do that, it's in the oath somewhere. He hands them back to me. "You say you're traveling on one scooter?"

He's just a little cop, really, not much bigger than we are. Not much older, either. *Un tout petit flic, a copele.* Two scooters, officer.

"Well." He seems to have run out of cop questions. "And you're just passing through town?"

We're staying in a hotel for the night. Show him the room key. We'll be leaving tomorrow.

"Where you going now?" His tone and his diction have become less official. But he never looks back at the other one.

Figured to get ourselves a spaghetti dinner.

"Spaghetti." He almost smiles. It's all right now.

Then the other one gets out of the car and comes toward us. He moves very silently. The young cop turns to him then and says, "They're just going on through, going to California," but the other one does not answer. His face is heavy, lumpy, colorless except for a bright swirl of broken veins on one cheekbone, as unmemorable as a news vendor's face, but for the blue cap that lends it line, but for the eyes. They are diamond-shaped, the color of cement, and not eyes at all but windows onto a blank stone wall beyond which there is no flight.

He speaks. "You boys got any money?" The terrible thing is that it might almost be a beggar's voice. The young cop will not look at him, or at us.

Not much cash. Traveler's checks. We show them our thin blue sheaves, and that, after all, is the end of it. Without moving, the other cop seems to have stepped back into shadow, disappeared except for his eyes, which still wait. The young one actually does smile—my lord, he looks like a camp counselor! "Okay, boys. Just checking." They climb back into their fuzzmobile and drive away. The other one's eyes brush over us once as they make a U-turn. He almost smiles himself, but it's not the same thing.

"That one would remember us," Phil murmurs. It is all either of us says about the encounter for a while, until we are through with supper. I suddenly realize that I am very much afraid to go out of the restaurant into the blue evening, and I say, "Phil, it's a dangerous world, just to walk around. It's a dangerous world."

He nods. "Damn lucky thing we had the scooters and the money. They were wondering if it was worth the trouble to pick us up for vagrancy. Might have, if we hadn't had the traveler's checks. Cash they could just grab, throw us in the can for as long as they liked. Nobody'd know where we were. Just lucky. Lucky that young cop wasn't a bad guy. It was the other one pushed him into stopping us. They pair them off like that, you know, so they embarrass each other. That other one. Oh, my God. I bet they broke him for something, and I bet I know what it was. Boy, lucky."

"Lucky we weren't vagrants," I say. "Lucky we weren't black." What I understand at that moment is unpaid-for; it will be gone after a good night's sleep in a warm bed. "If we'd been black," I say. "Jesus."

We leave Salina early and make almost two hundred miles, stopping often for Phil to do gouaches and pastels. We are in cattle country now, green and yellow, with a strange pinkness in the distant hills, and the Black Angus cows come close to the fences to watch Phil work. One of his gouaches, a tiny one of orange earth and blue road and telephone poles going away, pleases me, but he says I have a *Reader's Digest* mind. "Or they have yours. Hard to say."

We stop for lunch in Hays, in a tiny restaurant where the waitress reminds me frighteningly of Enid without really looking like her. Long hair, high cheekbones, a soft voice, a way of moving—I browse through an old newspaper and try not to stare at her. I seem to have spent a lot of my life trying not to stare at people and things.

There are two other men in the diner. Thirties, top-coated, with pink, large-pored faces. Southerners by their voices, but not Deep South, maybe Tennessee. They are telling the waitress jokes about Negroes in friendly, matter-of-fact voices. There is a joke about two Freedom Ride buses crashing and burning, and a joke about Mack Parker, who was lynched, and there is one about Emmett Till, the fourteen-year-old boy who was murdered in Mississippi for whistling at a white woman. "When they finally dredged that boy out of the river with all that tire chain around his neck, old deputy just looked down at him and said, 'Now, ain't that *just* like a nigger, tryin' to steal more chain than he could swim with?' " They laugh, and the waitress chuckles softly as she refills their coffee cups. Phil and I walk out with our meals half eaten. We get on our scooters and drive out of Hays.

We have climbed almost two thousand feet between Salina and Oakley, where we stop for the night. Oakley is a quiet, pretty town with a Laundromat and two motels. We zero in on that Laundromat miles away and stop at the motel nearest to it. Both motels are owned by the same man, a Friar Tuck sort with a rippling red face who knocks a dollar off the price because, "you're traveling a mighty long way on them tiny little things." When we have signed the register he gives us a little card with a pea-sized hole in it and asks us if we can push a dime through it. Phil pushes a pencil through the hole and moves the dime that way. "Take the card with you," the man says. "Tell 'em where you got it."

In the room we take off our Thermal underwear, our Thermal socks, and our Thermal sweatshirts and walk barefoot to the Laundromat. While the washer is doing the best it can (poor thing, we put the Thermals through it twice, and all it manages to do is distribute the stains a little more equitably and shrink the sweatshirts) we wander up and down the main street in the cool evening, watching children playing with homemade unicycles. They watch with interest as we go by, but without the usual scrambling rush to look at the beatniks. "That's because we've washed our Thermals," I tell Phil.

"No, it's because it's a nice town," he says. "I like Kansas. You ever notice, the farther west we go, the more old toys the kids have? Stuff we haven't seen for ten, fifteen years. When was the last time you saw things like those unicycles, like stilts, like that kid with the skate-board? I bet all the toys we keep looking for and can't find got out here somehow. Like all the old cars you see around. This is where they go."

Once my dreams were full of small square packages from cereal companies, and he and I cheated each other out of magic decoders and old golf balls. "Cultural lag," I say, having been to school since then. "If you listen to the radio here you can probably pick up old *Captain Midnight* programs, still floating around in the ether."

"Lamont Cranston. Somebody with a name like Lamont Cranston doesn't just disappear. I bet their comic books are pretty unhealthy too. I have a feeling about Kansas."

A dog barks at us out of somebody's back yard; it is too dark to see what size dog it is, but just on principle Phil and I both decide to walk on the outside. This is not easily accomplished, not in this physical universe, but we almost make it. "Some general!" I grunt, bracing my feet to keep from being pushed back onto U.S. 40. (This is a new game, developed somewhere between Saint Louis and Kansas City, that is on the way to replacing the Lone Ranger's idea of domesticity. Phil is the brave general. I am his loyal men.) "This is what they taught you at general school, is it? How to Hurl Your Men to the Wolves. You must have was an honor student."

"Men, old boy," he responds coolly, "in general school I was taught the immortal words of von Santaclausewitz, which go, 'When abandoning Novgorod to the Boyars, do not stop to count the kulaks.' You are a necessary sacrifice to my general's pension. Also, get your finger out of my nose."

"Nevertheless. You are my general, you own the baseball. I follow you everywhere, from negotiation to negotiation, singing, brawling, carousing, living off the land, faithful and sentimental. All us men. Give the beast a good kick in the slats, how's about it?"

"Don't nag me. I got the only men in the whole world that nags."

"You told my mother you'd take care of me and see I never caught cold. You said we'd sack towns and rape girls, and all like that, and commit atrocities and everything, and all that happened was I caught cold. I am your comrade-in-arms and loyal as could be, but I would sure like to rape somebody pretty soon, before I get too old to be brutal."

"If you're so loyal, you could whop that dog one, instead of climbing up your general. Anyway, I lied to your mother. I just wanted somebody to come with me to the war. It ain't all atrocities, being a general, you know. It gets lonely."

Two little girls skate past us, making a soft, hollow roaring on the sidewalk. One of them loses a skate; it drags behind her like a lobster clinging to her foot. She sits down to put it on again, trying to look at us at the same time. I say, "I would follow you anywhere, give or take a little."

"Good, good," he answers happily. "After you."

The next day begins rainy enough for the *bubbe* suits, but we drive out of it; by the time we reach the Colorado border the sky is completely clear. A woman who runs a diner in Sharon Springs tells us that this is the story of this spring in the West. A freezing winter and a dry, windy spring—it has been the same all along the way we have come. Every day we can see the wind blow topsoil along the highway as we drive along, and watch the earth just beginning to crack and pull away from the farmhouses.

"A little bit of rain for Kansas," the woman says, "and nothing at all for Colorado or Arizona or any of them. A friend of mine in Colorado, he says they're starting to talk dustbowl there, you know, like in Oklahoma. I wouldn't be surprised. Two years, three years without any rain at all, and you could just pick Colorado up and throw it away." She is a soft-faced woman in her fifties, who runs the diner by herself. She makes fine pie. "The rain makes the difference," she says, "not the wind. It's always windy out here."

Across the diner, at one of the tables, a lean man is cursing the government to a bored-looking friend. "If the god-damn country's so set on giving all that money to them god-damn black niggers," he demands, "why ain't they giving anything to the real Americans? Why ain't they giving that money to the Indians, that's what I want to know." I turn to look at him, and he catches my eye

74

and includes me in the tirade. "My wife's Indian," he explains to me. "One hundred per cent Cherokee, and the finest-looking woman you ever saw. We been married eighteen years." A boy of three or four is sitting quietly next to him; he has the look of being perfectly willing and competent to solve the problems of everybody in the room, to make things all right for everyone if we will only not crowd him so and give him a minute to think things out.

Before we leave I have to go to the bathroom, and on my way back the lean man gets me. I knew that would happen. His friend has disappeared somewhere, but he goes on talking to me as casually as though he had not noticed. I can't make him out, and I don't want to. He brings the taste of the two joking men in Hays back into my throat. I would push past him, but I don't know how to push past anyone, so I smile and inch. The little boy stands behind him, holding onto his pants pocket with two fingers, but not pulling at him.

He asks me if we are going to a particular town in New Mexico. I haven't said we were going anywhere; this could be the one man in Kansas and points east who hasn't been immediately told all about our trip and invited to contribute advice, wistful admiration, or sandwiches. As it happens, the route will take us within a very few miles of the town, and so I say, "Sure." He smiles delightedly. He has even white teeth, the kind that have a suggestion of blue about them.

"My people built that old town," he says. He tells me his name. "My people are good people, Americans. They built a hell of a lot of towns, but that's the only one they named for them. You go through that town, you remember you met me here."

"Yes, I will." I smile at the boy, who moves a little closer to his father and grips his pocket with three fingers. Phil pays for the coffee and pie and nods at me. The lean man still blocks my way. "You remember my name, now," he says. "What's my name?"

I say it. He insists on shaking hands; his grip is dry and light, like Earl's, gentle, as if there were no flesh inside the rough skin. "Good-by," he says. "I hope you get where you're going and do whatever you want to do."

"I'm going to see a girl." Why do I tell him, of all people? I don't know. I didn't know I was going to tell him. He peers down at me, squinting, bringing his face close. I say, "My girl. She's Indian too—part Indian. Iroquois."

"A girl?" the lean man asks in a very soft voice. He begins to shake his head slowly. "You going all that way to see a girl?" He keeps shaking his head, not laughing, but repeating, louder each time, "All that way to see a girl?" I expect to hear him laughing when the door closes behind us, but there is no sound except the wind moving in the scrubby brush and blowing sand against Jenny and Couchette.

Somewhere between Sharon Springs and the Colorado state line we see our first Rocky. It is a very sudden vision: we go around a sharp curve and realize together that what we have taken for a shaggy white cloud on the horizon is actually snow, and that the black mass wearing it like a torn piece of cloth caught on the horn of a bull is the first of the little green pimples that splatter the western half of the country, according to the map. We see that single mountain before us for the rest of the day, and its aloneness makes it completely unreal. Miles and miles of Kansas and Colorado, rising, gently, deceptively—and then this solitary blackness, fierce and barren, its roots lost somewhere beyond our sight, its crown making the sky around it seem bluer than it is; an intruder from Disneyland, a comic strip's idea of Art. "I think the mountains ought to be/Taught a little modesty." James Stephens laughs inside me.

We make about a hundred and seventy-five miles today and camp outside a town called Limon. It isn't much of a campground—a plot of sand and gravel about as big as a baseball diamond—but it has running water, toilet facilities, and fireplaces. The ground is covered with strategically placed clumps of weeds, the water comes out of the pipe the color and texture of brick and never really becomes domesticated, and the soil between the weeds is dry and powdery. Putting up the tent, we pound the poles and stakes down until it looks less like a pup tent than like a turtle tepee, and still they do not take hold. That tent is up on sufferance, and we both know it. For food we have a jar of mayonnaise and a package of spaghetti. I fill our pot with the slightly abrasive water, Phil lights the gas stove in the tent to keep it out of the wind, and, crouched on all fours, we stare at each other across the silent pot. Twenty years of competitive incompetency are in that stare. I say, "This isn't going to work, you know."

"No, of course not," he agrees absently. "But it's something to do, it's something to do. And it does keep us off the streets."

"When did the tent start snuggling up to the oil can?" There are dark, soggy patches on both walls and the flap. Phil shrugs. "Who knows? So it's wet on your side as well as mine. I don't much care."

"It'll be waterproof here and there, anyway." We look up to see a car pulling into the campground and parking a couple of fireplaces away from us. A young man and a girl get out and begin unwrapping packages of food on the picnic table. We rear back on our haunches, sniffing, quivering, almost pointing that food. "Give a look, the goodies," I whisper. "Maybe we could comb our hair forward and be war orphans."

"Nah, just show 'em your legs. These goddamn G.I.s only want one thing." The young couple look over at us, smile and wave, and unwrap more good things. Phil sighs. "Well, you can't have a miracle every suppertime. I got to go to the john. You could command the spaghetti?"

"Why not? Ain't like scrambling eggs." I crawl into the tent to inspect the pot and find the water bubbling in a swampy manner. It looks like rust soup. Propped on my elbows, I begin to break the spaghetti into the water

77

and promptly encounter my first problem, namely, second-degree burns. The situation is mathematical in its simplicity: you can have water in that pot, or you can have spaghetti. Not both. Not for very long, anyway. I lie on my stomach and stir the spaghetti as delicately as I can with a jackknife, sliding the strands into the pot one by one, listening to the silky sounds of the tent pulling loose, and trying to remember the Fool's story in *King Lear* about the cockney who put her eels i' the paste alive. "She knapped 'em o' the coxcombs with a stick, and cried, Down, wantons, down!" I wonder what you can do to jazz up mayonnaise.

A voice outside the tent asks my ankles, "Excuse me, but are you in?" I scramble out backward and discover the young man with the food. He is very tall. His height does not especially diminish when I stand up. He says, "I just dropped by to see how you boys were managing for supper." A Kentucky voice. I don't know many accents for sure after Bugs Bunny, but I know Kentucky.

"Well, we are in some slight difficulty," I begin cautiously. I exhibit the Spaghetti Machine; by now it is almost entirely dry and seems to contain a pale ball of yarn. He nods soberly and offers a suggestion. "What you have there," he says, "is a flowerpot, and not a very sizable one, either. What my wife and I have is too much food and no company, and we'd be pleased if you'd come on over and eat with us."

Phil returns from the john in time to catch the bit about eating. Instantly he is all business, all conditioned reflexes. We know what to do when offered food. "Oh, we couldn't," he says. "We'll be all right, we've got lots of food, really. We sure do appreciate it—" But the young man does not react like other people. "Never mind that. You put out that spaghetti and come on over." He turns around and walks briskly back to his own fireplace. We blink at each other, throw nothing into the air with spread palms, and follow the young man from Kentucky. Suppertime miracles, you're the only miracles for me.

"My name's George McCown," the young man tells us, "and this is my charming wife, Flo." They look like each other, despite the fact that George is sandy and angular and Flo is a small, pleasantly *zaftig* creature with thick red hair. They have the same dark blue eyes, the same effortless way of moving, and the same curiously carnivorous smile. Gentle faces, but tough and humorous at once, and happy with whatever agreement there is between them. George and Flo have been married for three weeks and are spending their honeymoon driving from Lexington, Kentucky, to Long Beach, California, where George will report to a naval base. "I'm to be an officer," he explains gravely, "and wear white all the time, except for going ashore, when I will change to dress blues. It all sounds very promising."

Dinner with George and Flo is as luxurious and dreamy as one of the animals' picnics in *The Wind in the Willows*. They produce baskets of fried chicken, sausages like night-sticks, cheeses the size of pizza pies, enough packages of lunch meats to play cards with (the image strikes us both at the same time: Phil whispers, "I got the ace of salami," but I trump him with a low liverwurst), pillowcases full of potato chips, and a portable cooler for soft drinks. "Never know when you'll get hungry," Flo says brightly, to which George answers, "I do." Phil and I contribute our venerable jar of mayonnaise, and, eventually, the spaghetti. George and Flo are very kind about it. "Sinewy stuff," George says.

So we sit, and we talk, and we eat, and within the dismal enclave of the campground it is very much as if we had come a long way to spend the evening with old friends. But it begins to grow dark, and George and Flo have to make Canon City; they plan to spend the night with one of George's numerous maiden aunts. We help them to repack their baskets, and they leave us things like loaves of bread, whole salamis, and, somehow, a fresh jar of mayonnaise. They also leave us their address in Long Beach. "I don't figure on going anywhere for the next couple of years," George says, "and you look as if you might be. Come by."

We watch them drive away, waving until Flo's red head disappears inside the car, like a banner being hauled down at sunset. The light is going fast now, and the wind is rising. As the light fades, the road seems to recede from us, until we are sitting by ourselves at the table, watching tiny trucks go by like glowing fish. It is almost impossible to see the tent from where we sit, but we can sense its dark form bucking in the dark as though we had the wind tied up inside.

"I tell you," Phil says at last. "Nice people piss me off."

"Me too, boy. I almost wish they hadn't left that food. I think I know why we forgot to take Kisa's curry with us."

"I wish we had an aunt in Canon City," he says.

The hysterical tent proves to be fairly warm when we insert ourselves into it, and our depression begins to lighten. We lie on our backs and talk quietly for a while. "Tell me where we are," Phil demands. He always wants to know. Told, he shakes his head firmly. "No we're not. I just asked you to see if you'd lie. We're in the Bronx, and tomorrow we have to get on the subway and go downtown to do something stupid. Why do you lie to me, you think it'll make things easier. It won't make things easier."

"We're going too fast. I feel bad about it. I wish we could go slower." This is his usual complaint; I have no idea why I should be voicing it now. But this evening he says, "Don't worry about it. I'm getting my drawing done, and that's all that counts for me. Just now. Stuff I've been doing lately ain't too bad, either. You like that thing I did this morning?"

"Yes, I do. I can't really tell you why, but you know that. I do like it, though. It has—I don't know—a lightness, I guess. Whatever that means."

"I wish I could get you over that," he says. "This goddamn silly block you seem to have about pictures. Give you a pencil, put you in front of a painting, and I can see you get paralyzed. That's a waste. It doesn't have to be."

"I don't know how to look at paintings. I like them, or I don't like them, or I'm not sure. In any case, I can't get inside them. I wish I could."

"You have this idea that painting's another world, you think it's a totally different way of looking at things. It's not. It's just a way of making you look at things. I don't think it's much different from what you do. Maybe I'm wrong."

We have said all this before, many times; and I go on staring at his drawings and paintings and saying, yes, yes, I see. "When you read something I've written, you have at least as good an idea as anyone of what I'm trying to do. But I don't know what you want, or how you're reaching for it, or if you got it at last. That's a lot of you not to know."

"Learn to see," he answers. "You sit around waiting for some kind of miracle, the great magic day when you'll wake up and understand paintings. It doesn't happen like that; it's unlearning everything you've been taught all your life about seeing, and learning all over with your own eyes. Writing must be like that."

"Yes, it is." I turn on my back, because there are too many clods under me. "It doesn't make any difference. It's the same thing. I look at people and I can't see them. I can't go inside them, any more than I can a painting. I see a thing, something, someone, something beautiful, something ugly, and I can't get my hands on it. I can't understand, and I can't just accept. I don't know if anything means anything to me. A painting or a person is like a wall in front of me. I can't see the wall, because I'm blind, but I know it's there and I know that if I take another step I'll bang my nose against it. My nose hurts already, thinking about it. That's all I know how to write about, how my nose hurts. I don't want to be blind. Maybe you don't think I look hard at your drawings, but I do, I try to see them each time. Like the way I used to look at the paintings in my house for hours when I was a kid. I try to

81

see. I hate being blind and constipated and stopped up. I try to see."

Have I said all this aloud in the tent? Or any of it? Or have I only been whining in my head again? I don't know —each of us talks to himself for the other to hear, and so we have our conversations. Phil is saying, "Gee, I liked Kansas. I'm going to go back there sometime."

"Yeah, okay. I'll come with you." The wind finds us again with a little whine of delight, and we pull our sweatshirt hoods up around our faces. "Good night, brave general."

"Good night, my valiant and loyal men. Don't try deserting in the night neither, you rascally old men, you. The encampment is ringed with bear traps. Ours and the bears'. Good night."

When I wake from a very sound sleep my head feels badly in need of defrosting, and there is something limp and oily crawling up my back. This turns out to be the tent. I nudge Phil. This accomplished with some difficulty, as he is small in the sleeping bag. "Phil," I say. I hesitate to bother him, because he doesn't get very much sleep. He never has. "Phil. The tent's down."

"I know it."

"Oh, you're up. What do you think we ought to do about it?"

"I'm thinking."

"We ought to do something, Phil, really."

"I know. I've thought about killing you, but I'd have to turn over to do it. I guess we ought to get up."

"Okay. You first. You should have been up all night, anyway, guarding the sleep of your weary men, namely me. In general school—"

"God damn it, for this I could turn over!" We get up in some confusion and stand barefoot on the cindery soil of Limon, looking down at the unconditional surrender of our tent. The pegs have all torn free, and the tent is splayed out like a fallen pterodactyl. It's hard to see each other in the dark, and it would be harder to see the tent, except that the wind stirs it against our legs quite often. The wind is very cold.

"Yep, that tent's down all right," Phil says, nodding his head. "I don't think I've ever seen a tent quite as down. Not this down."

"Not from a standing start. I don't see how we're going to put it up again, either. Look at the loops on the poor thing. Like a page torn out of a looseleaf notebook."

"Let's go find coffee. I always get coffee when my tent falls down on me." Hand in hand we blunder to the highway and start walking up the road toward Limon. We speak very little. It's a cold night, and our tent has fallen down, and it doesn't even feel unusual. "It's us, all right," Phil mutters sadly. "It is definitely us."

There is an all-night diner about half a mile from our campground; it is a few minutes after three o'clock when we get there. We order coffee, and when the waitress brings it we mention hopefully that we're camped down the road a piece and our tent just naturally blew down on us. Funniest thing. You could adopt us if you wanted to; we're public domain. Not this waitress. She looks as if she's adopted people before. Phil sips his coffee and stares straight ahead of him. I consider calling Enid, whose voice has been helpful on cold nights for a long time, decide against it, and find a week-old sports section of the Denver *Post*. Spahn lost. Damn. It's a bad night all around.

We sit in the diner for over an hour, barely speaking, almost asleep in the humid air. The place is a truck stop; heavy-set men, pale as soap with weariness under their beard stubble, come in, order coffee and fried eggs. One of them stays for a long time, sitting at a corner table with the waitress. The lights are very bright in the diner, and they show up the sagging pads of her cheeks and the folds in her neck that make a collar when she lowers her head. She seems happy talking to the truck driver. When he leaves, he pats her shoulder and says, " 'By, hon. See you

Thursday." But she won't be on duty this time Thursday. It will have to be the Monday after, then.

I have some idea of sitting out the night in the diner, but I am too groggy to argue when Phil gets up at last and heads for the door, wobbling on his axis like a toy gyroscope, but determined. We wander down the highway, almost drowsing in the headlights that come rushing toward us; we find the campground; and we put the tent back up. It is a one-night-only job, as secure as an anchor in the fog, but it is up and it will do. The sky is just beginning to get red back toward Kansas when we have finished. Early dawns they have around here. The hell with it, we're sleeping till checkout time. We writhe back into the tent (it's not *very* up) and fall asleep quickly.

Sharp on the stroke of six the wind arrives, and this time it is not fooling around. Oddly, it does not blow the tent down on us again; instead it rattles and cracks the sides against us until, half asleep, we feel ourselves skidding around inside like peas being shelled. Jenny and Couchette, parked broadside to the wind, seem secure enough on their stands, but they are shivering against each other with a sound like muffled cymbals. We load them up and get out, delaying only to find my socks. They have almost made it to the highway, so it's very convenient.

From now on the wind will always be against us, and it is a skilled, professional kind of wind. When the scooters are able to go fast, it simply buckles our windscreens and rakes at our faces; but when a hill has slowed us to a second-gear crawl, then it has us at its mercy and can hit us everywhere at once, ripping at every crevice in our clothing where it can find foothold, like an angry cat, blackjacking us with sudden gusts too cold to breathe, and always polishing us with cold, rubbing away whatever bits of warmth may cling to us, as though it were determined to make something perfect out of us. It is a wind to snap off steeples and borrow brood mares—and it will get worse—and yet nobody seems to notice it but us. It is obviously our wind, our winter, and neither of us is especially surprised.

It's a great mistake to try to cure a man of paranoia, for it gives him just as clear an understanding of the innards of the universe as physics or religion.

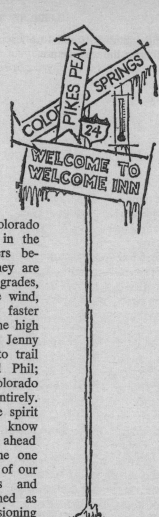

Between Limon and Colorado Springs a real discrepancy in the performance of the scooters becomes steadily apparent. They are both having trouble on grades, apart from the force of the wind, but Couchette is climbing faster than Jenny and staying in the high gears on slopes which force Jenny to drop into low. I begin to trail farther and farther behind Phil; over the last forty miles to Colorado Springs I lose sight of him entirely. It makes a difference in the spirit of the journey, although I know that I'd be sailing along ahead myself if Couchette were the one losing power. It's the nature of our friendship that our tastes and talents may be as unmatched as they please without occasioning jealousy, but our few dear possessions—scooters, guitars, women— had better be equal in quality or there will be trouble, foolish, brooding, childish trouble, no less real for never seeing daylight. This is the way we are.

Colorado Springs. I have wanted to see this town since I first heard:

If I was a headlight on some Western train,
Lord, if I was a headlight on some Western train,
I'd shine my light on cool Colorado Springs. . . .

It has been a cool, blue imagining in my head ever since, a kind of sanctuary where nothing bad can happen to anyone. The last couple of miles are almost straight down, and on a scooter you have a feeling of spiraling slowly into town, like a vagrant feather. Phil is waiting for me at the first traffic light, and together we set forth to see Colorado Springs. Phil knows the song too.

It is not a city. It is a conglomeration of used-car lots, of pink stucco houses, of stores that sell Indian dolls, of Arthur Murray places and Vic Tanny places, of cheap chain restaurants and drive-ins, of insurance offices and funeral homes made of hard candy, of movie houses, of shopping centers, of guided tours, of motels designed like Christmas cards—all of which would make it no uglier than many other tourist towns, except for the fact that the Rocky Mountains are all around it, and that it lives off their reality. Ringed by that ruinous loveliness, Colorado Springs has no chance at all; but nobody would notice it in California.

"God, what a vile town," Phil says wonderingly. "All the people look like sandwich men." He begins to read the steel signs that arch over Nevada Avenue. "See the Garden of the Gods. See Pike's Peak. See the Balanced Rock. Give a look, the Cliff Dwellings, with real dwelling Indians, they dance five times a day from sheer joy. Pike's Peak, this way. Also the North Cheyenne Canyon, Colorado's own Grand Canyon. Visit the Cave of the Winds. Pike's Peak, hey. You could still make the dancing Indians, if you hurry. Boy, this town doesn't do a damn thing but pimp for the scenery."

We park the scooters and go into one of those plastic restaurants that specialize in boiled coffee and quick service, which is no favor. I ask the manager about the quickest road to Gunnison. I have people-to-look-up there, and a small hope of reaching them tonight. "Quickest way'd be to take Twenty-four out of here, going through Trout Creek Pass, and out back onto Fifty at Salida. It's a straighter road—you don't have to do all that winding along the river. I always go that way myself."

We take his advice and switch over to U. S. 24, not without some misgivings at abandoning the Triptik, even for a little while—it feels too much like Dante running on ahead of Virgil. The road begins to climb sharply as soon as we are out of Colorado Springs, taking us directly into the Rockies for the first time, but it is tangled up with a snarl of the pink stucco houses and has to drag them along too. With them, clenched tightly to the road and sucking sustenance from it, like ticks, come peach-colored plywood-and-plaster motels; clutches of souvenir shops; a roadside stand for every pine tree; restaurants that look like the dining halls of summer camps; summer camps that look as spacious as Automats with riding stables; a handful of pathetic and ghastly attempts to create fairytale amusement parks out of tacked-on scrollwork and wooden toadstools; and one junkyard. After a while, like Colorado Springs, the Rockies themselves begin to seem two-dimensional, painted and propped up the night before.

Pike's Peak fills half the sky between one curve and the next, looking as soft as breaking water. The wind is growing bolder, and I feel myself becoming more and more sensitive to it, instead of inured, or even numb; a knife-lick across my wrist will set my whole body shivering and twitching, almost doubling over the handlebars. I cannot see Phil anywhere.

The road begins to slope sharply downward. I slide past a sign that says HARTSEL—15. Then I go around a steep, blind curve and find myself descending to a plain without place in the world, a wide orange desert that has no business existing outside of someone's old and polished nightmare. There are mounds and pillars and monoliths of sandstone welting up in all sizes, from anthills to cliffs, their colors shifting from orange to purple to a pale green that hurts the eyes. A mist is blowing down the road now, and shapes come and go in the wind like monkeys and like clouds: looming up and vanishing, scuttling alongside and vanishing, wrinkling across the bone road and vanishing. It is a science-fiction magazine cover conjecturing the surface of Mars; it is as garish an unintentional parody as Colorado Springs, and, like it, a landscape to flee across every night, tiny and screaming.

The road across the plain is fairly level, but the wind slows Jenny down to thirty miles an hour, and less when I try to push her. The cold is even worse on the plain, and I can hear myself sighing and gasping nervously, as children do when a make-believe is getting out of control. My hands are almost too numb to shift gears or twist the throttle—how much gas do I have? I never did get Jenny's reserve tank fixed. The idea of being afoot in this drifting, freezing, endless nowhere would panic me completely, but for a cheerful corollary: if I froze to death here, I'd keep. I'd be fresh as a TV dinner if they found me before spring.

The miles strain by on the speedometer, but there are no more signs for Hartsel. That's all right. I never believed in Hartsel, anyway. No cars pass me in either direction; the only signs of life are cattle grazing a long way off, barely visible in the mist. I stare at them with real, venomous envy, for they seem not to mind the wind at all. There is only one spot in me that is as warm and placid as those cattle, and that is the part that knows quite surely that I will always be cold, that there will always be a wind hunting through me, and that I will always be hurrying before the coming darkness in search of a place that is not there. One other thing about paranoia. It's warm. It's never warm enough, but it's warm.

A long way ahead, I can see the road beginning to climb again, but I can also see the sudden end of the Martian plain; the pine trees mark it off as surely as a shoreline, and even the road seems to change color. There is a gas station, and something that looks like a general store. Hartsel. No wonder it's not on the map. It'd fall off. Couchette is parked outside the store, and Phil comes out to wave to me. He has to help me put Jenny up on her stand; I couldn't do it alone. It is dark quite suddenly, the way night comes in the West.

The old couple who run the general store delay closing up until we have grown at least warm enough to hurt. We ask them about hotels, and they point out the other building in town. It is a two-story red and white house with a Welcome Inn sign over the door. Phil and I begin to giggle softly.

"Comfort Coast to Coast," I say. "The good brothers have a mission here."

"Congratulations, brothers. You got us." Leaving the scooters, we stagger up the road to the red and white house and fall through the door in fine last-reel style, partly due to genuine exhaustion and partly with the understanding that it would be a good thing to arouse the manager's sympathy. Welcome Inns are not brownstones, and some kind of adoption is plainly in order.

The manager is a young man named Ed Bird: late twenties, build of an athlete gradually letting things sag, round blond face with oddly flat and muscular lips. He gives us a room very cheaply because it is the first room he has rented in several days. "Tourist season's a little slow getting started this year," he explains cheerfully as he takes us to our room. "Most of the year we aren't really a hotel. More like a sort of a social club. What I mean, the cowboys come here to drink. Drink and fight." He shows us how to turn on the heat in the room and then decides to do it himself. "It's pretty tricky. The gas isn't working right just now, and sometimes it gets—yeah, *there* you go. Now I guess you'll want to wash up. Well, the water's kind of froze up in the pipes, the cold water is, so if you have some difficulties, that'll be why. About the men's room—don't try flushing the toilet in there. In fact, maybe it'd be better all around if you just used the ladies' room. Don't forget to knock."

He tells us that we can park the scooters in his garage and is about to go downstairs when Phil asks him, "Just out of curiosity, what's the temperature today?"

"About twenty-six, twenty-seven," Ed says. "Hard to tell, with our thermometer the way it is."

When he leaves, Phil sits down on the bed and stares at me out of maroon eyes the size of raisins. "Twenty-six, twenty-seven degrees. Damn near May, and twenty-six, twenty-seven degrees. Everywhere we go, we get there just in time for the winter. Oh, Beagle, how you lied to me."

"Quiet," I say, fondling the heater. "Enjoy this thing while it still works."

After a long while we force ourselves outside again to bring the scooters up and park them. We sneak the bounty of that long-ago last night to our room (Ed probably wouldn't mind, as the manager, but he also seems to be the hotel cook and kitchen staff), and construct, conquer, and consume sandwiches you could practice *karate* on. We consider going downstairs to talk with Ed for a while, but our rapidly overheating room appears to be the only place in the hotel that is warm at all; walking down the corridor to the bathroom, my feet curl in their shoes on the cold floor. It turns out not to be a good idea to flush the toilet in the ladies' room, either.

"The hell with it," I say, cuddling up to the heater again. "*J'y suis, j'y* flaming well *reste.*"

"Well spoken, my men. Do not plaster yourself all over that thing quite so, but give your old general a humble corner in the ashes, or I'll whop you one." We simmer and sigh for a long time before we peel off our steaming, stinking Thermals and climb into bed.

The room gets steadily hotter during the night, and I

wake in the morning feeling almost feverish, but the deepest cold is still inside me. The wind is waiting outside for us. I can hear it before I ever look out of the window and see it, pawing the earth and flattening bushes. The sun looks very small in the bright sky, lemon-colored and impotent. Phil is not awake yet. I dress, wash up, don't flush, and go downstairs.

No one else is awake in the hotel. The huge dining room where we came in last night (Ed was having supper when we arrived) is closed off by a sliding pine partition. For a moment I get back the exulting feeling of secrets that I used to have when I was a child playing by myself at dawn. I go outside to see if Jenny will start. She's been giving trouble the last couple of days. It is as cold as night, and yesterday stretches bleakly ahead of me. Jenny will not start, though I try every home remedy in my hornbook; she is not about to go anywhere in this weather. Neither is Couchette. When Phil comes out to work on her, her starter turns over quite well, but her engine will not catch for longer than a hiccup.

"They're good girls," Phil says with a sigh, "but they ain't totally crazy. Unlike some. What do you want to do?"

"Let's have breakfast. Try 'em again afterward."

"All right." As we are walking back to the hotel he says, "Let's not leave right away after breakfast, huh? I want to look at this place for a while."

"Okay. You want to draw?"

"Maybe. I just want to look. It feels interesting."

"Okay, sure." I am a little sullen and more ashamed. That's my fault. What's to become of us, who never needed reasons? My fault, my fault.

Ed is awake when we go back inside, tugging sleepily at the dining-room partition. "Hi, fellas," he says as we come in. "Sorry to be up so late, but some of the boys from Hartsel were over last night and they didn't knock off till about three. The noise bother you any?"

I remember dreaming singing a long way out of my dream. We shake our heads. "Good. I put you up at that top room 'cause I knew they'd be coming over to drink, but I got a little worried about the time the fight started. Now, what'll you have for breakfast? I was figuring on making scrambled eggs and cinnamon toast, and maybe some home fries. How's that sound?"

Musical, Ed. We meet his wife after he goes off into the kitchen. She is tall, with very thin legs and a thin, nursy-looking body. Her hair is fair and looks as if it would smell sweet, but at eight in the morning her face is stiff under the kind of make-up designed to make it not her face at all. She has a good smile, but when she is not smiling she looks vaguely frightened. Her name is Suzy, and she teaches French at a neighboring school.

Ed brings us our breakfast very quickly and sits down to eat with us at one of the big tables. Phil asks him our Question, the test phrase we would radio to Mars if we were the first to establish communication: "Does it always get this cold around here?"

We are ready to sing along with the explanation about the bad winter and the late spring, the warm day that went by here a few minutes ago and will surely be waiting for us over the next mountain, but Ed considers only a moment and then says judiciously, "Yes, pretty much. Hartsel's a cold place. We're in kind of a valley here, and we just get the wind from everywhere. I've been running this place since last July, and I've never seen it get much warmer. You're lucky you didn't come through here just a few days ago. There was snow on the ground from here to Salida, and the pass was just choked. Why, there was a blizzard off around Cripple Creek yesterday, fella in a car told me. You've been lucky with those little scooters, you don't know. It gets cold."

"Snow," Phil says to me. "Remember the guy we met in Salina, in the parking lot. He warned us about snow. Cut straight down to Wichita, he said, never mind about Colorado in the spring, he said. And you told me, snow is a New York thing, they don't have snow out West. You're a terrible person, Beagle. You lack seriousness."

93

"It'll get a little warmer around eleven or so," Ed says, and so we stay in the big dining room, drinking cup after cup of coffee, playing chess, going outside every now and then to do technical things to the scooters, and coming back for more coffee. It is only a little more than a hundred miles to Gunnison, but the way is mostly straight up; the climb climaxes in Monarch Pass, 11,312 feet up, twice the elevation of Hartsel. Ed thinks the pass is open now, but he isn't really sure.

Cowboys come into the dining room from time to time, mostly from outside, but a couple from the rooms upstairs. "They stay over sometimes," Ed says. "Nice having company." Hartsel, he explains, is actually not a town but a cattle ranch large enough nearly to constitute a town. It dominates the area, which is called South Park; almost everyone Ed knows either works for Hartsel or supplies it. The cowboys are uniformly lean, friendly, and timeless-looking—strong but not young; worn and knowledgeable but never old. They are the most competent-appearing men I have ever seen, and I have seen some really good plumbers in my time. We spend part of the morning talking to a tall hook-nosed cowboy named Gil, who is having breakfast while his two-year-old grandson, dressed exactly like him in dungaree jacket, Levis, and boots, plays around his feet. Gil's face is richly lined but not at all wrinkled; the lines are wearing it away, as rivers do a plain, and leaving no slack flesh behind. He is quietly irritated at having been called back from his vacation because the man in charge of a recent branding operation involving a few thousand calves has got things totally confused. "That man," Gil says, speaking slowly but distinctly through a mouthful of bacon, "has somehow accounted for nine hundred extra calves, which I know we don't have in this world. So I got to come back from Raton, where my wife's people live, and figure has he been borrowing those calves or just losing count, or has he got a few of them branded on both sides, or just what. Man's probably gone and counted the lambs in there too. *He* don't know."

When Gil leaves, Phil takes his sketchpad and goes to sit by the window, leaving me to talk with Ed. Ed used to be a racing-car driver and a good one; the clippings of his victories fill two good-sized scrapbooks. He has seen an amazing amount of the country from a cockpit, having raced as far west as Fresno, as far east as New York. A few summers ago he and two friends left Chicago with one stock car and something like thirty dollars between them and came home to Canon City by way of Mexico. "We'd just travel around looking for races," he says, "same way you fellas go around looking for things to paint. We'd always take something—not first-place money, maybe, but second, third money—and we'd go on and find another race. I liked it fine. I didn't want anything better than that." He is twenty-nine now and had been racing professionally for eleven years (with two years off for the Army—"and I used to come home and race on furloughs") when he married Suzy a year ago and contracted to be Welcome Inn's man in Hartsel. "It was either that or be a cop in Canon City and have to arrest all my buddies. Now I don't know who told those Welcome Inn people that Hartsel was such a great place for a hotel—why, hell, most of the year I make more money selling beer to the Hartsel boys than I ever do from the rooms—but it suits me fine. It's quiet, but I like it, and there's always company around somewhere. Evenings, a couple of the boys usually come over, and we just sit around and drink beer, talk, maybe play some chess. Only thing ever bothers me is the weather. The cold just gets to me sometimes, you know."

Business at the hotel ordinarily being so slack that he and Suzy are able to handle everything themselves, Ed has more leisure time than he is equipped to dispose of. He hunts and fishes a little, because everybody does around here, but what holds his imagination is a strange, confused dream of being a speculator, an operator, a man of angles and secrets. He has fingers, or fingernails, in the most peculiar assortment of cement pies that ever broke teeth. Some of the deals are merely wishful, like the arrangement with the old miner who claims to have discovered a rich vein of silver on someone else's property. "He won't tell anybody where it is, but I kind of figure if he ever takes anyone up there, it'll be me. He's a real old mountain man." Others are complicated variants of every sucker game anyone ever fell for, from chain letters to peddling pimple salves for premiums, to lonely-hearts clubs. There is one that I would swear sounds like an avatar of the old Spanish prisoner dodge; he is nervous about that one, but he does not want to back out of the deal. "It's not just the money," he says earnestly, "it's the contacts. I don't want to lose my good contacts."

He never makes any money out of his attendance on these machinations; he is always just about to. In all fairness, he has managed to avoid investing any real amounts of time or money in any one project. At the moment he is the local representative (acknowledged but uncontracted) of a real-estate firm that owns land in South Park and is trying to attract upper-middle-class tourists. Phil and I had noticed a couple of their billboards referring those interested to "our Hartsel agent," but neither of us had ever connected them with Ed. He has lost interest in the outfit, and his promotional efforts consist entirely in handing out their elaborately printed brochures to whoever wants them. He shows me one, and it seems as honest as any real-estate literature I ever saw: that is, it describes the basic plot of land as "the size of five football fields," which is as comprehensible as exact acreage to the average tourist, and prettier; and it swivel-hips neatly around the bumptious fact that there never has been much water in South Park and that there is liable to be less in the next few years. "You can't live here cheap," Ed says. "It looks like you can, but you can't. I don't think they're going to sell much land to anybody, but you never know. I like to have a few little extras going all the time. You never know. I'm not going to just stay here all my life."

Phil comes back with a few sketches of the mountains and the road; they are more notes than drawings, but Ed is extremely impressed. "Now that's something I like," he says. "I've seen a couple of fellas try to draw the mountains from here, but you're the only one who really got them the way they look." He shows the sketches to Suzy, to the cowboys. "That's what I like," he says. "That's pretty."

It is almost noon and as warm as it's going to get all day. Phil and I go outside for another try at starting the scooters, and at last the engines begin to fire. We warm them up and then go back to our room to get our luggage. When we come downstairs again, Ed has a proposition for Phil. He is hesitant and circuitous about presenting it, as though he fears he might be offending against foreign customs; the gist of it is that if Phil will do a drawing of the hotel for him he will not only consider us his guests for breakfast but will pack us a lunch to take along. The sandwiches will be ham and cheese, and it would be nice if the drawings were to be in color.

Nothing like this has ever happened to us. We have both sold our work, for one price or another, but this is special, this is real in a way that money has never been real to either of us, this is *barter*. Phil accepts the commission joyously and goes outside with his gouache box, while I explain to Ed that I have not quite finished breakfast. He goes into the kitchen to prepare the lunch, and I eat for both of us during the half-hour it takes Phil to do the drawing. It turns out to be his best work of the trip so far, and it saddens him to part with it. Ed is completely satisfied, and Suzy promises to mat the gouache properly before putting it up.

I have never seeen Phil really happy after selling a painting, but he is delighted with this bargain. "Damn, *that's* the way to live," he says as we are loading the scooters. "You do a drawing, the guy gives you breakfast, or a place to sleep, or maybe does some work on the scooter—that I could understand, that makes a little sense.

That's all I want. The other business—the dealers, the galleries, the shows, the critics trying to figure what's coming in and going out, the women who want to buy a hundred dollars' worth of painting, it shouldn't clash with the rug, scared, stupid people begging you to cheat them, looking for shortcuts, running your life. Of that I have had enough. But this way is nice. Damn, I feel good."

Before we leave he notices that the tables and chairs in the dining room are all of one design and falls to inspecting them. "This is all the same as the stuff upstairs," he says presently, "the bed and the bureau and everything. Is it like this in all the rooms?" Ed nods. "Boy, it's fine workmanship. Who made these?"

Ed isn't sure. "It was all here when I took over. There's an old fella in Colorado Springs makes most of this stuff. I always liked it being all one set. Why, is it worth anything?"

"Yeah, I think so. Not right now, maybe, but you wait long enough and it will be." Phil is squatting in front of a chair, touching a joint as though he expected it to make music. "It's a beautiful set, and it was made to last a long time. I'd hang on to it if I were you."

"I sure will." Ed is quite excited, but he tries to conceal it by leaning down to examine the chair gravely. "Yes, I can see this is good work," he says, tracing a floral design with his finger. "Sure." He reminds me of nothing so much as me in front of a painting. He gives us the lunch and walks out to the garage with us to watch us start up the scooters. As we shake hands his smiling face grows puckered and worried, making him look like a blond monkey. "I sure wish I could remember that old fella's name," he says.

We drive abreast for a little while, going up the road, and Phil says, "I hope he doesn't try cashing those chairs in now. There ain't much money in it for him, but there's a pile there for his kids or his grandchildren. That really was fine furniture, Pete. Somebody took a lot of time with it. Damn, it's a pleasure to see good handmade stuff like that. I got to try making some chairs and things one of these days."

"Old Ed's liable to trade it all in for the rights to a doughnut mine. Anyway, we're a couple of meals to the good."

"Aren't we just?" he says. "I work and you eat. The economic arrangements seem to have got themselves a trifle disheveled."

"Seems fair to me. Where do you detect the inequity, my general?"

"Well, if you would be so kind as to lean your nose a couple of points to the starboard, I would detect you an inequity wouldn't do you a bit of good." He begins to laugh so hard Couchette wobbles with it. "Oh me, what a world. Hartsel, Colorado. Dear, dear, dear." He leans back against his duffel bag and sings in his richest accent, " 'I see by my outfit what I am a cowboy.' " I take the second line, " 'I see by my outfit what I am a cowboy, too.' " Then together, in harmony:

"We see by our outfits what we was both cowboys;
    If you had a outfit, you could be a cowboy, too."

It is our national anthem.

UTAH COLORADO
ARIZONA NEW MEXICO
80
GUNNISON
DOVE CREEK
CORTEZ

Going over Monarch Pass, everything is deep green and white, deep green and white, very much like one of Hokusai's views of Mount Fuji, Phil says. There is snow on both sides of the road now, though the road itself is clear; yesterday there was only a kind of white deposit that looked more like sediment than like snow. This is old snow, when you look at it, porous and dirty, February snow on an April afternoon.

The wind means nothing to the pine trees; now and then a single row of them stirs all together, sending snow spilling down their feathery branches as slowly as a waterfall seen from far away. There are patches of dark ice on the road, and the cars that pass me are not going much faster than I am. One car is full of nuns, and several of them scramble onto the rear seat to look back at me, smiling and waving. They are all young, with pale, parched faces. It begins to snow; not even flakes but tiny, stinging specks that vanish before they have even touched the hot flanks of Jenny and Couchette. The snow doesn't last long; it was just a question of making a point.

The nearer we get to the pass, the sharper the contrast between green and white becomes. There is snow all around us now, piled in huge, hard drifts, occasionally framed into fields as deep and tumbled as a giant's bed; under the gray sky, the snow looks as though it had never melted since the mountains first wrinkled out of the ground. The mountain pines follow us all the way to the top; there is no real timberline here, only a kind of tonsure near the very summit. At some points they are packed so closely together that the seagreen becomes almost blue. I begin to dislike pine trees and to suspect them of actually being insects or some form of fungus, anything but real trees. Real trees die in the winter.

A small sign tells us when we have reached the summit of Monarch Pass, and by unspoken agreement we pull the scooters over to the side of the road and stop for a moment. The descending road offers us the fragile illusion of being within grasp of the horizon, and for a moment we feel as though we could reach every place we might ever want to go before sunset. Then I ask Phil, "Would you care to say something humble, old chap?"

"Let's get coffee in Sargents," he says. Sargents is the town at the foot of the pass. "Also, you could call your people in Gunnison. Better they should have time to make a big supper."

"Common courtesy. After you, laddy."

At the point where the road begins to slope away there is a large restaurant, and the nuns' black car is parked outside it. The young nuns are playing in the snow, hurling snowballs at one another and laughing like children. They wave again as we go by, and I look back over my shoulder to see if they know how to make snow angels. But we curve out of sight too quickly, and the road demands all my attention. When I can take my eyes from the road

101

for a moment, I catch picture-puzzle flashes of the trees and the mountains and the white sky. The world as seen from a Ferris wheel, and more like our usual pace than the patient ascent, looking around at everything.

I call Mike and Joanna Silva from Sargents. Mike Silva is a transplanted New Yorker, an old friend of an old friend of mine who had written to him that we were on our way. He tells me how to get to his house and adds that the color of the roof is turquoise and that the house will smell of macaroni and cheese.

We drive the last thirty miles to Gunnison. It is getting very cold now, and the wind holds both scooters back, especially Jenny. When I look back, the mountains have merged into a solid, featureless wall, green verging on black, the color old coins turn. Small black and white birds flap across the road now and then, swift and flickering as torn shreds of newspaper blowing along the road. I'd stop and look if I weren't so cold.

Gunnison is a small town and well laid out; it is no problem at all to find the street where Mike and Joanna live, but I drive right past the house. Who knows from turquoise roofs when even your hair hurts with cold? Fortunately Mike is waiting for us on the lawn and calls us back. He knows it's us. We park the scooters in the driveway and stumble into his house.

The next half-hour is a warm confusion of faces, voices, sounds, and smells. There are children, any amount of children, and there is Mike, no mistaking Mike, outlined so clearly in burnt-sienna crayon. There is a sweet-faced woman with dark curly hair who must be Joanna, for there's only one other girl there, and she is somehow too plump and beaming to be Joanna, although she seems very nice too. Boy, that's a lot of children. A balding young man sticks his head in the door, says hi to everybody, and disappears again once or twice. What child is this? There is a dog too—I would swear to that dog—but it's gone when things quiet down. The house smells good, faintly gingerbready, but mostly macaronish, as Mike said. I start to plunge my hands into the steaming casserole on the table, just to get the circulation going again, but get sidetracked talking to the boy who has a bandage on his ear. He hurt it playing baseball, he says. Oh, it's so good to sit down on something that isn't moving. Yes, I'd love some.

I am talking when I become fully aware of myself again, which is not uncommon. All of the Silvas' guests are gone, and the macaroni is gone too. The children are in bed, I guess. They must have a lot of beds. Mike is here, and Joanna, who winks gravely at me as she pours the coffee, and the plump girl—her name is Connie, I think. Phil is here too. That's how come the macaroni isn't. My lord, I'm tired. And yet I feel good, as though I had finally arrived somewhere.

Joanna smiles at me. She has nice skin, somewhere between sallow and golden, at once a woman's skin and a little girl's. It is very familiar skin, very reassuring, though I do not know why. I must have liked somebody with skin like Joanna's when I was little. Maybe a social worker. I loved social workers. "Well," she says.

"Well." It may come out as a tired, comfortable grunt, and that's all right too.

"Come on into the living room," Mike says. "There's a couple of kids on the sofa, so we'll have to talk quietly. Will you for God's sake take those Superman sweatshirts off?"

We spend that night, and all the next day and the next night, in their house, and it is different from any way we have been since the journey began, but it is not an interlude. The Ferris wheel never stops turning, and life still wheels and blinks by us, bewildering even in the quiet times. Mike leaning in the doorway of the spare bedroom talking about the mountains, and about coming out here and going to college, and about how to treat people, and about Joanna; Joanna cooking breakfast with some children late for school and some underfoot, a token confusion in her words and gestures, but a deep serenity in her pancakes; Joanna sitting in the kitchen with every last child

103

asleep, talking about Mike with her chin resting on her folded hands—these moments are happening and passing swiftly, and both of us are sharply aware of this. It is as though Mike and Joanna were alive and we were ghosts against their windowpanes; again, as though they lived without notion of time, while we were drowning in it. And perhaps we both cry, "Save me," to them, for our different reasons, prepared to deny it if we were heard.

We are very active that next day and evening with Joanna, despite the late breakfast and the long, easy supper. In the morning we drive outside Gunnison in Joanna's jeep, taking the two younger daughters with us—there are really only four children. Joanna drives us into a stony little gully cut by the Gunnison River, and she and I and the children walk slowly along the riverbank, while Phil wanders off in another direction with his gouache box. We talk about the country, about religion (Joanna is as joyously Catholic as the animals in *Prayers from the Ark;* she is the only person I have ever met who could say, "I'm very devout, but Mike has doubts," and make it sound completely trusting and natural), about the fact that Gunnison is allowed to take only a comparatively minute quantity of water from the Gunnison River, about the possibility that the daughter currently wobbling an inch or two away from the river may fall in; but mostly we talk about Mike. He has left early this morning to work in Grand Junction—he goes to school half the year and works the other half for Joanna's father, who is an electrical contractor—and Phil and I will be gone before he returns, but we spend our day in Gunnison learning about Mike, whether Joanna is actually speaking of him or not.

To my eye there is a strangely autumnal quality in the gouaches that Phil does by the river. The reds and yellows of the earth are at once bright and sad, and there is a cold wind blowing out of that hard blue sky. Only the blue-green river feels young and fertile and promises to stay so for a long time. Spring comes late here, Joanna says.

As we begged her to this morning, Connie has found us a guitar, but only one; so after lunch we sit in the living room, improvising piano and guitar duets—ragtime, boogie, blues, something like Leroy Carr and Scrapper Blackwell, and something, in the words of James Thurber, "very much like something that no one had ever seen before." It's a completely new way of making music for us, and it's fun, but it is not a relaxed kind of music we make; instinctively we have settled on a nervous, fast-moving form, for we do not want to waste the day, and we do not know how to keep the day from being wasted, or even what "wasted" and "keeping" mean today. We are relieved when Joanna determines to take us for a drive to a town called Crested Butte, thirty miles north of Gunnison.

It's a good ride through the blue land that does not really begin to steepen until we are about ten miles from Crested Butte. Warm and sprawling in the back seat, I am able to look at the country with wider eyes than I was when the wind was chasing us through it. The spaciousness of it astounds me; this is the kind of country you dream of running away to when you are very young and innocently hungry, before you learn that all land is owned by somebody, that you can get arrested for swinging through trees in a loincloth, and that you were born either too late or too poor for everything you want to do. Nobody lives here. You could be anything you wanted to be in this land, and nobody would know. Phil drives the jeep, and I pick out tunes on the guitar. Joanna sits in the front seat with her legs tucked under her and looks out of the window. I point out the black and white birds to her, and she says they are magpies.

Crested Butte is a tiny, old, pointy-roofed town lodged in the mountains like a bit of meat between great teeth. Walk the wooden sidewalks of the main street, and you'd swear that the mountains were sprouting out of the next street over. It's a true ghost town, totally quiet in the warm, dry afternoon, but somehow friendly, unlike the

frightening towns we have passed through that were still
with people, silent with breathing. There can't be more
than thirty people in this town, but they live here all year
round. Joanna says that a lot of Gunnison people come
here to drink, and indeed the only place in town that seems
to be open is a tavern. We park in front of it and go in.

It is a long, high, echoing place, big enough to hold
three times Crested Butte's probable population. There are
ten or twelve people inside, all of them sitting at the bar,
and all of them drunk in varying degrees. There is a
strange dissimilarity about them; they do not look like
people you would find drinking in the same bar. They are
nearly all middle-aged to old, and all retired. Joanna
knows most of them: this one was a horse-trainer, that one
was a pediatrician, a stonemason, a coal miner, a water
witch. Hunched and chattering, shrunken as newborns
under the high ceiling, turning as we come in and blinking
in the snowy sunlight slanting through the door, they seem
to share only the sullen knowledge that others have also
come there to die.

We sit down in a booth to drink beer and play the
guitar, and several people come over to listen, among them
the woman who runs the bar. The coal miner offers Phil
a Yugoslavian instrument that looks something like a long-
necked tenor guitar but is tuned like a mandolin and
made to be played with a pick. Phil, who could get some
kind of music out of a banana, even if he'd never played
one before, tunes it to the guitar, and we lean back to play
Brassens for Joanna. The song she likes best is the one
that goes:

Au bois d'Clamart,
Y'a des petites fleurs, y'a des petites fleurs.
Y'a des copains
Au, au bois d'mon coeur, au, au bois d'mon coeur. . . .

It is the saddest and loveliest song in the world.

Once, when I turn my head, I see an old man in a

long black coat standing very close to me. I do not know where he came from—he was not at the bar when we walked in—or how long he has been standing there. He is very old, much older than Mr. Abel in Kansas City; he seems as twisted and naked and far from home as a bit of driftwood. His face and his hair and his eyes are the same slushy color, but his transparent hands are as spotted and as delicately veined as the wings of butterflies. Smiling at me, he draws two little flutes from his coat pocket and shows them to me. I made them, his face says.

One of the flutes is made of wood, the other of some kind of clay. I balance them gingerly on my palms, for they feel as fragile as the old man's fingers, and hand them to Phil, who pipes a few notes on each. "Chromatic scale," he says wonderingly. "Be damned." He gives them back to the old man and says, "Play something, please."

The old man puts the clay flute in his pocket and begins to play on the wooden one. The sound he makes is shrill and thin, but it has seconds of sweetness as real and sharp and lost as the seconds of honey hidden in red clover. We try to follow his music with our instruments, but there is no tune there, only notes that waver and wail because the holes are not placed right, only the old man's whining breath exulting that it still moves in his mouth. His buttoned-up black coat sways gently around him, and he casts the shadow of a bell as he plays. When he stops he smiles and steps away, never quite out of sight, but never coming forward again. He is always there, but we have to look for him, and we forget to.

The proprietress tells us that he is Italian and speaks only a few words of English. "He comes in every day," she says, "and sits around." He is ninety-three years old—she knows this, but she is not sure how she knows. Somebody told her.

The water witch is very drunk, loud and desperate, unbuttoning herself. She wants to know if we can sing "When It's Springtime in the Rockies," and begins to sing it herself before she is through asking. She runs over to the bar

to lead the other customers in the song, and comes skitter-
ing back, applauding us and herself and everybody. "Don't
let me tell you what to play," she keeps commanding us.
"You go on playing just what you like, you're fine. Can
you play some of that real Spanish music?" We do
"Coplas" for her. This may or may not be a Mexican folk
song; at all events, it is to be played at noisy parties after
you are quite sure that nobody there knows a *rascado*
from "God Bless America." If the girl you are playing at
happens to be any kind of Latin, it is a good idea to play
something else, possibly "Railroad Bill." It's been a long
time since we had any fun playing "Coplas," but there is
a mean, rainy enjoyment in watching the drunken woman
try to beat out flamenco rhythms on her thighs and do the
arrogant steps. I don't know why the pleasure is there,
but it is.

At first we banter stiffly with her, but this becomes bor-
ing in the same way that amusing an aggressive child does,
and we take to smiling and ignoring her. At this point, like
a child, she grows demonstrative, although her husband is
nearby, watching. She begins to pat and fondle me, mostly
because she can't reach Phil, but partly because I always
seem to attract older women, while Phil is constantly pur-
sued by determined virgins. This has never proved to be of
the slightest benefit to either of us. I dodge her as much
as I can and keep playing. This is not easy and absolutely
ruins "Crawdad." Finally—perhaps about the third time
she chucks me under the chin and pulls my beard—I say
something so casually cruel that I have forgotten what it
was by the time I begin to regret it. I watch the orange
mouth begin to crumple—exactly like a child's—and the
bewildered grownup eyes try wearily to rearrange whatever
it was I said into something nice and maybe a little flirta-
tious, and I think, This is not fiction, this is not something
you can have one character say to another and then cross
out later on if it spoils the scene. This is real, that was a
human being you just hurt. You do remember the differ-

ence, don't you? Her husband sits and drinks his Jack Daniel's, and watches, and says nothing.

We are alternately gay and sad driving back to Gunnison, now singing, now silent. Phil doesn't like the gouache he found time to do in Crested Butte, but he knows why he doesn't like it, which is something. Joanna plans supper and hums "Au Bois de mon Coeur." I nurse my rapidly fading high and try to remember what it was that I wanted to tell Joanna, knowing that I will remember it when we are gone. I watch the mountains drawing nearer as the shadow comes from the east to take them. It feels like Sunday evening.

After supper we take the two children who don't go right to bed for a ride on the scooters. Phil takes the boy, Danny, and I carry Sheila, who is ten and the oldest child. She is serious, as befits her position in the family, but she is still a child and may be the only person we have met so far who fully understands why we are driving scooters across the country. She is definitely the only one who does not ask, "When will you be going back to New York?" She asks me to drive around Western State College and points out every building on the campus. This is where Mike goes to school.

We do not go to bed until around two in the morning, and yet we have done nothing more with the evening than sit in the kitchen, talking with Joanna and Connie. At midnight, as though it were some sort of New Year's ritual, we all go down to the cellar and help Joanna shovel the ashes and clinkers out of the furnace and put in fresh coal. I have not lived in a house that had a coal-burning furnace for at least twelve years, but I remember how it works, and how a lot of other things I haven't touched for a long time work, and I decide, that's it, that's why I like this house so much, why I become so stupidly wistful, that's what I meant to tell Joanna. So I tell her, and of course that's not it.

Going to bed, Phil and I talk about Joanna. "That's a good woman," he says. "That's a sweet one. I like her."

"So do I." At times I resent the fact that Phil's enthusiasm often makes mine seem a little irrelevant. I say, "I felt good about her as soon as we walked in. That doesn't happen to me very often."

"A sane woman," he says. "She's crazy, sure, out of her head, but she's sane." I nod. What we mean by "crazy" is difficult to explain. The people we call crazy have a kind of freedom within themselves that takes many forms, somber and joyous. Some of them may really be insane. "A delight," he says. "A woman. This is a good house. I wish we could stay here longer. I almost wish we lived in this town, so we could come and visit them."

"It's a real them, too. You say one name—Mike, Joanna —and you think of the other. How many couples you could say that about?"

"Not many," he answers. "That's the funny thing. This is a hell of a sweet, warm, full-grown woman, with whom I couldn't possibly live. That aggravates me. I suspect Enid'll probably be like that."

"Maybe." I think about them meeting, the two people closest to me, the two people I can feel being alive even when I am not there, the two people in whose aloneness I truly believe. "Be funny if you hated each other," I say.

"I should be so lucky."

In the morning it's like the day we left Alex and Kisa's house in Ann Arbor, if we were ever there. We rise late, stall over breakfast, drink a second pot of coffee, and make funny, clumsy efforts in the direction of something called "helping Joanna around the house." But it is stalling, and the humor is at once desperate and lifeless, and it is actually a relief to be standing in the driveway with our Thermals and sweatshirts and jackets on, waiting for the scooters to warm up. Joanna looks tired. It was hard getting Danny and Sheila off to school this morning, and now the two younger children aren't feeling well. "I got used to having the two of you around," she says. "It felt very natural."

A lot of people on whose living-room floors we have

spent a night or two have said the same thing. I almost wish Joanna hadn't. I almost wish we didn't adopt so easily. "We'll be back," I say.

Joanna gives us each a swift, warm hug to take with us and says, "Be careful. Call us if anything goes wrong." I don't know what else she says to Phil, but to me she adds, "Write to me, tell me what happens with Enid. I always want to find out how things come out." Me too, Joanna. Good-by.

Beyond Gunnison the country is still grazing land, but mostly for sheep now. It must be shearing time, for the pastures are full of bald animals, purple as undercooked steak, with numerals written across their sides in green paint. Some of the tiniest lambs are inscribed from tailtip to nose, and there are indications that the tallyman ran out of lamb just as he was getting into his stride. It makes me think suddenly of all the green and yellow and off-white IBM cards I have filled out since I was old enough to think I understood what I was doing: all whittled and nicked as neatly as player-piano rolls. Who has them now? the university? the Army? the government? Maybe some undersecretary somewhere really does take them all home and play them every night, stomping on the pedals and laughing. Maybe I'm somebody's music box. I'd like that better.

Late in the day we reach the Colorado 80 turn-off, which is supposed to take us into Cortez. It's a godawful road: dusty, oatmeal-colored, packed with holes the size of bathtubs; a dinosaur racetrack. Jenny and Couchette have excellent shock-absorbers, but when they hit those baked-in potholes they come up with a crunch that makes us wince for them. Indeed, the most agonizing part of this ride (and it goes on for almost thirty miles) is not the steady, rhythmic jarring of spines and kidneys, or the meek-looking little ridges that jolt you clean out of the saddle, or the dust, or the feeling of endlessness, but the awareness of the beating Jenny and Couchette are taking, no matter how slowly and carefully we drive. The engines are working much too hard in the low gears; the shocks are taking the kind of merciless smashes that give them no leeway to absorb them; and God knows what's happening to the tires. Human, we feel that we are suffering less than the beautiful machines under us, which is a genuinely stupid attitude, a limb of the deadly middle-class sentimentality that led us to name the scooters in the first place. At every jounce I murmur, "Sorry, Jenny, sorry, love." Her speedometer cable breaks on this road.

It is night before we hit blacktop again. It feels incredibly, physically sweet, like stepping into cool grass on blistered feet. But Cortez is a long way from here, perhaps fifty miles, and the cold is spilling over us like thin blue fire. Now and then we run through pockets of warm air, ridiculously voluptuous—you always find those on a scooter, even on the coldest night, just as you find the small, cold winds on a summer day. The road is very dark, but driving close together we light up the whole road for a long way ahead; and separated we reach out to each other when the wind makes the trees and the grass and the clouds move at us and the whole chimerical world is made of quicksand. *God pity all those with no money on a cold night like this.*

And at last there is a fork in the road and a sign that points dead left and says DOVE CREEK—2. It is not really very late—ten, perhaps—but Dove Creek is small and dark enough so that we might drive straight on through it, looking for it, except for a gas station where we find out that we are, after all, here. Dove Creek has two hotels, one of which is full, surprisingly enough; there's a big livestock show going on in Cortez. The other is a strange place on the edge of town, an old house run by an old man for old men. It feels like a cross between a hunting lodge and a flophouse. I doubt if it does very much transient business; the other hotel probably gets all that. These old men must live here all the time. They look very small as they sit in their fraying armchairs, watching us sign for our room. Naked and robbed, like the lambs we saw this

112

morning, they stay very close to the pot-bellied stove, as though it were all that was left to them and might vanish too, at any moment, if not loved enough. They begin little motions with their hands and heads and never complete them; they say words and let them fall meaningless; they are moving, all together, very slowly, swaying as though a current were stirring them on the bottom of the sea. " 'Nobody knows how their days will cease,' " James Stephens says to me, but then he contradicts himself with the soft and terrible wail, " 'O, God, He knows, and God, He knows, and surely God Almighty knows.' "

Upstairs, in a small clean room, we use up the last of George and Flo's waybread: the tuna fish, the mayonnaise, and an onion. Getting undressed, Phil says, "First thing tomorrow we ought to take the scooters apart and clean them up good. There's half of Colorado 80 in there now, and that dirt'll bake right in if we let it."

"We can do that in Cortez, find a motorcycle shop and clean them there. If we bust something, I'd sure hate to be stranded here. It's only about thirty-five miles to Cortez."

"All right." He lights a cigarette and asks, "Where were we this morning? Where did we leave from?"

"Gunnison. Don't you remember?"

"Gunnison," he says. "Mike and Joanna, that was this morning?" And then, slowly and wonderingly, "My God, everything seems so long ago."

We spend almost half a driving day in a Honda shop in Cortez, cleaning Colorado 80 out of the scooters. Then we head southwest instead of straight south into New Mexico, on the advice of the Honda mechanic, who warns us against the Triptik's route to the Grand Canyon. It's a bad road, he says, and just at this moment those words would frighten us off a freeway. Twenty miles out of Cortez, therefore, we veer off onto Colorado 40, making for the Four Corners Monument where Colorado, New Mexico, Arizona, and Utah nose at one another like dogs. It is all desert country now, but we can still see the Rockies when we look back, a shrunken crescent behind us, power-less as senile enchanters, quite pretty once the awful immediacy of being among them is gone. "Now it will be warm," I say to Phil.

The Painted Desert is pink, just the shade shirts used to be eight or ten years ago. The fascination here is not in the colors but in the way the mesas and canyons break up the land and build the horizon, and in the way the move-ment of the sun, the shadow of a cloud, can change what you are looking at into something different, horns into hollows, monoliths into barrens. From far away the red mesas, the wind's castles and whetstones, look as man-made as the huge housing projects with which New York City is replacing poverty. Phil stops a couple of times to draw but eventually says, "We might as well go on, I'll be at it all day. Man, would this be a maddening country to paint. I could do you a series of painting you could tell time by."

The Four Corners Monument looks much like any other state campground, except for the large round dais in the middle. Concentric rings of stairs cut into the dais lead you up to the monument, which is a bronze disk divided into four equal slices. Each wedge bears the coat of arms and the motto of the state it represents. A sign on the monument informs us that this is for real, that all those big square states actually touch in this bronze disk, and as far down as you want to go. Up too, I guess.

"I can imagine writing a mystery with this as the kicker," I say, sitting down in Utah. "Kidnaping and ex-tradition and jurisdiction and all like that. Maybe a movie; Hitchcock would like it. The climax would be Cary Grant and Claude Rains dodging around and around the monu-ment, each one trying to trip the other into a state where the cops can get him. Then you get the real kicker: Steve Reeves has sneaked up in the night and spun the whole monument like a *dreidl,* just for laughs, so nobody knows where the boundary lines are any more. Total confusion and panic, until Doris Day stands up in court and reveals

I SEE BY MY OUTFIT

that she has the real boundaries tattooed across her—"

"Call me when you're quite through," Phil says. He squats on the small disk-within-a-disk from which the state lines radiate away into the desert. "Meanwhile I would sit here and fart on four states for the price of one. They seem to be on Special."

We have a couple of cupcakes left over from the delicatessen lady in Kansas City, and we sprawl across the states to eat them. Phil is starting over to a wastebasket to throw the wrappers away when a car turns into the circle and stops near the scooters. A man and a woman get out. The woman is carrying a dog that appears to be made up of equal parts of Pomeranian, cat, and tarantula, and that obviously has to go. She takes it over to a relatively unhallowed area of the circle and sets it down to relieve itself while she loads a camera the size and approximate shape of a bazooka. The man is middle-aged, freshly tanned, with a freckled scalp and a very small mouth; a pleasant, friendly man from Seattle. We talk for a few moments. He is driving the opposite way from us, toward Cortez, but according to him the nearest town on this route is Kayenta, some eighty miles from here. "You're heading into the Navaho reservation now," he says. "You'll like it. It's real exciting, seeing the way they live and all. Pretty nice people, too."

His wife calls him over to take pictures just as Phil comes back. We decide to camp at Kayenta tonight, which will leave us an easy drive of a hundred and fifty miles to make the Grand Canyon tomorrow. As we start up the scooters the wife is posing her husband crouched on all fours in the bronze disk, his feet in New Mexico and Colorado, his hands in Utah and Arizona. This leaves him no way to hold the dog, which is apparently supposed to sit still under his belly and look as if it were having a good time in agreeable company. Not that dog. It is not having a good time at all, and it is struggling hard to get the hell away from there and go die. "Smile for Mommy, dear," the woman calls as she backs away, adjusting for windage and elevation. "You smile too, Nelson." The man seems to want to wave to us as we pull away, but he can't because his hands are in Utah and Arizona, and besides the dog would get loose.

Sundown catches us on the road to Kayenta, and we eat our canned spaghetti in the desert. It occurs to me as we set off once more that we are realizing another winter dream tonight, the one about racing across the desert in the violet evening, two small, swift shadows going West, lighting up the empty road all the way to California. At this point in the dreaming we would sit very quietly for a little while, and then one of us would say softly, "*Psst-psst,* long gone," and make his two flat hands be two scooters going West, going away. The other would say, "Long gone. Hoo-boy." We had, of course, dreamed it without the wind and the canned spaghetti, but we always do.

It is quite dark when we get to Kayenta, but a nearby café sheds enough light for us to set up the tent a little way off the road. Then we go into the café for coffee. It is a bigger place than it looked from outside, and it is full of young Indians, couples and foursomes on dates, stags of both sexes eying one another in the doorway, others coming in to stand on tiptoe and look around for someone and then go away again. They are a handsome people, remarkably Oriental-looking; at this moment in their lives many of them are homely with loudness and acne, but their features are so beautifully cut that they make the faces of the white people in the café seem soft, ill-defined, indecisive by comparison. But there is a strange tautness in the way they move—for all its grace—and in the way they speak and stare, even in their laughter, as though they were holding tight to something invisible that was fighting to get away from them. The girls have the saddening beauty I have seen in the faces of very young Puerto Rican girls in New York.

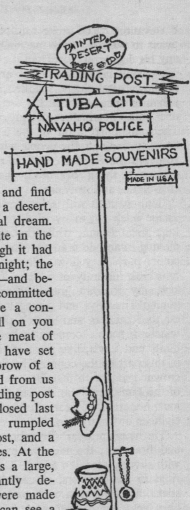

PAINTED DESERT

TRADING POST

TUBA CITY

NAVAHO POLICE

HAND MADE SOUVENIRS

MADE IN U.S.A.

It's strange to wake up and find yourself in the middle of a desert. It's like beginning the real dream. The sand is painfully white in the sun, and as clean as though it had just drifted down in the night; the sky is a rich, deep blue—and between those two totally committed expanses you yourself are a confusion, with the sleep still on you and your ego groggy, the meat of a nothing sandwich. We have set up the tent just on the brow of a small hill. Across the road from us are the café and a trading post which must have been closed last night. Behind us are rumpled desert, another trading post, and a handful of huts and fences. At the bottom of the hill there is a large, handsome motel, elegantly designed to look as if it were made of wood. Beyond that I can see a post office and a very new school.

After breakfast at the café we go into the trading post next door to see about the big straw hats we have been advised to wear crossing the desert. It is a large place, as full of candy machines and cheap sunglasses as any rural general store, and it smells faintly of fried meat. The really important goods are hung from the ceiling: saddles, belts, chaps, blankets, dresses; they dangle just above our heads, so thickly arranged that they stir against one another when somebody comes through the door. There are mirrors on all the walls, and even one on the floor, so that with the people who are really there, their reverberating reflections, and the reflections of the robes and dresses swaying overhead, the trading post seems as crowded as a subway car.

Old, old men with skins as dark and wrinkled and soft as the buckskin many of them wear sit on the steps and look for the sun, while the old women chuckle inside, moving in an odd cramped way in long dresses heavy with color: purples, yellows, blacks, greens, blues—they make me think instantly of a dress I once saw, or dreamed I saw, my Russian grandmother wear when I was very young. The boys and young men lean their elbows back on the counters and stretch their legs in front of them, watching people come into the trading post. They wear boots and Levis, like most of the young men we've seen in this part of the country, bright embroidered shirts, flat-crowned hats with the sides curling up. They may well be of the same people as the older men and women, but they look hundreds of years descended from them, instead of eighteen or twenty-two.

The women wear silver brooches, earrings, necklaces, and bracelets; the men wear heavy leather belts scaled with silver plates like armor. There are cases and cases of rings in the counters, as casually exhibited as the Chapsticks, as uniform in color and design as though they had been spat out of the same machine in half an hour, as though they were made of glass and plastic instead of turquoise and silver. Even the poorest-looking Indians wear some kind of jewelry.

We buy a water bag here, but we do not find the big

straw hats. The good ones are too expensive for us, and the cheap ones seem to be woven of confetti. I fall in love with one special hat, but it happens to be on the head of the old Indian who is waiting on us. It is an old black hat, broken with white lines where it must have been crumpled and stepped on and kicked, and its brim droops like a hound's ear all along one side, but it is a wonderful hat, a magic hat. D'Artagnan wore a hat like that when he came up from Gascony, and Don Quixote wore a hat like that when he went home at last. Around the crown its owner has placed a thin silver band, as simply made as a wedding ring. They do look long-married, the old man and his black hat.

There are only four people in the other trading post: the middle-aged Indian couple who run it, an Indian boy of about seventeen who works there, and a small sandy-faced white man in a postman's uniform. They are sitting together when we come in, talking in calm voices. The manager looks up and smiles at us. "Good morning," he says. "Yes? What can I do for you?" He speaks slowly and clearly, not so much with an accent as with an odd rhythm, a hesitancy, as though he himself were speaking behind the beat of his sentences. He and his wife look very much alike. They have the same light orange skin; the same wide-set, wrinkle-lidded eyes, tortoises' eyes; the same heavy lines of forehead and cheek and jaw, too strong for sagging flesh to blur; and the same amazingly sweet smile, completely without greed, without bitterness, completely unguarded. You forget how rare smiles like theirs are—because you have to—until you see one.

The boy, as cheerful and slangy as any New York stock-boy with a summer job between college semesters, takes us to the back of the store and shows us heaps of hats, towers and totem poles of hats, out of which we have a certain amount of trouble picking two to fit our shaggy heads and seedy wallets. The one I settle on is light-colored with a dark band; Phil's is gray with a light band. We clap them on our heads, turn to look at each other,

and say simultaneously, "My God, do I look like you?"
In the full-length mirror on the wall we see two small
hairy figures staring at us. They wear chino shirts (over
each top button and out of each sleeve there peeks something as limp and tired and snot-colored as the old cloth
Band-Aids used to get), properly battered Levis, and torn
suede shoes, in which they slouch like marionettes. One
of them has bloodshot brown eyes; the other's are bloodshot blue. Their briary beards have the same tantalizing
hints of past form as an abandoned bird's nest; their wind-
burned faces are just about to tan, and won't. They will
never be able to comb their hair again, but that doesn't
matter now, for they both have cowboy hats.

"Jesus God," Phil says very softly. He points at the
foolishly grinning face beside him in the mirror. "Look at
you, Beagle. Roy Rabbi."

"Please to regarding small self, honorable wise bastard.
Billy the Boychick, with glasses yet." I have never worn a
hat in my life, and the image of myself peeking wistfully
out from under this straw sombrero, a kind of hat which
even Gil's infant grandson wore with more dignity, will
remain with me for a long time. All the ridiculous ones
do, and this one is a stayer, even with the cream of twenty-
four years to contend with. The idiot in the mirror waves
at me.

The Indian couple are Mr. and Mrs. Bonino—at least,
the name sounds as Italian as that. Mr. Bonino is extremely curious about New York. No, that is not the right
word, not for a wonder about something as totally unreal
as New York is to Mr. Bonino. The idea of the city means
something to him, like a poem. "I would like to know
about New York," he says. "They tell me that people live
badly in New York. Is that so?"

"Lousy," I answer flatly. "That's why we came out
here." That is not entirely true, but it is spontaneous.

"Ah," murmurs Mr. Bonino. He glances around his
store and through the open doorway, where the white

desert trembles in the sunlight. "Is it all the people, they all live badly?"

"They live in boxes," Phil says. He points to a stack of orange crates on which the postman is resting his feet. "One on top of the other, like those. The rich ones live in very expensive boxes, the poor ones live in boxes you wouldn't keep a dog in. The middle ones are in the middle boxes. Nobody can breathe."

"Told you, Louis," the postman says amiably. He was born in Phoenix but lived in New York for a couple of years after the war. "Didn't I tell you?" Mr. Bonino smiles but does not answer. Mrs. Bonino says, "The children fight a lot, I think. They get drunk and run around and they have accidents with their cars. I hear about it on the radio." She has a light, swift voice, much younger than her face, as her face is younger than her hands.

"It's a bad city to raise children in," I say, "especially when you have no money."

"What is a good place to raise children?" Mr. Bonino wonders. "We are just like New York here. The young boys, even the girls, they drink and they get into fights, all of them, all the time. I don't know what happens to them. They don't care about anything. I don't know why."

He looks straight at us, waiting to be told. We shrug, we mutter, "It's that way everywhere, a lot of reasons, the cold war . . ." The postman says, "No money, Louis. Never any money. You know it as well as me."

Mr. Bonino nods politely, but the unanswered question in his face turns the nod into a dissatisfied headshake. "Yes, I know about money," he says. "Tell me this, if you would. They say that it is very bad for the Negroes in New York, they beat them up all the time. Is that so?"

There is a certain mad logic in the idea of two middle-class Jews telling an Indian what it is like to be a Negro in New York, but it has to be seen from farther away than the Indian's grave black eyes. I begin cautiously, "Well, it's bad for Negroes everywhere, New York or any other town. They don't have to beat you up; they can starve you or put you in jail or make you live in a house with no heat, with the rats. . . ." but it sputters out and dies. That *you,* the old bear trap for the liberal, killed it.

"I don't understand that," Mr. Bonino says. "I don't see why they should treat anyone like that. I hear about it all the time, but I don't understand."

Phil and I know very well why New York is a hard city to live in for most people and most possible combinations of colors or ancestors. The knowledge, arrived at in our own long ways and times, is part of our lives, but it is also as much a number in our repertoire as Routine B, or the Lone Ranger bit, or "Au Bois de mon Coeur," and we can use it as we use all our bits, either to make another New Yorker laugh ("Now it is not easy to make a prisoner laugh," boasts Wilfred Shadbolt, the head jailer who wants so badly to be a strolling jester) or to tell each other a truth without breaking the rhythm. But somehow we cannot answer Mr. Bonino as we might anyone else. We cannot make him laugh, nor do we dare to offer him the very few truths that have not turned to quicksilver inside us. The first choice would not satisfy us, and the second would never satisfy polite, puzzled Mr. Bonino. He sits with his head held a little forward and his broad hands spread flat on his knees and asks us questions about the way the people of New York live, stranger's questions that we have answered wittily and warningly before and will again. But what Mr. Bonino truly wants to know is not in his words, and we are not the people to know where else to seek it. We will try, at least, not to pretend to be.

In time the subject changes to the Navahos' relations with the United States Government. The Navahos are not a wealthy people—at least, neither Mr. Bonino nor the postman knows of a Navaho who owns much more of value than his silver ornaments, his underfed livestock, and an occasional pickup truck—but there is money somewhere, enough to have put a couple of lawyers through school and to retain them in Washington on salaries of up to thirty-five thousand dollars a year. "Once or twice in a year," Mr. Bonino says, "they come back here and they say, 'Everything is fine, but we must have more money.' They always get the money." Mr. Bonino is somewhat skeptical about these lawyers' devotion to the cause of their people, but he is not bitter, only a little amused. "Maybe they are as honest as any lawyers we could get," he says, and he smiles. "Who knows?" The postman snorts.

The last two dry years have hurt the Navahos badly. The difference between very little water and less water is as immediate to them as the difference between one eye and none. "The horses and the mules are dying," Mr. Bonino tells us, "and we can't do anything if we have no horses, you know. There are not many roads through the desert, and only a few of us have cars or machines. We need the horses. The other animals are dying too." One of the Navaho lawyers recently went to see whoever it is you see about Indians' horses dying of thirst and explained the situation to him. "And the man said, 'Well, why don't they just take taxis and buses, and' "—Mr. Bonino rubs his head for the word—" 'and take streetcars, like anyone else?' " The postman, who has obviously heard this story before, still grows furious, and Mrs. Bonino shakes her head sadly, but Mr. Bonino laughs so softly that you might mistake it for a sigh. "The man didn't know," he says. "How do you explain? Most of the people on this reservation, they have never seen a taxi in their lives, they don't know what a taxi is. Maybe the children, because they read about it in school." He is silent for a moment, and then he chuckles again and says, "Maybe the man had never seen a horse, either."

When we finally pay for our hats and say good-by, Mr. Bonino says seriously, "Well, I am very glad I had a chance to meet you. I like it sometimes when someone from a big city comes in here and we can talk. I sit here in my store and I listen, and I think, and I learn about things sometimes." He wishes us luck on our journey, and when we look back at the trading post he and his wife are waving to us. The blinding sun turns them into shadows behind the beaded curtain, moving as jerkily as the electric-light cartoons on Broadway.

We see only one sign of life as we scramble down the hillside, an old woman in a black dress hanging out laundry. She is struggling with a huge, beautiful quilt, as vividly black and gold as a tiger swallowtail, which the wind keeps trying to take away from her. The old woman is very small, and the drape puffs out so powerfully in the wind that I would not be at all surprised to see her carried off into the sky, like a little cricket clinging to a black-and-gold balloon, to drift away forever, or anyway until the rapacious birds got over their astonishment at seeing a cricket in the sky. But she is so stubborn and so determined! there is not the smallest cry for help in the way she moves her stiff old body. She defeats the wind this time, pins the quilt firmly to the clothesline, and goes back into her hut.

The hats turn out to be one of our better ideas: besides the fact that they shield us from the direct rays of the sun, the shadow over our eyes eases the glare of the desert itself. But the wind, like a fantastically powerful child, wants those hats as badly as it wanted the old woman's beautiful cloth, and very nearly gets them. I lose count of the times my hat comes loose and, held only by the cord, tugs at my neck with real strength (imagine a country where they hung people from kites, so as not to have to bury them), or flaps wildly into my face, like an outraged hen. I begin to develop a habit of driving with one hand and cramming my hat more firmly onto my head with the other. Paladin does something like that all the time—it's a Character-Building Detail—but I don't think it's because his hat is too small for his head. Mine is.

We stop at every trading post along the way to look at jewelry. Both of us have always lumped Indian jewelry with export-only Mexican silver and African folk art with a seam down the middle, but some of the jewelry in the trading posts is as fine as any either of us has ever seen, and the art as a whole is vividly alive and thriving among the Hershey bars and the Indian-chief postcards. There is a delicacy and a second-glance simplicity to some of the gaudiest tie clasps and belt buckles; there is a feeling of continuity and variation among the motifs and techniques of the different tribes; and there is a sense of individual workmanship even in a caseful of apparently identical pieces. We will stare at hundreds of rings and clasps and brooches during the next few days without growing dulled and numb to them, or insensitive to their individuality.

The multiplicity of patterns and designs brings *The Lord of the Rings* back into my thoughts again. There were twenty rings in that epic, scattered through three different worlds like seeds of good and evil, but only one ring was master of the others. It is that ring that Phil and I are both seeking in an absent-minded way. We dream of finding it in some tiny shop glowing like foxfire on a dark street with narrow sidewalks, in a strange country; the shop, preferably, to be run by only an old man and his familiar, and to smell of iron and leather and all kinds of good wood, the kind of place where Phil would find his pocket of Martins and I all the lost little boxes from the cereal people. The Ring will be there, and the old man will know its value and not care, because of what else he knows. Then the only problem will be finding another one to match it, and finding two foolish girls to give them to.

Most of the Indian jewelry is remarkably cheap in comparison with its actual worth—there are pieces going for thirty-five dollars that would fetch at least five times that amount in New York—but almost all of it is too expensive for us. I eventually buy a ring for Enid, a simple pattern of turquoises set into what at first seems to be some polished black stone and is actually only carved emptiness. It is a pretty ring, and soothing as blue water in the blinding sunlight. Curiously, it is the only one of its kind in the store.

Naturally the rest of the afternoon is spent looking for

a ring just like it. None of the rings he sees in other trading posts grab Phil the way this particular arrangement of stones and thin silver does; every time he comes across one he likes even a little, he drags my left hand out of my pocket, studies the ring on my little finger, grunts sourly, and says, "Come on, let's try the next place." I had no special feeling for the ring when I bought it, but his covetousness gives it a value beyond price tags. By the time we reach Tonalea I am explaining loudly why this ring is so perfectly chosen for Enid, and by Tuba City I may not give it to her at all. The Master Ring was supposed to have that effect on the bearer.

On our way into Tuba City we are stopped by a patrol car with a Navaho Police insignia. The driver is an Indian —homely, intelligent face, Chinese-looking, maybe thirty, maybe less. He looks like a TV character actor. "Where you fellows coming from?" The bright-cop voice. Cops have two kinds of voices, very distinct from each other. I think they must distribute them at the police academy. "Kayenta," Phil says. "Going on to the canyon. Heading for California." It has become a reflex with us to reassure a cop that the hideous crimes we are obviously bound to commit won't be committed in his territory. Cops, like everyone else, hate responsibility.

"What part of New York are you boys from?" the cops ask.

"The Bronx," we answer, as cautiously as you can say the Bronx. This has all the earmarks of a Clever Trap, especially since the exact addresses are on our licenses, but the cop smiles disarmingly. "Oh, yes, sure, I see. Selwyn Avenue, Gunhill Road. Where the hell is that now? Must be around Westchester, huh?"

"Some distance, actually." The cop nods and smiles and props his arm lazily in the window frame. "Well, let's see, how do you get up there from downtown? Take the old Third Avenue El, I guess."

The El has been gone below 149th Street for a long time now. This is beginning to remind me of the long day on an Air Force base in Evreux when everybody arrested me on suspicion, including a noncom who decided that I was a Russian spy, undoubtedly well briefed on most aspects of American life, but certain to fall down on such subjects peculiar to the American Way as baseball and jazz. I don't know much about jazz after Jelly Roll Morton, but I know baseball as only an incompetent can. I think I recited to him, among other things, the roster of the 1927 New York Yankees, complete with averages. He arrested me anyway. "No, we both take the IND," I say to the cop, "the Concourse line. He gets off at a Hundred and Seventy-fourth Street, and I go all the way to the end of the line, Two Hundred and Fifth Street. We take the I. R. T. sometimes"—I intend to overdo things—"you know, the Woodlawn line, but it's a little more of a walk home."

Strange, strange and silly, to be standing in the pink desert reciting the weary old New York names to an Indian cop. He is beginning to grin, though; he says, "The Woodlawn line, that runs out to Two Hundred and Forty-second Street, doesn't it?"

"No, you're thinking of the Lexington Avenue line, runs to Two Hundred and Forty-first Street." The cop frowns slightly, and Phil interrupts, "No, he's not, he means the Seventh Avenue subway, that one goes to Two-Hundred and Forty-second."

Woops, so it does. *Ausgefundet*. Ruined by insufficient indoctrination. But the cop puts his notebook away and hands us back our licenses. "Okay, fellows," he says. "Sorry to bother you, but we got word of a couple of guys on motorcycles causing trouble back around Tonalea, and we had to check everybody." He waves toward Tuba City. "Consider yourselves our guests," he says.

At the trading post I give Phil the ring to take inside, and sit down on the porch to wait for him and watch people. A very old man in a red shirt and Levis eases himself down on the porch next to me, handling himself as gently as if the smallest noise, the wrong vibration, might send

127

him cracking and sifting down the steps like a tiny ava-
lanche. He wears moccasins and a tall peaked William S.
Hart kind of sombrero, and his face is very dark with the
polishing of age. I look at him out of the corner of my
eye, turning my hat nervously in my lap—who knows how
much of what I have read, this old man was? For a moment I sit in the cold shadow of history in a way I never
did when I sat on the parapet of the Ponte Vecchio and
watched the children swimming in the brown river. Then
the old man turns his face to me and smiles with long,
tapering teeth and asks, "How fast will that machine of
yours go?"—pointing to Jenny. His voice is high and
shaky and very Western.

"About seventy," I say. The old Indian nods placidly.
"Saw a fellow come through on one of those things a year
ago. How much'll one of them run you, new?"

I feel faintly disappointed, as I always am every time
history snickers at me and turns into people, but I always
enjoy telling people about Jenny. We are sitting on the
steps, discussing scooters, when Phil comes out of the
trading post. Nothing there, he says, giving me back my
ring, but there's a place a couple of miles down the road,
come on. I say good-by to the old man and follow him.

The trading post down the road is not part of a town;
it is a wooden house in the middle of the desert. There are
no other houses anywhere to be seen. Indians simply come
walking up out of the desert or piling out of pickup trucks.
When we go into the trading post there are several of them
at the jewelry counter before us, but the beaming white
woman who runs the place shoos them jovially aside, clap-
ping her hands as if she were chasing ducks. "They're
lovely people," she explains to us, although we have not
asked. "I mean, I've known them for years, and there's
not a better people anywhere, but they just come into the
store all day and just *lean*. You, Billy Soredaughter!" She
snaps her fingers at him. "You move on away from there
now, that's a good fella, the gentlemen want to look at the
jewelry." The middle-aged man with the skinny legs and

the disproportionately powerful chest and shoulders gives us the same look of indifference beyond contempt that you sometimes fancy in the eyes of a baby, and walks away. "Tell the little 'uns to come on by, you hear?" the woman sweets after him. "I been saving a lollipop for each one of them, the kind they like, with the chocolate inside."

Smiling fondly, she turns back to us. Yes, that certainly is a pretty little thing, isn't it? No, I don't think I've ever seen anything just exactly like it, although I do have something here that's more or less the same kind of work. Like most of the trading-post managers and clerks we have talked with, she neither pushes nor haggles; she is genuinely proud of her Indians' work and likes to talk about it. She wears a couple of attractive turquoise pins herself, and she has several sets of earrings at home.

She shows us a case set aside for personal jewelry. Most of the ornaments there must have belonged to men; there are armbands and heavy bracelets, and always the belts, the silver gray behind the glass, and the leather frayed or torn like paper. They look as though they were made by another kind of people, a species that died out thousands of years ago, leaving nothing but a few broken skulls and their idea of beauty. "They wear their best stuff themselves," the woman says. "I feel real bad when they have to come in and pawn them. Most of these here are real old."

From time to time she interrupts herself to shout something like, "Hi you, Moses Black Elk, don't you go playing with those dishes if you aren't going to buy any, you know better than that"—very much in the manner of a harried but patient baby-sitter—or to sell someone some canned food or coffee. She talks to her paying customers in a *bêche-de-mer* of English, Spanish, and Navaho, always asking about their families and occasionally about their livestock. They answer her in monosyllables and single sentences, which appears to satisfy her, for she always smiles happily. "I kind of make it a point to know what's going on," she says.

We do not find a ring for Phil here, but as we come out of the store a movement of mesas catches his eye, and he takes his sketchpad from Couchette and squats in the sand to work. I lean back against the building and brood about small things, just to keep in practice. The middle-aged Indian that the woman chased away from the jewelry counter comes out of the trading post and stops in his tracks to peer over Phil's shoulder. His face has the dignity and sorrowful slyness of an elephant's face. Two other Indians, a father and a young son, come out of the trading post, hugging heavy bags of groceries against their hips, and they too stop to watch Phil. Neither says anything, nor do they look at one another or at the third man. Other Indians come drifting out of the desert with the wind behind them, as though they had been wandering for a long time in hope of seeing Phil drawing, and in a few minutes there are eight or ten Indians, men and boys, standing between us, none of them moving or making a sound. I can barely make Phil out among all those straight backs; just enough to see that he never looks around. For a moment it is like watching a scrawny, intent cave painter working on a wall, while the rest of the tribe crowds attentively behind him, watching to make sure he gets the mammoth's tusks curved right, but never daring to kibitz for fear of offending this new and disturbing magic.

In time, only a few minutes, the Indians go away again, as quietly and definitely as they assembled. The father and son drive off in a station wagon, but the others really do seem to disappear back into the desert. The sand is driving hard enough in the wind to make me wince and blink where I sit in the shade, and yet the Indians move through it with the hurried, half-grotesque grace of seals returning to water. When I tell Phil about them, he says, "Be damned, I didn't notice a thing. Those Indians know how to watch painting. I wish you'd told me they were there. Rather draw them."

We leave the trading post around sunset and stop to cook supper in a tiny campground balanced as precariously as a waitress's pile of dishes on an elbow in the road; beyond the three-walled shelter in which we set up the stove there is a steep fall to shrunken sandhills that hold the red and purple shadows fast between them, like knuckles. We have a can of roast-beef hash and a can of spaghetti. We heat the hash first, tacitly hoping for another suppertime miracle by the time we get to the spaghetti.

"The guitars get there yet?" Phil asks. I shake my head. Our guitars—after Jenny and Couchette, our only valuable property in the world—are being driven to California by a friend who left from Washington, D.C., a few days before we left New York. He is supposed to deliver them to Enid, but when I called her last night from the café in Kayenta they had not arrived. "Good-by, guitars," Phil says, sad but positive. "Doubtless old Gordon got to driving with his arm around some chick and not watching the road, and she happened to be driving another car at the time anyway. Poor Gordon, the bum. Maybe they saved the guitars. Fat chance."

"They'll get there. Maybe he went through the Panama Canal a couple of times, you can't tell with Gordon. They'll get there, and we'll sit on Enid's front steps and play 'Crawdad,' and eat real spaghetti, and play 'Crawdad,' and drawl for the admiring neighbors, and play 'Crawdad'—"

"And after?" That is not a question we ask each other often.

"Hell, I don't know. I haven't made it up that far. What for you going *after* all of a sudden? A little fifth-column sabotage?"

"Ah, I just got to thinking today. For once we're going somewhere to get there, not just to make the trip, not even to visit somebody, and when we're there what the hell's

131

really going to happen? All this time I've been fantasizing like always—you'll find a place with Enid, and I'll get myself a studio for twenty, thirty a month and find some piece of tail doesn't mind modeling and cooking and sleeping in. And I'll paint like crazy and make little sketching trips all over, go down to Mexico, and now and then, like Monday through Friday, I'll mooch meals off you and Enid, and on weekends you could invite me over. And I'll sell paintings, and you'll sell stories, and we'll drink beer and grow fat and sloppy and lay around. It ain't gonna work like that. I won't do any painting in California. I'm gonna starve and get drafted. For that I could have stayed in New York and not painted there either." His face looks very small, greenish-white and pointed in the frame of his beard.

"I don't know. Maybe not. What can I tell you, dad? I had to go. You didn't."

"Don't be a schmuck," he says. "Also, look out for the hash." It is beginning to rise menacingly out of the can, like a bubble of gas swelling in a swamp. I lower the flame and batten down the hash with a knife. Phil says, "I wouldn't have missed this trip for all the paintings I could sell. Jesus, it'd take me a lifetime to paint everything I've seen in three weeks, everything that's in my head. I sit still and I can feel myself jiggling like a kid with all the things I want to get down on canvas. What's really pissing me off is that all I've got is thirty lousy drawings. That ain't enough."

"I feel lousy about that. Three weeks ain't enough. The real way we should have done this trip, it would have taken three months, maybe more. We did it wrong, for what we wanted, but I couldn't help it."

"You better turn off that damn hash altogether; it's crouching to spring." He shakes his head. "I feel like I'm pushing as much as you are. It's a funny thing. I got it in my head that something's coming to an end with this trip. Maybe it's not, but I feel it—the way you were just talking as if it were all behind us, a long time ago—and half the

time I want to drag it out as long as possible, and maybe
never get to California and Menlo Park and Enid. The
rest of the time I want the whole damn thing over with;
if we didn't have to stop between here and there, I
wouldn't. So it comes out even, we stop when we stop,
and I do a drawing or two drawings, and what the hell.
We'll make the other trip sometime."

The idea holds him; between spoonfuls of the venomous
hash he begins to talk it out. "What we ought to have, actually, is one of those big old Ford pickups and fix it up
ourselves. Good pine boards, maybe an aluminum roof,
throw a couple of air mattresses in there, a little stove—
you want to carry water for washing? Wouldn't be too
hard to do."

"No, it'd take up too much space, and it's kind of point-
less, the way we wash. Stop in gas stations, like always."

"Yeah, I guess so. You know, we really could do it,
Pete, we really could make something out of it." He
frowns suddenly. "Come to think of it, maybe we ought to
get two trucks. Figuring you'll want to take Enid, and I'm
bound to latch on to some trouble in California, even if
it's just for laughs and posing. Those old Fords don't cost
much. Probably have to do some work on them, though."

"Well, if we could afford one truck, we can always pick
up another one. Damn, that would be the way to do it.
Wander all over everywhere, nice and slow, maybe do
fifty miles in a day, maybe none. We could meet people,
and talk, and not have to leave the next day, take all the
time we wanted. Boy, I'd like that."

"Me too." We grin at each other, understanding perfectly well what we are doing, and why, and still believing
in it as much as we believe in anything.

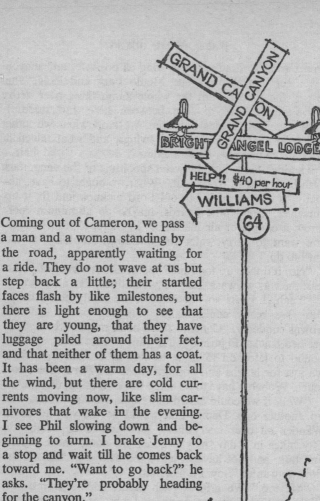

Coming out of Cameron, we pass
a man and a woman standing by
the road, apparently waiting for
a ride. They do not wave at us but
step back a little; their startled
faces flash by like milestones, but
there is light enough to see that
they are young, that they have
luggage piled around their feet,
and that neither of them has a coat.
It has been a warm day, for all
the wind, but there are cold cur-
rents moving now, like slim carnivores that wake in the evening.
I see Phil slowing down and beginning to turn. I brake Jenny to
a stop and wait till he comes back
toward me. "Want to go back?" he
asks. "They're probably heading
for the canyon."

"It's going to get cold." I turn
Jenny around, and we start slowly
back toward Cameron. The young
couple stands where we saw
them; when we stop across the
road with the headlights on them,
they freeze like deer. The girl

134

reaches out for the boy's hand but does not take it.

"Not everybody is ready for the mad grandmas," Phil murmurs. He calls to them, "Looking for a ride? We're going to the canyon." They come up slowly then, nodding, testing smiles, allowing themselves to touch each other now, since there is no danger. The girl looks nineteen or twenty; she has a long, oval face, short-cropped hair—dark brown lit with red, like plowed earth—long dark eyes, and a thin mouth. Her body seems to be all gristle, like an acrobat's body. The boy is our age, or a little older, lean as barbed wire himself, with a locked face and a good, seldom smile. He reminds me of the ranch hands back at Hartsel. His name is Jim; hers is Anna. They have been married seven months.

"Car broke down about a hundred miles back," Jim says. "We've been thumbing ever since. Been standing here about two hours now." They have only a suitcase apiece, but the things are bulky and heavy as fire hydrants, and we have to unstrap all our own luggage to load theirs on properly. The addition makes the scooters all but invisible from the rear and about as easy to balance as a button. Jenny's rear tire being a little low on air, and Couchette's having no more tread than a doily, this is bound to be a wobbly evening all around. By the time we finish loading, the last bit of warmth has faded out of the air, and Anna is beginning to bite her lips and hug herself. We rummage in our luggage again and bring out our winter coats (mine will do for a mild, springy winter) for them to wear. Anna, in Phil's coat, goes with him on Couchette, and Jim gets behind me. Well, hell, it was Phil's idea to stop, really, and it's a stupid thing to argue about, who gets to take the girl. I'd have to catch the little rat bastard to argue, anyway.

Jenny carries the extra load well; I was never really concerned about that. What bothers me is that she is clashing gears more than ever when she shifts, and there are times when she won't go into gear at all but roars and races and screams thinly until I have to put her in neutral and start over again. I blame my own clumsiness for this each time it happens, but it has never happened before, and it worries me.

There is a special wind up tonight for old customers and connoisseurs; a subtle wind, best appreciated by a paranoid palate. It is still determined to get my hat away from me and even manages to work the slipknot loose several times. Once, jamming the hat so tightly on my head that gangrene of the follicles begins to threaten, I mutter sideways to Jim, "I keep thinking, Real cowboys don't lose their hats."

Jim laughs quietly. "This one did. Soon as we got out of the car to start thumbing, the wind took it right off my head and sailed it off the road into a gully. Started to go down after it and then I figured, well, what the phooey, I'm sure not about to kill myself over a hat."

"What happened to your car?"

"Clutch burned right out," he says. "Gonna have to call home when we get to the canyon, tell my daddy he'll have to come get it. Sure wish we hadn't left it, but we couldn't stay around to get it fixed. That clutch is gone."

"Where's home?" It's really too cold to talk, but I feel curiously like a host, determined to make conversation, as though he were an unexpected guest in my house. Far ahead Couchette's taillight winks out around a curve, as though a nightbird had gulped down that queer, lonesome, glowing insect.

"Moab. Utah." Jim is going to be a wrangler for the Phantom Ranch, a tourist camp that runs muleback trips to the floor of the Grand Canyon. Anna will be a cook. The conversation ends there, more or less, though Jim asks what we do and I tell him. Why does Sigunick get to take the girl all the time?

The view opens out suddenly, and I realize that we are wobbling along a mountain road, narrow enough that I would hate to meet a fat firefly going in the opposite direction. All to the left there is nothing to see but massive, tangled darkness, dizzying because it is so close, and a

bluer emptier darkness that is the sky. To the right the
view is bright as cumulus by comparison; we are looking
down into a great pale gash stretching to the horizon,
scabbed with mesas and plateaus here and there, but over-
whelmingly raw still to the eye and the mind. In that first
glance it seems impossible that the thin river I think I see
far below, glinting like a hatpin, could have worn such a
wound into the earth; this is a clawmark, a bite, not a
diaper rash. The Pacific Ocean is supposed to roll in the
crater where the moon burst away; whose moon was
gouged out of this unhealed place? That might be the
earth's purpose in the universe, after all, to be torn into
other peoples' moons.

I nearly pass Phil at one point; he has parked precariously near the edge of the road to let Couchette cool off. I
hate having to stand still in the wind, but he's right, of
course. When we open the oil tanks a colorless feather of
smoke whisks off into the dark like an escaping genie. We
leave the scooters open, warming our hands quite ade-
quately over their innards, something like that part in
books about the Klondike where they have to kill the
sled dogs.

Jim and Anna are standing together, lighting cigarettes.
Phil and I turn our heads cautiously to look at the canyon,
hanging onto the scooters as though we would fall if we
let go. The canyon seems to light one rim of the world,
like dawn.

"Big, ain't it?" Phil says.

I nod. "Funny, coming up on it in the dark. You never
think of seeing places like the Grand Canyon at night."

"I'd like to paint it like this," he says. "Black and gray
and blue, and stupid little bits of pink." He puts a hand
on my shoulder. "Beagle," he says simply. His voice is
husky with phlegm.

"Sigunick." My voice is husky too, but I pat his hand
a little away from my jugular, because you never know.

"*Ma-a-a-a!*" We fall hysterically into each other's arms,
half laughing at the utter ridiculousness of the situations

in which we always find ourselves, half weeping because the ridiculouses are always, always cold. Our cowboy hats tock and scrape against each other, and our voices mingle in a high, shuddering babble.

". . . freezing, freezing, all our lives freezing, a man could die, you know, you freeze him too much . . ."

". . . I want to go home. I don't like it here a bit. Take me home this instant, or turn off the freezing, one . . ."

". . . Ooo-hoooo, the freezing, the suffer, the agony with the ecstasy . . ."

" . . . the misery, the awful, the cold, and also there's gravel on the road, you notice the gravel? . . ."

". . . Ooo-hoooo, the gravel. Listen, don't use your brakes for nothing, one time I braked, and the gravel, and the wind gives me a little *zetz,* and there I was, freezing at the bottom of the canyon, only dead . . ."

". . . and I could throw myself on your pyre in grief and despair and freezing . . ."

Jim and Anna look at us a little strangely. They are shivering too, but it seems almost dutiful, a social gesture made kindly to assure us that other people in the world feel the wind. We may be overdoing things a bit, dancing and wailing with cold, but that, too, is social in a way. We are traveling together for a little time, but we don't know one another, and we need not ever, unless we share something besides the same road, the same ride, like people in a subway. Laugh at us, then, share our silly suffering. It's cheap enough coin; we hand it out like Monopoly money, but it's all we have—except the other stuff, which nobody wants, including us—and sometimes it buys a moment of companionship which all of us can take away. Laugh at us; we'll go on from there. We know how.

Jim and Anna smile and agree that it sure is cold and offer us cigarettes. Anna asks us, "What nationality are you boys? I've been trying to place your accents, but it's got me beat."

"New York Jewish." We might as well have said Lilliputians or Hobbits, for all the help it is to Anna. She stands a foot away from me, pointed and androgynous in Phil's Navy coat, shoulders hunched a little—she is cold, really —eyes not focusing on either of us but crouched between us, pale mouth amused in a secret way, as though she had just told herself a joke. She locks her arm through Jim's and puts her hand in his pocket. First time I've seen her do anything like that; they are not a demonstrative couple. "Cold, honey?" she asks him.

"Doing all right."

"Look at old Phil," she says. She knows both our names, but she is looking at me when she says it. It comes to me that I have been staring at them with the vacuous concentration of a man trying to crack a safe. "I bet old Phil's wishing he'd never seen us." She smiles, to show she doesn't mean it, but her eyes are knowing as a child's in the matchlight. I mumble some meaningless denial she probably can't even hear, and walk a little way off to stand next to Phil. He is leaning on Couchette, looking down into the canyon.

"Guess what time it is," he demands. I shrug. "It's a little after one. Freezing at the Grand Canyon at one in the morning. Us."

"So a month ago we were freezing on West Fourth Street at one in the morning. One day I would write one of those travel books, how to freeze on five dollars a day."

A small giggle from Anna; we are the only people I know who talk to be overheard, even when there's nobody near. Phil says, "Yeah, but us. The roving Fuzzies, wandering the world, laughing, singing, making music, brawling in tearooms with broken biscuits . . ."

". . . buying glass beads and junk jewelry from the goddamn Indians . . ."

". . . pockets full of snowballs, and our noses running . . ."

Anna says, "Excuse me, Phil." Both of us turn. She is standing with her head tipped back slightly, looking at me. "Did you say something about Indians?" Her voice is as casually conversational as ever, more so.

I stare at her without speaking. Her eyes are wide and bright—the whites shine like gold—and expectant, more than expectant, eager. I hardly recognize her, she looks so suddenly alive; a minute before, she was only a two-dimensional design that owned a suitcase. I do not answer her.

"You see, I'm one-quarter Indian myself," Anna says. "Cherokee." Jim sits down on Jenny to tie a shoelace.

"Well, Indians are all right," Phil says. "If they're sexy." But she still looks at me. For a moment, she becomes real for me, standing there, standing still and smiling at the strangers, waiting for trouble.

"That's funny," I say. "My girl, the one I'm going to see, she's part Indian too. Iroquois. Not a quarter, though, just a little bit." My credentials are in order; as a liberal it's quite all right for me to use Enid's ancestry as a kind of skeleton key to sorrow. What bothers me is that I might easily be using it as a substitute for her being attractively foreign, or talented, or blind, or something. Suddenly I want to see her very much as I look at Anna.

Jim and Anna have a reservation at the Bright Angel Lodge, the second of two hotels we come to. We see it from a long way off, glowing like an ocean liner. Cars are crowded into the parking lot, like teeth in a comb. We park the scooters in a loading zone and unstrap the luggage. Anna's hands are so stiff she cannot carry her suitcase, so Phil takes it into the hotel. For all the lights, there are very few people sitting in the lobby. It is two in the morning, the way it is in an all-night diner near a bus terminal: bright, cold yellow, plastic, formica, chrome, air-conditioning, voices sounding small and prerecorded.

Jim goes over to the desk to register, and Phil disappears somewhere. Men's room, cigarettes—who knows? Anna sits down in the first chair she sees, rubbing her hands over each other. I take off my cowboy hat and push back my hood. I look sideways at Anna, stiff-necked and sneaky-eyed as a boy looking at his girl in the movies, and go "Whoo-eee," or "Wow," or "Whew," something relaxed and whooshy like that. We've been through a wind together, all us comrades.

Anna smiles and nods her head slightly. Under the bright lights of the lobby her head looks smaller and more delicately made than I remembered. She has some kind of rash on her forehead. I help her wriggle out of Phil's coat, and she says, "Thank you."

"What'll you and Jim be doing after this summer? Will you go back to Moab?"

"My God, I hope not," says Anna. In the two-o'clock silence her voice is as clear as though a mist had suddenly blown off it, bitter and fearful and a little humorous. It may not be Anna's real voice, any more than the other— time and the movies give people so many voices—but it feels as if a human being just went by in those five words, not an interchangeable shadow with a Cherokee grand-parent. I would like to think so, I guess. "I don't know," Anna says. "Maybe we will."

Jim comes back with the room key; and Phil, com-plaining that the hotel doesn't have a cigarette machine. Hell with them, let's try the other place, I wasn't done shivering anyway. We stand around for a moment to make sure that Jim and Anna don't need any more help. What-ever amused Chinese drafted that old folk custom about rescuers, he knew something about the nature of assistance in general. I think we shake hands with Jim and Anna when we leave them, but I am not sure.

Outside, there is the cold again, and the scooters with their straps dangling. We refasten our own luggage and drive back the way we came, to the first hotel. The park-ing lot there is up a short steep grade, and when I try to put Jenny into second gear she flounders in a jangling, shrieking neutral. It happens three times, and I finally take the grade in first gear.

As we drink instant coffee in the hotel lobby, nodding and blinking in the cold chairs, Phil says, "You know, all the way she had her hands in my pockets, and I kept thinking, This must be the most totally sexless contact I

141

have ever had with a woman in my life. That's the only memory I have of her right now, and I have a feeling even that'll be gone tomorrow. Damnedest thing."

"They probably didn't believe we were real," I say. "I wonder if they'll wake up tomorrow and not be able to remember how they got here."

"Wouldn't be surprised. I don't think they'll worry about it for long, though." He is almost asleep in his chair. He says, "We kill me. Hitchhikers."

We spend half a day in the Grand Canyon Village, the idea being to take things easy and do most of our driving tonight. It is a restless and unsatisfying time, for a combination of reasons. We have no money to throw into the canyon (a dollar is too much to pay for powdered eggs without being introduced to the griffin that laid them), and even if we had, I wonder if we would spend it on trips along the river. Both of us prefer our adventures as comfortable as possible, but both of us dread and detest tourism in all its aspects, from the primitive to the sneaky. You can't have it both ways, not on our incomes. Even so, hikes into the canyon cost nothing, unless you have to be rescued (this costs forty dollars, thirty-five if you manage to schedule your emergency before 4 p.m.), and we could always spend a couple of days wandering along the rims. We have all the time we need, but we do not have the feeling of time, and that is the end of it. I assure Phil that he can take as much time as he likes to draw whatever he likes, and he determines to barter for his time by driving late into the night; and so we pace sourly through the lovely country, getting neither drawings nor distance out of the day, seeing only what we cannot help seeing, cramped by richness, stretched too thin by lack, and so constantly aching somewhere. I think that we are often angry with each other without knowing it, and I know that we are angry with ourselves.

We do find a mate for my ring, though, and a case of rings just like it, this ring that we had not been able to match anywhere else. The Master Ring disappears quietly, and in its place appears the image of the Sacred Sword of Loralow in James Thurber's *The White Deer*. It lay forever between the paws of the Seven-headed Dragon of Dragore, which was mechanical and ran down occasionally, thus permitting a daring hero to steal away the Sword. A little man would shuffle out then and lay another Sword between the Dragon's paws.

"Might as well try a couple of sketches," Phil says when we leave the shop. "I won't take long."

At breakfast this morning he said flatly that he wasn't going to do any drawings of the canyon at all. "I've seen too many. Everybody does the damn thing in one of two ways, calendar art or the hotsy-totsy way, all pink and green and impressionistic, housewives in an art class trying to do a Monet like the professor showed them. Hell with it. I don't want to cause trouble."

Now I say, "Suit the self, little buddy, don't rush. I'll stroll around, write a few postcards, maybe just stand and look at the canyon. Pick out the geological strata and all. Take your time, dad."

"Write a couple postcards for me," he says as I am walking away, and I say, "Okay," before I think about it. I do write to four or five friends in New York, but it is difficult to know what to say and even to remember the addresses. In some part of my mind it is always winter in New York, and I hated getting letters from other seasons when I lived there.

Stared at for a long time, the canyon is less overwhelming than when I only sensed it in the darkness. I think the colors will break up and stream away, melting and fading like a sunset, if I watch much longer. Grayish-white limestone, red shale, sandstone-colored sandstone, a bitter-looking greenness that might be shale, one wide red streak that's probably shale too, but I wouldn't want to commit myself off a tiptoeing sense of color and a C in first-year geology. There are little telescopes, skinny as peppermint sticks, mounted along the wall overlooking the canyon.

They are gifts from colleges and institutions of geology, and you can look through them for nothing; you can pivot them into different notches and be assured that you are peeping at a particular point or plateau. You can't really see them, because the little telescopes have no lenses, but that's where they are.

Phil is having an infuriating time with the wind; every time I look over at him, he is snatching at a sheet of paper that is flapping like the laundry outside his window the day we left New York. Even when he does lay hold of it, it buzzes against his fingers, crumpling, smearing. I can feel his helpless rage where I stand—some of it, anyway. Twenty years counts for something, but not a lot, compared with what there is.

He gets a gouache out of that encounter: the blue horns of the inner gorge and the coppery greenness of the plateaus are what stay with me when he puts it away in his portfolio. Having watched him work, knowing his mood, I have a painful desire to say something about the gouache that would mean something, to praise or to help. I wind up saying nothing at all. It's a little better than being loud stupid.

"The goddamn wind," he says. "The miserable, stinking Western wind. Blows the gouache right off the paper. Wrong kind of paper anyway, the stuff'll all drop off tomorrow, probably. Hell of a mistiness about everything, too." He grins, looking for a moment as weary as he looked in the hotel lobby last night, and begins to tidy up his gouache box. "Hell with it. If you ain't fighting one thing, it's another. Time, place, money, people, materials, yourself, the wind. I wish I could paint. Let's get out of here."

It takes us almost till sundown to drive the fifty-seven miles to Williams, because we take our time about it and Phil does a lot of sketching. I stretch out in the grass and read the pamphlet a park policeman gave me. It tells about the history of the canyon, and about the flowers and wildlife, and about the Havasupai Indian reservation in the park, and all the wonderful observation points we passed last night, and what the park is like at other times of year. Seems like a hell of an interesting place. I wish we'd been there.

Once a little Renault with a Quebec license plate passes us, and a young man and woman wave to us, smiling. They are both handsome in the rare way that makes you feel good to look at it, and they wave to us for a long way.

We eat in Williams and go on, hoping to reach Kingman before we stop for the night. The evening is cool and dark as a clothes closet. Our headlights seem to vanish into the night like rain into the sea. There are few towns. Ash Fork, Seligman—they whirl out of the darkness like subway stations: sidewalks, gas pumps, motel signs, traffic light at the intersection. Three kids in an old Hudson, looking around. A patrol car moving slowly down the main street, a drowsy pike, "Going on through? Good,"—and the town left behind like a subway station. You run out of songs to sing, games to play, poetry to remember, sex lives to wonder about. You think about yourself, you ask yourself for reasons, and the requests grow slowly back into you, like wild boars' tusks. This is lonely and tiring. We spend the night in Peach Springs, forty miles short of Kingman.

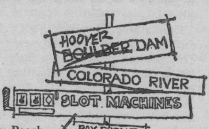

The country between Peach Springs and Boulder City—where I have people-to-call—is as lean and bare as I had always imagined Arizona to be, and it fits much more neatly into the place marked Desert in my head than the Painted Desert ever did. There is a deceptive sea-softness about the Painted Desert; the colors do that, and all the things that the wind and the sand have made together. This desert has no color, and all that the wind and the sand have done here is to scour each other clean and hard. This would be a good desert for a saint's meditations, except for the yellow and white desert flowers which bloom along the road with a totally irrelevant joy.

The Quebec Renault that passed us yesterday passes us again, and the young couple

146

wave and smile in recognition. They must have spent the night in Kingman. The girl leans out of her window, as if to call back to us, but if she does the words are lost in the wind and muffled in her own hair whipping across her mouth. Again the sight of them makes me oddly happy, but this time a little lonesome as well, and I find myself first straining Jenny to catch up with them, and then slowing down to let them get well out of sight.

About ten miles from Boulder City the desert begins to cloud up with broken black hills. We climb them carelessly at first, expecting the road to flatten out soon, but it grows almost as steep as the road to the Grand Canyon in a much shorter time. Swept through the hills and the narrow stony valleys by gravity, like marbles in a pinball machine, we get occasional glimpses of the land below us: ashes and cinders, clinkers and slag, coffee-ground black and dusty asphalt gray, scooped and spilled into the shape of hills and canyons and pits. The garbage hills, barren as a burned match, cold as the dark side of Mercury in the afternoon shadow.

Then, very suddenly, we are dropping down toward the Colorado River on a road steep and winding enough to have us leaning far out of the saddles to bank the scooters, warping them around like little boats. We turn off at an observation point, park the scooters, and, suddenly very tired, lean on a stone railing, looking down at Boulder Dam. I know they call it Hoover Dam now. It looks very tiny from here, white and peaceful. "When I was a kid," I say to Phil, "I was crazy about Boulder Dam."

"You had the hots for Linda Darnell too. It all ties in."

"No, really. I had a book about Boulder Dam, and I knew the whole thing by heart, all about the river, and Major Powell shooting the rapids, with one arm yet, the whole thing, what kind of special boats he had. I even knew how the dam worked, me, I couldn't open a pack of cigarettes without a hemorrhage. When we went to the beach, summers, I used to make models of the dam in the sand, with cracker boxes for the powerhouses."

"What kind of crackers?"

"Social Tea Biscuits, or arrowroots when we had them. They had to be long boxes. See, I do remember. But it ain't the way I thought it would look. I don't see the powerhouses at all. They must have changed it a lot since the book was written."

The river is the borderline between Arizona and Nevada, and we cross it on the crest of the dam. We stop at the first place we come to, a roadside bar. There is a pile of gold stones around the door, and a lot of llamas tied out in the parking lot. The nuggets are painted, but the llamas are quite real. Phil points to a pay telephone and says, "So go call the people in Boulder City. I could do with a good meal or two."

"Let's get a beer first." I'm stalling because I'm nervous. It's one thing to marvel at our magnificent *chutzpah* in charming room and board out of tenuous acquaintanceships, and quite another to project all that wistful charm over such a pitiless instrument as the telephone, especially if you happen to be a shy and chicken person with a taste for picaresque literature. Phil and I share a vision of ourselves as a couple of foolish, joyous con men, which is just true enough to be terribly misleading, and we know it all the time.

"I'd call first, was I you. It's getting pretty late."

"All right. Gimme a dime." I wish they were his total strangers; he hates telephones. I tiptoe through the phone book, more or less looking for the number of Larry Beckman's parents. My God, I met Larry once, two years ago, and we talked all one perfectly pleasant evening, and then he went into the Peace Corps. Granted, his best friend married a cousin of mine, and it happens that Larry's parents are pretty friendly with my aunt and uncle, but my God, is a sandwich really worth it? Maybe they don't have a telephone, hoho. James Beckman, Boulder City. Well, maybe they won't be home. I'll give them five rings. On the fourth, a man's voice, deep and a little hoarse. "Yes, hello?"

"Mr. Beckman?" Smooth now, relaxed, as though you had more claim on his time than a Jehovah's Witness. "Mr. Beckman, my name's Peter Beagle, and I'm a kind of distant friend of your son Larry." Chuckle. "That is, I'm Naomi Soyer's cousin, Rob Coe's wife, that is, *she* is"—chuckle—"and I knew Larry before he went into the Peace Corps." Chuckle like crazy. "Anyway, I'm just passing through town, a friend of mine and I are, we're crossing the country on a couple of motor scooters"—pause for admiration; at least I can still hear him breathing—"and Naomi's parents, Israel and Sue, they thought we ought to drop up as long as we're passing through. So I thought we'd. Drop up. If it's all right with you. If you'll be home."

Mr. Beckman says quite kindly, "You'll have to speak a little louder. I don't hear very well since my stroke."

Oh dear. Oh dear, dear, dear. Maybe if I said, oh, I'm sorry, I must have the wrong Larry's father, and hung up, and told Phil nobody was home . . . no, Phil's watching, he's seen me talking. I take a deep breath and recite my little speech over again. Word for word.

"Well, any friend of Sue and Israel is a friend of mine," Mr. Beckman says. "You're quite welcome to stop in, if you'd like to." What a nice voice he has.

Careful, now, don't spoil it, don't make nice Mr. Beckman sorry for his offer. "Well, we have to drive all the way to Jean tonight, so we couldn't stay very long, but yes, I'd like that very much. How do we get to your house? We're at the dam now."

"You'd better talk to my wife about that," Mr. Beckman says. "She has the sense of direction in the family. I'd just get you so lost you couldn't find yourselves. Friends of Larry, dear."

I manage to condense my speech for Mrs. Beckman by leaving out the chuckles. Her voice is softer and older than her husband's as she tells me how to get to their house. Her name is Jenny.

"So?" Phil asks when I step out of the booth. I pat his

collarbone jauntily. "The old boy still has it, little friend. Let's go get that beer."

"Gimme back the dime, then, you're so smart," he says, holding out his hand. "You think I forget so easy?"

"What are you talking about? That's a twenty-cent call to Boulder City, you little misery."

"You ain't so smart," he says coldly. "A real bum would have called collect. You check the telephone? Sometimes they give you the dime back by mistake."

"I checked." We go into the bar. I break a five-dollar bill ordering two beers and get back as many silver dollars as I have owned in my life. There are not many people in the bar: three or four tanned young *schussbummers*, and one thin man in his forties, playing the slot machines. I watch him in the mirror with great interest, because he is the first man I have ever seen playing them. He slouches on one elbow, like a bored student, and feeds coins swiftly into three machines before he plays one—a dime, a quarter, a silver dollar, zipzipzip. But he drags the handles down very slowly, leaning his weight on them. The handles make a soft, crunching sound as they come down, and then go *klock* as they spring up again. Now and then a few coins come rattling down out of the dime and quarter machines, but he is already playing the dollar machine and never looks up or even scoops the money up until he needs it to feed the machines again.

"They say about a meal?" Phil asks. As a matter of fact, they didn't, but I answer, "A snap, a breeze, a nothing. You mere got to be charming and lovable, like always. They got all the sound of natural-born adopters."

"Oh, I like that kind," he says happily. "I would be so lovable. This would be the definitive lovable, it would be the National Bureau of Standards, my lovable. Jesus, Beagle, do we ever make me sick."

"Why? Ain't like we don't give value received. For a sandwich and a cup of coffee we would sing for them, we would tell funny stories, we would be boyish and wondering, we would take their trip for them, escape their escape, leave them something to talk about, the way we do for everyone. Better than TV."

"Yeah, I know, but us? Us rabbits?" The thin man's family come trooping into the bar: wife, two small boys, and the kind of stylishly withered old woman you see on cake-mix boxes. They greet him with open palms; the heap of change in front of him vanishes like Stalin's monuments, and he has to break a bill at the bar to get more. His family have already begun to play the machines when he gets back, and he has to nudge and tug and make faces to get a chance to play himself. The children are obviously playing for the fun of the gadget, pulling the levers with all their strength and putting their faces up close to the flashing wheels. But the old woman plays swiftly, with anger in her movements, yanking at the handles as viciously as a wildly frustrated laboratory rat in a Skinner box. She gets less reinforcement from the machine than any of the others, but it does not deter her from putting more money in, although she makes little peeping cries between her teeth every time the wheels chitter to a stop without loosing a single coin to her cupped hand. As for the mother, she plays with a military economy of effort, marching up to the machine and pulling the handles as briskly as if she were going through the manual of arms. She has a big, glassy face and a crescent smile that ought to be spinning up there on the wheels of the slot machines, along with the lemons and the cherries and the oranges.

Starting up the scooters under the aspiring-to-arrogance gaze of the llamas, he says, "There's nothing you can't do to people. They'll do it for you."

"I had a toy slot machine once. Plastic, yellow with a red handle. I wonder what happened to it."

It is growing dark by the time we get to Boulder City, and the air of the town is as softly blue as shadows on snow, as coldly blue, although it is a warm evening. The Beckmans live on a quiet dead-end street where low apartment houses sprout in rings, like mushrooms, around well-kept courtyards, five houses to a court. A middle-middle-class arrangement—thus do we also do in the Bronx—and oddly pleasing to discover in this November-colored town. I had not realized that I was a little homesick.

"Here we go, little buddy. Lovable?"

"Lovable. Lovable like all getout." Good talk, books, and gentle jokes. Her name is Jenny—save that for the proper occasion, don't waste it. We stroll across the grass and enter the first apartment house on the left. The vestibule is open on two sides, and the blue light coming in casts violet shadows like latticework all the way up the stairs.

The Beckmans live on the second floor. Their door is open, and Mr. Beckman is waiting for us, a man of sixty, maybe more, wearing a red and black bathrobe and carpet slippers. He has a curiously broken face—not mashed, not as if he had been hit, but unconnected, wandering, as though his skin were all that held his skull together. Gray-green veins slide up his forehead to disappear in his thin black hair.

"Mr. Beckman? I'm Peter Beagle, I'm sort of a distant friend . . ." To my horror I hear myself beginning my telephone recitation, like something in a dream, but Mr. Beckman nods and says, "You're the young fellow who called. Glad to see you, come on in," and turns around to lead us into the apartment. He walks very slowly, left foot scraping the floor softly.

The apartment is a strangely spare place, neither bleak nor especially spacious, but furnished as though the Beckmans had never allowed themselves to own anything that might put a claim on them. What furniture they have seems to be tucked away around the edges of the floor, and most of it is as functional and anonymous as the furniture that comes with a rented summer cottage. They have lived in this house a long time, I know, but it feels as though they could move away tomorrow and leave very little of themselves behind.

Mrs. Beckman is sitting on a couch in the living room.

She apologizes for not getting up; a cyst has recently been removed from one of her ovaries, and it hurts her to move. At first glance, she reminds me of a great soft wingless white bird. We sit near her, Phil in a straight uncomfortable chair and I at the foot of the sofa, and Mrs. Beckman and I begin almost immediately to talk about her son and my cousins. There is nothing else to talk about. Mr. Beckman sits in an armchair across the room and watches us.

Larry is still in Ghana. He has met an Indian girl there and will marry her next month. Yes, I know. Rob and Naomi will be going to Europe this summer to meet them in London. Yes. We were a little worried about the marriage, but I guess we've sort of come around to it now. Yes, I think it'll work out fine. You have to figure he knows what he's doing. Oh, Larry usually knows what he's doing. Yes, I liked Larry the couple of times I met him, only a few times, really. To be honest. Yes, he knows what he's doing. How are Israel and Sue? Very well, the last I saw of them, fine. They write to us a lot, you know. Yes, I know. You're probably more up to date on Israel and Sue than I am. Yes, they do write a lot, but Rob and Naomi haven't written in a couple of months, and they always write so promptly. Well, I'll see them in Berkeley, and I'll certainly remind them to write. Yes, do that. Yes, I will.

Watching Mrs. Beckman's eyes as she talks, I become certain that she understands horribly well that I don't care a damn about her, or her husband, or her son, or anything except a meal. I wonder if my face tells her that I don't even need the meal, that I am not at all hungry or desperate. What shoved us into the evening of these absolute strangers was the delightful image that has carried us so far so sweetly, the one about the rambling men, the cheerful *schnorrers;* but the most essential skill of any kind of debonair nogood is the willingness to climb the wall of anyone's privacy, and I keep forgetting that I hate to do that.

The number of names to be asked after and mumbled

bare dwindles like a melting candle. When they're all gone we'll sit here in this living room and stare at one another, stalled, short-circuited. I keep my head turned away from Phil. I feel foolishly responsible for his being here, and I don't want to know what he's thinking. He has not said a word since Mrs. Beckman and I began to talk, except once, to ask for an ash tray.

Mr. Beckman himself has hardly spoken at all. He is quite deaf and hears only whatever his wife translates into his decibel range, but he dominates the room if you look at him for long, in the way that a two-dimensional butterfly can make the twig it lights on, and the tree the twig belongs to, seem unreal. Now and then I turn toward him and raise my voice to include him in some particular inanity, but volume makes it sound even stupider than it is, and my voice becomes so soft with nervousness that even Mrs. Beckman cannot hear me. Once, when I mention something about the novelty of being given our change in silver dollars, Mr. Beckman fumbles in his pocket and brings one out. He snaps it singing off his thumb and smiles pleasantly as he catches it. Abruptly he hurls the coin to the floor, where it clanks dully, bounces, and clanks again, toneless as a brick. "This floor is a phony," he says fiercely.

Mrs. Beckman tells us that he has been ill for the last few years—a couple of strokes heading a fetid swarm of old man's ailments. Since the last stroke his mind hasn't been quite right, she says. She is speaking in a normal voice, but her husband's smile grows wide and sweet, merry as the moon. "See, I can say anything I want," he explains, "because I'm not all there, so it doesn't matter."

Mrs. Beckman asks us if we would like something to eat. It's what we came for. Why, yes, to be perfectly honest, yes, we would. If it wouldn't be imposing on you. No, it wouldn't, but we'll have to fix it up ourselves from whatever we find in the kitchen. Mr. Beckman cooks for them now and does whatever housework needs to be done, but

he gets tired. Oh no, of course not, we'll be fine. Thank
you very much. You just sit where you are.

We dart for the kitchen and begin clattering around like
a couple of happy little elves. Phil fries eggs, makes coffee,
and inflicts a few flesh wounds on a scarred old ham, while
I wash all the dirty dishes and utensils I can find. We take
our meal back into the living room and eat very quickly. I
remember to tell Mrs. Beckman that my scooter's name is
Jenny too. Beagle the raconteur.

As I watch them together, there is an odd unworldli-
ness about the Beckmans, as though they were stranded
Martians working with desperate seriousness at being con-
vincing human beings with a full life of human experience
and memories rooting them to this world. The way they
talk has a lot to do with it: they speak in a slow back-
country way (in the kitchen Phil muttered that they re-
minded him of Lum 'n Abner) that feels too back-country,
almost studied; and when they talk to each other they
often seem very near to slipping into another language, one
of soft inquisitive gutturals and muted harshness. There is
obviously a great dependency between them, a fitting together of weaknesses and strengths, some of it physical
—if she is his ears, he is her eyes and legs—and some of it
a knowledge of each other that must be almost painful.
And yet I cannot say whether they like each other,
whether they are glad to need and know each other or
not. He calls her his keeper several times.

We are drinking our coffee, jockeying silently for the
precise time to apologize for eating and running, when
Mr. Beckman suddenly gets up, shuffles across the room to
kneel beside a cabinet near my chair, and withdraws a
football-sized object wrapped in cotton and tissue paper.
"Show you something I like," he remarks without looking
up, but with an impatient note in his voice, as though he
had been wanting to do something he liked for the whole
interminable evening. He peels away the tissue paper and
reveals an empty whisky bottle stained a smudgy purple
from neck to arched bottom. The color is as deep as

155

grapes, but peculiarly flat and lifeless. I turn it slowly in my hands and hold it up to the light and murmur, "Boy, yes, well," in a thoughtful manner.

"You probably don't know what that is." The old man is watching me out of wary penny-colored eyes as I study the purple whisky bottle. "That's desert glass. Glass turns that color when it's been lying out in the hot sun for a long time. You find it all over in the old ghost towns."

"What a weird thing," Phil says, peering over my shoulder. "Let me see it, Pete." I pass it over to him, asking Mr. Beckman as I do so, "Is this the only color it turns?"

"We used to have a few yellow ones. Might still, I don't know." He looks inquiringly toward his wife, but she shakes her head. "There weren't many of those," she says, "and I guess we just sold them all or gave them away. People liked those yellow bottles."

I recall her mentioning that they had run a souvenir shop for years until increasing ill health made it too exhausting for them. "Show them the other bottle, Jim," she says, but Mr. Beckman is already unwrapping it. It is the same color as the first one, but round. "Weird," I say. "Desert glass."

Mr. Beckman is rummaging in the cabinet again, muttering to himself. Phil and I twiddle the purple bottles and look at each other without expression. It beats talking family, anyway. The old man opens a ring box and hands me a small fragment of stone, pale as a winter sky, shading into gray at the edges. It is smooth to the touch and almost translucent; when I hold it against the light I can see dark, feathery formations within it. "That's moss agate," Mr. Beckman says. "Montana moss, it's called. Larry found it a long time back. He must have been about nine."

Phil nearly climbs over me to get the stone, and I let him take it because Mr. Beckman is holding out another stone that seems to breathe with colors as he turns it in his hand: blue, green, red, rose, yellow, purple, tumbling over one another in the light. "Opal," he says. "Found it up north around Denio, in the Virgin Valley. This is the kind they call black opal, but they aren't really black." Phil and I leave our chairs and crouch on the floor, huddling over the stone as though it could warm us. "Opal will petrify wood, you know," Mr. Beckman goes on. "Agate'll do that too. We had a big chunk of wood opal once, but I guess we sold it." Mrs. Beckman nods slightly. "I used to remember every stone we had," he says, "and where we found it, and where she put it, which was the tough part. Now I have to ask her. She's learned to remember, though, so it works out all right."

"I wish you'd get around to making a ring out of that opal," his wife says. "You and Larry were always going to mount it, but you never did."

"Well, I'm still always going to mount it," he answers. "I'll get to it one day, maybe when Larry's home." He laughs then, a sound like a car struggling to start on a cold morning but as full of unmalicious delight as are his eyes when he looks at us. "I don't know, though," he says. "These days, I just like having it around to show to people."

We ask to see more, and he shows us a dark green piece of uncut jade. "Now I found this on the bank of a river in California," he says, "not far from San Francisco, as a matter of fact. Went there to look for agate; river beds are great places to find agate. This is Monterey jade, Wyoming jade, whatever you want to call it." He brings out another green stone, darker than the jade and freckled thickly with coppery-red spots. "This is bloodstone," he says. "You find it wherever you find agate or jasper. It's all part of the same family, chalcedony." He opens the boxes slowly, handing me a stone and not unwrapping another until I have made inarticulate dove-sounds over it and passed it on to Phil: a sard, a tourmaline, a cinnamon-stone, two matched carnelians he means to mount as earrings, a violet amethyst, a piece of rose quartz, a hawk's eye—they march across the carpet like the single footprints of something ceaselessly beautiful, until, like Christopher Fry's Jennet at the jewel box, we wander

... away to the melting moody horizons of opal,
Moonstone, bloodstone, now moving in lazy
Amber, now sheltering in the shade
Of jade from a brief rainfall of diamonds.
Able to think tomorrow has an even
Brighter air, a glitter less moderate.

The agates are Mr. Beckman's special favorites, and he
has more of them than of any other kind of stone. They
have many different names: the banded agates are lovely
as bright fish and haunting with the remembrance of staring
long into marbles; and there is lace agate, where the clouds
of color seem to form designs of flowers and ribbons;
there is moss agate, like the stone we saw first, and one
called sagenite, clear as window glass but invaded with
opaque needles of deep black and deep red that crisscross,
however you turn the stone in the light. The one I look at
longest, however, is less colorful than the others: black
ferny growths, like moths' antennae, embedded in milk-
blue chalcedony, almost stylized in its simplicity. Mr.
Beckman calls it plume agate and says he used to have
much better specimens.

He has cut and polished most of the stones himself, although Mrs. Beckman and Larry have each cut several, as
well as several pieces of desert glass, which we take for
chips of quartz. Nearly half of his collection is mounted in
one form or another—ring sets or necklaces, earrings or
bracelets. Mrs. Beckman's own jewel box has horizons and
rainfalls to rival Jennet's. Turquoise is not one of the
Beckmans' favorite stones, but she has a couple of large
brooches that contain the finest pieces of turquoise we have
seen since we became aware of it three days ago, fierce,
vivid blue, veined thinly with the copper matrix. She becomes very fluent as she shows them to us, but she is
speaking not of the gems themselves but of the places
where they were found and the time when her husband
cut and set them for her. Larry was a baby then.

It is so with most of her ornaments, many of which have

belonged to her for ten or twenty or thirty years: she is
deeply aware of their beauty, but what matters at least as
much to her is the invisible country rock of time that
frames each one. Time is a distasteful concept to Mr.
Beckman ("I haven't the faintest idea, and I don't want
to know," he says when Phil asks him the hour. "Time is
a made-up thing, like money. Numbers running around in
a circle. There are plenty of circles waiting to make a slave
out of you, you don't have to make them up") but it is
real enough to his wife, as it is to most women. I think she
sees herself when she looks into the stones for a long time.

"If Larry were here," she says, "he could take you up
into the hills tomorrow to look for rocks. We don't skip
around as much as we used to."

"Hell we don't," the old man answers. "We just don't
skip so fast any more. Listen," he says to us, "you two
come out with me tomorrow and I'll take you rock-hunting
right around here. Go down into the Black Canyon, and
you'll come up with some of the prettiest almondite garnets
you ever saw. Or we'll go out around Searchlight, if you
like turquoise that much. Larry can take you all over
everywhere when he gets back, but I can show you a
couple of good places I can still get to. I'd enjoy that."

When we tell them that we cannot stay they seem genuinely surprised and disappointed. They had expected us at
least to spend the night. "We just haven't got the time," I
say, and Mr. Beckman slaps the arm of his chair with a
soft sigh. "Ah, there it goes again, sure enough," he says
sadly. "Time. You haven't any time. Well, you won't ever
have any time, because there isn't any such thing, and
you'll spend your whole life looking for some of it so you
can put it aside to do the things you want to do. There
isn't any time, there's just you. It'd be good if you could
learn that young. It took me my whole life to learn, but
I know it now."

"Yes, I know." Outside the window, behind his shoulder, the empty street is blue as ink. It's late, ten-thirty,
eleven maybe. I hadn't thought we'd stay this long. Phil

says, "We'd better go, I guess." The smile he gives Mrs. Beckman is very slight and shy. I have rarely seen him smile just like that. "I don't want to," he says, "but we'll fall asleep if we sit here much longer. I can't keep my eyes open, and we're supposed to drive fifty miles tonight."

He's leaving it up to me, really, and why not? He's walked out of a lot of warm houses into a lot of blue, cold streets to go somewhere that meant nothing to him, and there's no real reason to drag him off tonight; but the teeth of time are in me now, and I can't help him or myself. "We just can't," I say. "I wish we could stay too, but we have to go."

We say good-by to Mrs. Beckman there in the living room, because she cannot walk to the door with us. "Come back any time you want to," she invites us. "Larry's coming home in a couple of months, and he'll be sorry he missed you. Come and stay for a while." We say yes, we'd like to and follow Mr. Beckman out through the kitchen. He opens the door and turns on the light in the kitchen so that we can see our way down the dark stairs. "Good-by," he says. "Hope to see you again."

We shake hands with him. "I'll take you up on that," Phil says. "I'd like to go rock-hunting with you." So would I, I say.

"Yes," Mr. Beckman answers. "Good-by." He turns around and walks away. Mrs. Beckman calls to him from the living room, and he replies, but we cannot quite hear what they say.

The night is warm and feels warmer because we were expecting it to be cold. There is a sweet, elusive fragrance in the air; we can catch it only when we stand still. What is it? I don't know. What grows in Nevada? We walk slowly across grass and out into the street without speaking. Jenny and Couchette look very small parked at the curb; when we start them up they make a raw tinny sound, rattling between the quiet houses. We let them warm up for a little while.

"What lovely, strange people," Phil says wonderingly. "I really am going to come back here, you know."

I nod. "But can you imagine saying that after we'd been there five or ten minutes?"

"Oh, Jesus," he says. "Boy, I could have killed you, Beagle, the way you just sat there and talked family for the rest of my life. Can't you talk anything else to strangers but your goddamn family? Boy."

I shrug, a little irritated because I remember how I felt at the time. "Worked out all right. What a marvelous collection that old man had. I never saw stones like those."

"It wasn't just the stones," Phil says. "It was the cutting, the way he set them, the workmanship—just the way he was with them, I guess. I'd like to try that, get my hands on some good stones and see if I could design decent jewelry. Maybe I could, you never know."

"I don't see why not." The foggy old yearning to make something good with my hands hurts like ice for a moment and then subsides into bearable everyday envy. "Me too. I might try something like that sometime."

The scooters are ready to go now. The sky is very clear, almost translucent, as though we were looking up from the bottom of the sea, but a flight of tiny silver clouds is crossing the night, going north like summer birds. The envy in me spreads out to them, like a kind of love. They are so far away—they might as well be as long ago as starlight— and they move so slowly. You have to watch them pass something as near as a chimney to be sure they are moving at all. The Beckmans are like that, I think.

"Like what Joyce Cary wrote about Bill and Amy," I say to Phil. "They are truly private persons."

He looks away from me, shaking his head slightly. "I felt almost hypnotized in there," he says. "I really didn't want to leave. I felt like a thief. Scary damn thing. I'm coming out of it." We turn on our headlights, and the dark street becomes the same color as the clouds. "Let's go to Vegas, little buddy. After you."

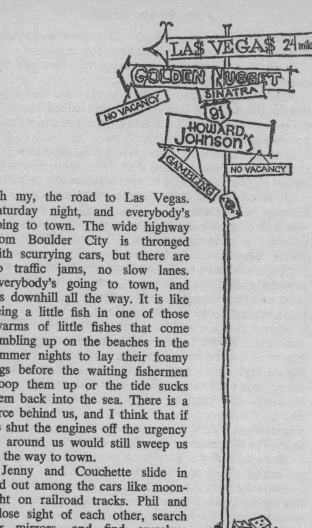

Oh my, the road to Las Vegas. Saturday night, and everybody's going to town. The wide highway from Boulder City is thronged with scurrying cars, but there are no traffic jams, no slow lanes. Everybody's going to town, and it's downhill all the way. It is like being a little fish in one of those swarms of little fishes that come tumbling up on the beaches in the summer nights to lay their foamy eggs before the waiting fishermen scoop them up or the tide sucks them back into the sea. There is a force behind us, and I think that if we shut the engines off the urgency all around us would still sweep us all the way to town.

Jenny and Couchette slide in and out among the cars like moonlight on railroad tracks. Phil and I lose sight of each other, search our mirrors, and find ourselves again; we wiggle our fingers in our old countersign of helplessness before the wind but we grin uncon-

162

trollably and whoop at each other over the roofs of sports cars. The joyous image begins to rise before me once again—perhaps, after all, it is brave to be a bum and ride in triumph to Las Vegas. The Beckmans may be slow silver clouds, but we will be a constellation and spin across somebody's sky every night. "Those are the Fuzzies," the lecturer in the planetarium will say, "the only constellation that has no fixed path but seems to skitter from horizon to horizon, forever seeking something in the skies. The ancient Greek legend says that they have dropped a dime." A few drivers point at us and smile—see, those stars are supposed to be the wheels of their scooters, and those are their cowboy hats—but most of them are looking straight ahead and do not turn when we peer in through their windows. Everybody's going to town.

It is twenty-four miles from Boulder City to Las Vegas, but the drive seems to take no time at all. For one clear moment we are rushing downhill, herded by shadows toward a distant meadow of light; suddenly the highway has tightened on us and the city swallows us with a roar of brightness. I wonder if this is how a candle looks to a moth come in out of the dark. The cars are parked together as tightly as cobblestones now. We wobble along in low gear, going with the traffic—as if we had much choice— trying to stay together. The sound of the street is a long *aaahhh* of unending, unbearable expectation, made up of the impatience of automobiles, the fiery crackle of women's shoes along the sidewalk, the silence of light, and the rising knife-like laughter of all the people who roll up and down the street like waves of mist.

A block ahead of us, illuminated on the roof of the Golden Nugget (we have been seeing their billboards for a thousand miles), stands a mechanical cowboy, huge as a balloon in the Macy's Parade, bowlegged, baboon-faced, one hand hooked in his belt, the other going up and down slowly to tip his hat. Timed to the tip of his coffin-sized hat, his voice groans out, "How—dy—pod—nuh—how—dy—pod—nuh," about once every fifteen seconds. His voice reminds me of the bear in the shooting gallery that roars faintly when you hit it. It is a chilling voice, bitter as iron. You would think it would frighten people who were out for a good time.

A convertible with four teen-age boys in it pulls along-side us at a traffic light. The driver yells, "Here for the convention?" Someone in a diner mentioned a convention in Las Vegas, but I can't remember a thing about it. "From New York," I call back, indicating our license plates. "Going to California." But California is very near now, forty miles or so, like going to Scarsdale. "San Francisco."

"You'll love Las Vegas," the boy says. "It's a great town. Have fun." The light changes, and the car jumps away from us. There is something going on up ahead, in the shadow of the cowboy: they have the block roped off to cars, and there are cops diverting traffic, and people packed on the sidewalk, as eager and alert as if somebody were about to jump out of a window. I guess that's the convention. We turn off before we get there and drive down a side street for a couple of blocks before we stop to park the scooters. Once we are away from the main drag, the street is surprisingly quiet.

"Okye," Phil says, locking Couchette. " 'Ere we are, Charley. Put yer 'at straight and let's go see the bloody town."

"Right-ho. Only let's not stay too long, huh? Mere poke around a little, see what there is. We got a way to go yet."

"Poke is all," he says amiably. "I always wanted to see Las Vegas, I don't know why. But I never figured to stay very long." There are a couple of pawnshops on this street, but both of them are closed and neither one has anything promising hanging in the window. We walk back toward the main drag, adopting an elaborately casual stroll, hands in our pockets, hats far back on our heads. "So this is Menlo Park," Phil says. "Doesn't look like it."

Once we are inside the crowd, the way we look at things changes. Now it is the lights boiling down the street that are unmanned and anonymous; the faces that swim and flap and float and drift by us are perfectly clear and easily characterized, exactly like a series of close-ups in a movie. We see all the bits: the tanned, loud, *nouveau riche* Texas couple and their retinue; the hard-faced blonde on the make; the honeymooners, tender and slippery; the college boys; the farmers come to town; the rambling, gambling men; the businessman on a bat; the clerk who saved up; the girl run away from home, or Berkeley, or someplace like that; the two girls come up for the weekend; the nervous little racketeer shuddering through the crowd, looking back. They may be making a movie here after all, we'd never know. Everyone looks made up for his or her part, and they all speak their overheard scraps of dialogue with fierce, tense preciseness, line-perfect every time. None of it makes any sense at all, but of course that's the idea: meaninglessness multiplied and jumbled to confuse the viewer and make him grateful to follow cool sanity, in the person of Laurence Harvey, down a quiet, deadly street to a rendezvous with Hope Lange, a schoolteacher turned dealer, who knows too much.

But who are we, then, bearded and naked, chest-high to everyone, blinking and shuffling and turning round and round like bears, to stare and to listen? We can't be the audience, because we're here in the movie, but we can't very well be Laurence Harvey and Hope Lange. We might just be two more extras cast as a couple of beatniks, but somehow I doubt that too. I think we're actors from a low-budget film, the kind you shoot in the closet because you can't afford a good camera, or sets, or make-up, or people who photograph like what they're supposed to be. Hoo, what a terrible movie that one must be. Let's just float through this real movie until they throw us out.

Bodiless voices all around us are talking about the convention, and I hear several people warning others to buy some kind of lapel buttons, because otherwise somebody can lynch you for being a killjoy or something. A man is standing in the middle of the sidewalk, selling those very buttons. He is dressed like a cowboy, but he's not a real cowboy. I detest him at first sight, and it pleases me to observe that he's having a hard time getting rid of his buttons. He splits the crowd like a rock in a rapids, drawling his demand that everybody be a good sport and buy his buttons, the money goes to a good cause, everybody's buying 'em, you're taking your chances if you don't have one by midnight, only one dollar, only a single silver dollar, and it won't cost you a penny more for those whiskers. We deep-fry him with the Withering Glances we usually reserve for each other, but I say, "No, no, thanks." Who knows what he turns into, come midnight?

We take our time selecting the proper gambling hell to visit—somehow we know there will be only one—and finally settle on the Golden Nugget, the iron cowboy's pedestal, because it must surely be the most hellish of all. Our image of places with names like the Golden Nugget is blended of only the most seasoned romantic ingredients: it is a kind of cross between the old Western saloon with the gilded balcony and the little rooms "upstairs" where the been-around entertainer carouses sadly with her boss, whom she does not love; and the outlawed back room that turns into a Goodwill store at the push of a button, where mean men with contacts play poker all night long, where the dealer wears a green eyeshade and the winner drives home in the cool morning with a pistol in his lap. We know better, of course, but what difference does that make? We always know better.

The Golden Nugget is a long, high room, upholstered in billiard-table felt and decorated with paintings of Western gambling scenes. The slot machines are ranked three deep near the front door; beyond them are the craps tables and the roulette wheels; beyond these, the card games. Every machine is being played, and all the game tables have people shivering with impatience, waiting to get in, but there are different rhythms moving here, not only from game to game but sometimes within the games themselves. The craps table is the swiftest, the noisiest, the most excited, but this applies almost entirely to the players making come or don't-come bets. The stickmen and most of the players are quiet and intense as the dice keep rolling. The stickman is always beautiful to watch, never hurried, never upset, striking with his hoe as gracefully and finally as a matador. The roulette wheel has a quieter crowd, but the soft hiss of the wheel, like the sound of tires on wet pavement, and the chittering of the white ball give it its own rhythms, a little like drums and gourds played delicately. The card game tempos vary from the *slapslap-slap* of twenty-one, quick and over, to the secret islands of the poker tables. And over it all, syncopated as Latin music in itself, but dominating all the other rhythms as absolutely as a heartbeat, comes the crunch and giggle of the slot machines. Once you start really hearing that sound, it's hard to hear anything else.

Whole families, like the ones we saw this afternoon, young housewife types who must be playing with their husbands' paychecks, middle-aged couples, old men with blue lips and double-breasted suits, old women like abandoned spiderwebs, almost too weak to get the coins up to the slot and to battle the handle down without being slung screeching into the sky to form clench-fisted constellations themselves—they all stuff money into the machines as though to keep them from crying terribly; they play one machine with each hand; they would use their feet and their mouths if they could; and yet there is no real feverishness about them, no sense of hunger or of daring or even of need. A very few, mostly the ones who drop in a couple of quarters and go away again, show some interest in their fortunes, and a few of these go off like firecrackers of exaltation or despair. But most of them play with the faces of men who run adding machines eight hours a day. Whatever they're after, it isn't winning; common to all of them is the reflex of plowing their scanty trickling winnings back into the slots without even looking at them. After a while they begin to seem as much a part of the machines as the handles or the money chutes or the melting wheels. Perhaps this is the thing they want, if there is something they want.

We clump around the Golden Nugget for a time, still with the sense of being in the wrong movie, trying to concentrate on the other games. But everything is moving too fast—it's like trying to catch a Bandersnatch or to read the label on a revolving record—and gambling is perfectly meaningless to watch, anyway. You have to pay to be involved. At last we nod at each other and shove out a side door into the warm night, where the cowboy on the roof greets us "nuh—how—dy—pod—nuh." The place must be soundproofed.

It's just after midnight by the Golden Nugget's clock. Whatever was going on in the street is still going on, only louder and with more people watching. I must be tired, but I swear I can't make out what's happening, although I can see a master of ceremonies skipping around with a microphone, just as happy. Well, who knows what entertains people these days? Maybe he strips. It occurs to me that I don't know how to get out of this town. We've missed a turnoff somewhere, and this play-street detour compounds the confusion. There is a motorcycle cop sitting on a sawhorse with his arms folded, apparently watching whatever it is. I walk up to him and ask, "Excuse me, can you tell me how I get on the road to Jean? Going west. San Francisco. Excuse me."

The cop blinks and sits up suddenly. "Wow," he says. He starts to rub his eyes and then stops. "Excuse me," he says. "What did you want to know? I'm asleep here." He has a young face, but his hair is beginning to gray.

I repeat the question. "Woo," the cop says. "Going west. That's Ninety-one you want. Well." He yawns and rubs his eyes. "You'll have to excuse me," he says, grinning. "They got me on special duty here, and I am worn out, I am through." He gives us the directions slowly but thoroughly, interrupting himself with great gullet-splitting yawns. "Wow, I'm tired. I've been on duty since eight o'clock yesterday morning." His eyes are focusing in a

168

funny way, and I'm not entirely sure he sees us. When we thank him he nods in the wrong direction and sits up very straight on his sawhorse, holding on with both hands.

We walk away down the side street where we left the scooters. I say, "Truthfully, I am glad to be getting out of here, little friend. I am not much for this town."

Phil's voice comes back hard and tight, almost stammering. "Christ, those machines. That wasn't gambling, that had nothing to do with gambling, that was a prefrontal lobotomy. I never saw so many people looking like that. Dead. I don't want to see any more of that."

"I'd have liked to talk to one of them. I'd like to know what they think is happening when they play."

"What think?" he says. "Meat, that's all, self-made, mindless meat. Fuck 'em, they deserve everybody who wants to take everything away from them. Let's get out of here, dad. I don't want to see any more dead people. I see enough of them. Let's get out of here, let's go to California."

The quiet side street pulses like an ember with reflected light, and there are shadows moving in doorways and parking lots, as there are shadows breathing in embers. A man is standing by the scooters, leaning close to look at them but not touching them. We quicken our steps a little. When we come up to him he turns and smiles with yellow teeth that gleam wetly in the light. "You fellas come all the way from New York on these machines?" he asks. He is an old man in an overcoat that looks like peeling bark, an insect-fragile man, not very tall, with clear hazel eyes, like my brother's. We say yes, yes, we sure did.

"I used to race them things," he says, "thirty, thirty-five years ago. Used to have a motorcycle, I don't think they make it any more, an Indian. I don't know if you have ever heard of the Indian motorcycle." As it happens, we both have; the strangest uncles and old family friends admit to having driven Indians. This pleases the old man, and he goes on. "I used to race for the company, the Indian people. All the motorcycle people used to have their own teams racing for them. Starting in nineteen-twenty-seven, they used to send us touring around the country every year, and we raced in all the big towns. We raced in Oakland, California, and in Denver, Colorado; in Salt Lake City, Utah; Tulsa, Oklahoma; Kansas City, Missouri; Cincinnati, Ohio; Baltimore, Maryland; Pittsburgh, Pennsylvania; and Buffalo, New York. The same towns every year. That was how I saw the country."

He asks about the scooters' electrical systems; apparently the wiring of the old motorcycles was liable to make you briefly incandescent at any given moment. He has not touched a motorcycle in over twenty years. "Got married the last year I raced for the Indian people," he says, "and my wife, she came along with me on the tour. It was a real honeymoon. She rode along on the back of the motorcycle, and we went to Oakland, California; Denver, Colorado; Salt Lake City . . ." He likes just to say the names. "Took a spill just outside of Baltimore, it was a bad road then," he says. "I got broken up some, and so did my wife." He taps his knee, bending stiffly to do it. "I got a silver plate in here, and the other one don't work right, either. My wife, she got broken up too, so we just quit after that. Never raced since, except once, when I got out of the hospital. I wanted to see if I could, you know." He has been working for a lumber company for twenty-nine years. His wife died two years ago.

We sit on the scooters, listening to the old man's voice in the quiet, glowing street. A pleasantly homely woman in her thirties comes up to us and asks us if we are parked here or not. "I hate to push you," she explains, "but it really is the only place we can find to park the truck. We're taking the kids camping."

"That's all right, bring it around," the old man says. "I'll stand right here and guide you in. I was just telling these boys about how I used to race motorcycles. Well, so long," he says to us. "You ain't got far to go now. Take it easy."

"Where are they going?" the woman asks him.

"All the way from New York City to San Francisco, California."

"Boy, that's some trip," the woman says. "We're from Hobbs."

Jenny moves away from the curb very slowly; the street slides past us like an empty merry-go-round. Mounted on the scooters again, we are no longer part of the action on the movie set, and it recedes from us as we pass through it. Faces puddle together again; voices reach us like the sea in a shell; nothing that happens to a single soul here can trap us or concern us because we are getting out of town. However they make the movie turn out, we will be long gone. Crossing the main drag, we nod at the sleepy cop, but he is directing traffic now, gesturing as though he were wading unhappily in lip-high water, and he does not see us. I wonder where he's sending all those cars.

U. S. 91 is Las Vegas Boulevard, the Strip. Here, according to the Triptik, "eminent entertainers display their talents in new luxurious hotels and colorful casinos." Yes, I know about this part of town. I have been to so many movies, seen so many night-club acts televised, memorized and chanted so much show-business mythology, that I could probably draw a map of the Strip without mislaying too many colorful casinos. The magnificently tasteless façades float by, shivering like mirages of cuckoo clocks and wedding cakes, of gingerbread houses and funeral homes and Howard Johnson's. The floodlit names go by too: Sinatra, Horne, Martin, Rooney, Hackett, Fisher—so they do exist, or at least the names have found real people to wear them. I'd like to see Sinatra. But I never seriously consider stopping to see if they'd let us in. I knew a three-year-old boy once—he looked like a beautiful turtle—who was taken to a movie when his mother couldn't find a baby-sitter, and he liked it quite well and thought it was the only one in the world. Whenever he was asked if he would like to go to a movie, he would answer gravely, "No, I've been to the show." The phrase has been one of ours for a long time.

I notice that all the Strip hotels—the Sands, the Sahara, the Dunes, the Desert Inn, the Flamingo—have the NO VACANCY sign out, all of them, down to the motels that look as if even their proprietors must be made out of plasterboard. Whatever in the world is going on in this town, it's keeping a lot of people happy. Never find out now. The highway is getting wider and darker as the lights fall away behind us; like the white, windy road that we battled into Columbia, Missouri, it is divided by a deep trench that makes the other side seem very far away. No clubs now, no motels, very few lights along the road. Jean tonight, Boron tomorrow, then Kingsburg, then Menlo Park. We worked out a schedule last night.

I had thought that Jenny was running smoothly and swiftly, judging her pace by the speed of the traffic around me, but Phil, a long way back the last time I looked, is suddenly even with me and then passing as easily as though we were going in opposite directions. He throws a concerned look over his shoulder as he goes by, and a moment later Couchette's taillight flares as he brakes her to a stop on the shoulder of the road. "What's the matter, dad?" he asks. "How come you going so slow?"

I feel a flash of anger at him for no reason at all, except that Jenny was running with the throttle wide open and I love her very dearly. "Nothing; it's all right. She feels like taking it easy, is all. Come on, Sigunick." I pop Jenny into first and roar off like the Wild One, without waiting for his answer. Take your time, baby, any way you want to run. God damn him. I wonder what's wrong with her.

He is by me before I can get her into second gear, because she will not go into second gear. Something is broken; I know it as I am trying third and fourth gears, shifting into neutral, and starting over. The clutch disengages when I squeeze the lever, but the shift twists too easily, and the gears will not take hold. There is only first gear now, wherever I turn the handle. I bellow after Phil, but Phil is gone. I let Jenny roll onto the shoulder again, and she stalls out as soon as she comes to a stop. I turn off the headlight, so as not to drain the batteries.

"Well, that's it," I say aloud. "That's it."

This is what we feared, this is what we knew would happen, the stranding, the hamstringing of the dream. Everything around me looks different now, so suddenly and sharply that I might have been changed into another kind of creature with differently made eyes. The warm sky and the wide road, the thorn-colored night, the headlights whirling by, are all become bitterly insignificant to me, distant as a song I have whistled and wanted to hide in. It's all over. Think of something else. A corner of the Triptik pokes up at me from the scooter bag, the page that has the street map of Las Vegas. It tears loose as I stuff it back out of sight.

It isn't the end, of course, and I know that too, sitting by the road with the gearshift as loose as a broken neck in my hand. It's only a cable that's broken, and we have others, because we were afraid of so many things when we left New York that we took along enough spare parts to build two new scooters. We don't know anything about installing shift cables or adjusting them (which is the reason this one broke, I think, remembering the warning signs at the Grand Canyon), but we can surely get to a service station and figure out something. But the strange certainty will not go away. The journey is over, stupidly over, here on U. S. 91 just outside Las Vegas. Already it seems to have been over for a long time.

I could be talked out of this if Phil would come back, but he'll probably get all the way to Jean before he begins to wonder where I am. Twenty-five or thirty miles each way, and a dark divided highway to hunt over—he might not find me till morning. The nearest turnoff is eleven miles from here, for a town so small it isn't even on the map. I might try to inch that far in first gear; there's an outside chance that Phil might have got worried and stopped at the turnoff to be sure of me. It's something to do, anyway. I can't stay here. I disengage the clutch to start Jenny, let it in again, and she moves off along the shoulder of the road, roaring sadly, trudging like a queen who has never had to walk.

It takes me perhaps a quarter of an hour to cover two miles, and then I have to give it up. I remind myself that I might just as well wait for Phil as burn up all my gas looking for him, but the truth is that I would rather walk than let Jenny shake herself to pieces any longer. An agony of affection comes over me once she has stalled to a stop again. Her sides are so hot. Never mind, I say, it's not your fault, never mind, never mind. I'll think of something. Rest a while. I put her up on the kickstand and sit down on her to wait for Phil.

I have always prided myself on accepting with humor and patience situations I cannot change. You have to pride yourself on something. Tonight the patience consists in sitting cross-legged on Jenny and blinking my little flashlight whenever a single headlight goes by on the other side of the road; the amusement in the fact that this flashlight will throw a beam of light as wide as a strand of spaghetti the distance of a fairly urgent piss for about as long as it takes to say, "That'll teach you to buy forty-nine-cent Japanese flashlights, you damn fool," twice. I suspect that the light it produces doesn't even travel with the speed of light. It'd be a great flashlight for a spy who didn't really want to know anything.

The stars are falling. I didn't know April was their autumn. They scratch the night sky as they fall, but the sky is as unresisting as a great pillow; the marks are smoothed out instantly, and you cannot remember where the star was. I sit still on Jenny, watching the stars fall and waiting for Phil to find me. I have no way of knowing how long I wait: long enough for the traffic out of Las Vegas to thin to a trickle of trucks; long enough for the night to turn a little colder; long enough to memorize every swirl of pebbles and shadow of grass I can see from where I sit; long enough to start wondering if the miserable little bastard had any occasion to look back before he went to sleep in Jean. Once I would swear I see him, unmistakable scooter, duffel bag, hat, hunting face, and all, hurrying toward Las Vegas. I switch on Jenny's lights, wave the flashlight, which goes out, jump up and down, and scream like a peacock. He passes without seeing me, but my faith is renewed. I apologize to him as humbly as I can without making him insufferable, and sit down again to calculate how long it will take him to reach Las Vegas, turn around, and come prowling back on this side of the road. It gets a lot colder before I decide that it wasn't Phil after all, the miserable little bastard.

It is the cold that makes me move at last, a mingy, niggling kind of chill that nags like a child. I push Jenny a little farther off the road, lock her up, walk a few steps away from her, and turn around again. I can barely see her when there are no cars passing. With her front wheel turned all the way to one side, she looks small and injured. In Western movies it is usually the wounded cowboy who has to send his reluctant horse for help. "I'll be back," I tell her. I turn away again and start walking toward Las Vegas.

Walking warms me, but it doesn't wake me up. I meander along, watching my feet go with a certain interest and not thinking of anything. When something goes by, I flap my flashlight at it. Cracking my knuckles would attract more attention. I try to keep my eyes away from the crevasse that divides the highway, because if I look at it too long one of us seems to be sidling toward the other. I walk for a long time, back to the place where Jenny's shift cable broke and beyond, but there is no light that might be Phil going either way, and nothing to tell me that I am any nearer to Las Vegas than I was, except that I can't see Jenny any more. I wonder what I'll do when I get there. I keep on walking, singing a little and stopping when I hear myself.

A small pickup truck, coming along the road very

slowly, passes me, stops, and begins to back up before I can make myself move toward it. The runningboard is level with my thigh, and it seems to take a long time for me to scramble up and stick my head through the window. An awful voice, something like Mel Allen talking into a tin can, says, "Hi, got a busted scooter back there, and I can't find my buddy. He's on a scooter too, but he's lost."

"Yeah, I know," the driver says. "I passed you before, sitting on your scooter, but there was too much traffic, I couldn't stop. Had to go clear to the next turnoff, go on back to town, and come around again." He has a strange floppy face, neither young nor old, white as the hard part of a lettuce leaf, and seemingly made all of cartilage, like a nose or an ear. Looking down at the floor, I notice that he is barefoot, the dank soles ribbed with calluses from driving the truck. "Get in," he says.

Docilely I climb into the truck, and he begins driving back the way I have walked. I had some vague idea that I was going to Las Vegas, but I guess not. It seems logical enough to be being carried back to my starting point, doubtless to start all over again. Life must be like that for a baby. The driver thinks he saw Phil on the other side of the road a while ago, but I know somehow that he's a little crazy. I have a hard time knowing things for sure when I'm fully awake, but I'm all right when I can't hear myself talk.

"Shouldn't have left your machine out on the road like that," the driver says. I tell him that she is locked up and in no condition to be anybody's getaway car. "Don't mean shit. Goddamn kids around here, they'll strip her right where she stands, won't be nothing left but the tire tracks. Those fuckin' lousy kids, I had a flat one time and I went to call up, and when I got back, those bastards, they'd tunneled right straight through my car, just like a bunch of termites. Broke in the front window and busted into the trunk through the back seat, didn't even leave the goddamn seats. Right in broad daylight too, cops driving by all the time, they didn't give a shit. Buddy of mine, he caught those fuckin' kids taking his car apart and they busted his head with his own tire iron, wouldn't nobody stop for him, cops, nobody. That's why I stopped for you. I figured a bunch of those kids come along, they'll strip your machine, bust your head, and those goddamn cops won't do nothing about it." All the way back he fills me with horror stories about the dark alliance between the cops and the kids, until I am peering out of the window in a real panic, fully expecting to find Jenny down and thrashing under a swarm of black-jacketed carnivores who would as soon bust my head with a tire iron as look at me, or listen to me play the guitar and sing in French, or anything. The fear wakes me up, though. It does that every time.

Phil is still nowhere in sight when we come up on Jenny—alone and unharmed—but he arrives almost immediately after we stop, hunched like a racer over Couchette's handlebars, but driving slowly. I lean out and yell to him, and the driver honks his horn and blinks his lights, but Phil has already picked out Jenny in his own headlight. He stops a little way farther on and comes back along the shoulder; he is neither grinning nor waving, but his whole body seems to express a long, deep sigh. "What's the matter, dad?" he asks.

I climb down from the cab. "Shift cable busted. Where'd you come from? We didn't pass you on the road." We might have lost each other for only a few minutes at a traffic light.

"Saw Jenny and crossed the divider." He squats on his heels to inspect Jenny's crankcase. Presently he says, "Good, it's only the nipple that's broken off; the cable's all right. I got a spare nipple. We can fix it."

"Not here, we can't. How did you figure on getting her back to Vegas, coast?" Even when I'm ridiculously glad to see him, that damn professional air of his drives me mad.

"No sweat," he says calmly.

177

The truck driver interrupts. "Well, if you boys got yourselves fixed up, I'll be on my way."

"Thanks very much for the lift," I say, "for going all the way around and everything." He nods and drives away. Watching his taillights sailing into the darkness makes me feel momentarily nervous and alone, even with Phil. I don't really believe that we know how to fix a shift cable, and what if those goddamn kids show up now? "Who the hell was that?" Phil asks. "You got the strangest friends."

"Weird cat who picked me up when I was walking back to Las Vegas. I was looking for you, I think. What happened to you, little buddy? I was worried as hell."

"Jesus God," he says. "Beagle, I thought you were dead, you know that?" He uses the word "dead" for so much that bores or disgusts him, it is strange to hear him say it like this. "I got all the way to Jean," he goes on, "and I pulled off the road and waited for you, and I waited, and I waited, and I lay down on Couchette with my hat over my eyes like a real little cowboy, and I smoked a few cigarettes, and I waited some more. I got pissed off as hell after a while. I kept thinking, what's the sonofabitch nursing her along like that for, he won't get here till next Wednesday, and I'm tired. Mad as hell. So after another while it crosses the mind, could it be a disaster has befallen my little friend, like maybe he got killed, and I jump up and start trying to flag down trucks, cars, anything. Hoo-boy." He lights a cigarette. In the matchlight his face looks yellow and translucent as a leaf that is not quite ready to fall. "Beagle," he says, "nobody stops for you. Half an hour of jumping up and down beside the road, and nothing would stop. They speeded up as soon as they saw me; they went past, *bam, bam bam*, tough bananas, friend. Finally I drove off the highway into town, and I asked, where's the cops? I didn't want to do it—if I have to holler copper, you better be dead—but what the hell. Anyway, the only cops were in this truck-inspection station a little way down the road, so I went there, and I said, hey, would you know about it if somebody got killed on the highway? Like, do they tell you these things? You can't take anything for granted with cops. So he said, yes, yes, we'd probably know, chances are—anyway, we haven't any deads tonight that I know of. He said to stick around and he'd ask the next truck-driver coming in from Las Vegas. So I stuck around."

He is smoking the cigarette in swift little pecks, jerking his head slightly with each one, like a bird drinking. "Forty minutes of that," he says, "waiting in a booth the size of a rumble seat, big bright lights, like cops always have to have, listening to them chewing the fat with truck-drivers. Forty minutes, maybe more, before a guy comes in from Las Vegas and says he's seen a scooter parked by the road about seven miles out of Vegas. Nobody on it. The heart goes *ooof,* you know? So then he adds, he did see a guy walking down the road toward Las Vegas, guy with a beard and a cowboy hat. I damn near kissed him about the neck and ears, only he wouldn't have understood. Oooh, Lord, walking to Las Vegas. What'd you want to do that for, you jughead?"

"Wanted to play the slot machines. Don't nag me, Sigunick."

"That's right," he says. "Be a wise guy. Make life a little harder for me, contribute your bit. You schmuck. Anyway, I get on Couchette and back I go, and any time I see something that might be Jenny I cross the divider, giving little happy whoops of delight and recognition. Only that side of the road is about ten feet lower than this side, and I don't see so good in the pitch-black anyway, so it always turns out to be a clump of grass or something, and I have to cross back again." He moans softly. "Oooh, is that a divider, hoo-boy, such a divider. Back and forth, back and forth, like a yoyo—ho*ho,* what a divider. I must have crossed that goddamn gully five or six times before I found her. Recognized the windscreen. So

179

now you tell me how you spent the evening, old friend. I am agog."

"Worrying, mostly." We topple slowly into each other's arms in a simple, manly embrace of great relief and great weariness. Presently I say, "*Effendi,* how are we ever going to get back to Las Vegas?"

"Do not fret, old soulmate of my puberty," he replies. "The same thing happened to me the first day I had Couchette, only worse. See, the cable is connected to the shift bar, the shift bar's connected to the crankcase—wait, wait, help, get me off this. Thank you. I'm tired. Anyway, the whole shift bar fell off, and Couchette was locked into third gear, and I had to drive her all the way home from Queens, you remember. I jump-started her at every traffic light, and I pushed her up every hill, and it took me a long time. Same thing, really."

"Not entirely. This is first gear Jenny's locked into. I don't really want to drive her seven miles in first gear."

"So who said you would have to? You would mere use first to cross over to the other side—you'll like that—and then we would hold the clutch in and turn the shift bar to third gear by hand. Sensible?"

"I guess." I walk out into the middle of the road and stare down into the lopsided gorge that divides it. The darkness makes it impossible to judge depth or width, but it looks like a housing project for dragons. I walk back to the scooters and ask, "Isn't there another way?"

"Well, you could always drive all the way to Jean in third gear and cross over there. Of course you would not find me here when you got back, but you certainly could do that. It's an alternative."

"All right, don't nag me. I'm scared." I start Jenny again and take her slowly out into the road. Phil cautions me about one particular spot that looks like the easiest place to cross. "No slope right there," he says. "It's a nice straight drop, plunk, like three coins in the fountain. How I know, I thought it was a natural crossing myself. Did Couchette not have brakes like a truck, you could have walked all the way back to Gunhill Road before you saw me again." I ease Jenny over the lip of the gully and let her start down.

Gravel and stones and dry clumps of weeds, all violet in the bucking headlight, and a rasping sound under the noise of the engine, as if Jenny were ripping the earth like Douglas Fairbanks cutting his way down a mainsail. I make two mistakes, or perhaps one big one with subdivisions. The first mistake is to give Jenny a little gas, instead of using first gear to hold her back, and the second is to try to check her wobbling rush down the slope with the foot brake instead of the hand brake. The rear wheel locks and skids, and Jenny slews violently, to the right, to the left, and almost in a circle as I fight her delicately balanced weight to keep her from going over. Only reaching the bottom of the ditch brings her out of the tailspin. Climbing the other side is easy after that. I bring her to a stop as soon as she is over the crumbling edge, and she jerks forward once and stalls. Couchette bounces up beside me a moment later, and Phil says, "Some divider, ain't? I bet they have two of them running parallel to keep you from passing on curves."

"They must be building a moat. What do we do now?"

"Now you hold the clutch in and twist the handle to third." He squats beside Jenny and reaches under the cowling. Whatever he is doing to the shift bar makes the handle shiver in my hand; he says, "See, it's just the upshift part that's broken. Once I get her into third, you can shift down if you have to. There, that ought to do it; start her up and I would push you some till she gets some speed up. No, Beagle. You push too. That's right."

Driven, a Heinkel is probably as maneuverable a scooter as there is, but the only thing harder to push around by hand must be a fully armored knight on ice skates. I huff along beside her, holding the clutch tightly, listening to Phil make moose noises behind me. When I feel him let go—and it is as unmistakable as any double rupture—I tumble into the saddle and let the clutch out.

Jenny nearly stops dead right there; she keeps moving, but at a slightly slower pace than when we were pushing her. She stutters and totters along the road, giving every indication of being within a breath of conking out, and keeps going. In the time it takes Phil to walk back to Couchette, start her, and catch up with me, Jenny has picked up enough speed to be out of danger, and we run abreast on the empty road all the way back to Las Vegas.

The town looms up on us once more like a fire-bright ship approaching over an obsidian sea. The royal names of the Strip sail by again, the colorful casinos, the spun-sugar palaces, the floodlit fountains, and all the NO VACANCY signs, in all styles of lettering and all the colors of cake icing. Needing something from a city makes it a little more real, and we see Las Vegas differently from this end of the night. We hurry on down the Strip, trying at once to gauge our speed to the light changes and to peer at every hotel on both sides of the street. Every single one that we can see is full up, and only a few signs say they're sorry about it. You can actually hear the neon filaments creaking their delight all together, like night insects. Saturday night, everybody's here, everybody's come to town, and the money's moving. I have a feeling that it's not a very good idea to need anything from Las Vegas.

Finally we turn off at a service station and ask the night manager if we can leave Jenny there while we go looking for a hotel. He is an agreeable young guy who says we can leave her till morning if we like, but he is dubious about our chances of finding a place. All the Strip hotels are booked solid, because of the convention, and he suspects that even the wrong-side joints will be filled tonight. He gives us a few addresses and tells us how to get to them. When Phil asks him if he knows anybody with an arc welder, he goes to the trouble of calling a couple of other stations to find out if they have one. One place, a few blocks back up the Strip, has a welder, but it belongs to one of their men, who won't come to work until nine this morning. It is almost three o'clock now.

"What do you want to do?" Phil asks. We are standing in front of the gas station, watching the night men do their work.

"I don't know." We have to keep stepping aside to let people hurry by; seen from above, they would seem to be moving through the bumping, shuffling dance by which bees talk together. The sky is strangely light for three in the morning, almost milk-colored. "We might go on to Jean and look for a place there."

"Jean's a small town," he says. "It's only got a couple of hotels, and you know they'll be filled up tonight. I can't see driving all the way out there just to come all the way back in a few hours to work on Jenny. I think we've got more chance of finding something here—hell, a flophouse would do for the night. Might even find a cop and ask him if we could sleep in the jail. They let you sometimes."

"All right. Up to you." A police car stops for a light at the corner, and I step out into the street, taking off my hat and smoothing my beard. I tap shyly at the window, and the cop rolls it down. "Yes?"

"Officer, I wonder if you could help me. My friend and I are passing through on a couple of motor scooters, just passing through, and we've had a little accident." A tanned young face, familiarly handsome, but somehow basically shapeless, as if it had been patted out of gum arabic. It is a movie star's face, a public face, and I'm sure he knows it. He looks at me as though he were staring into a camera.

"My Gawd, no!" he answers. He pulls his head back and wriggles his eyes to express amazed and contemptuous rejection. "No certainly not, you couldn't possibly sleep in the jail." The voice is late Tony Curtis, after the diction lessons. I'd give anything to see him make an arrest. I bet he charges admission.

I ask about flophouses, and he smiles coldly. (*The*

183

Marshal smiles coldly.) "We don't have any of those here," he replies. "We keep them out." (*We got a clean town here, mister. We aim to keep it that way.*) Well, could he possibly offer two stranded travelers any advice or assistance? It's good public relations for cops to help people. He suggests that we camp somewhere along the highway, far enough off the road so that he or some other cop won't have to see us and arrest us. That's all he can do for us, sorry. (*You'll get your guns back the day you leave town.*) He spurs away into the traffic, a hard man, riding herd on his town, with fine lines etched around his eyes. It's a chancy job.

Phil, who has come up in time to hear the cop's last words, stares after him and says, *"Creo que no.* He probably makes half his quota that way. That's amazing. You should have gotten his autograph."

"Let's check out those hotels, then. I'm tired, Sigunick. I'm so tired I feel drunk."

"I'm just tired," he says. "Like we were cold in the mountains, when we knew we'd never be warm again, that's how I'm tired. All right, let's go look. You better direct me. I can't really see."

So the real night begins. We hunt along the stagnant back streets of the city, plodding from the brownstones to the converted frame houses, moon-white, dry as dead insects, clean with rot, to the flophouses—there are three of them within a block of the police station—where old men in their underwear fret and shiver awake on yellowing mattresses to stare at us like the ghosts of monkeys and of moths. There is no room for us anywhere. In one hotel, just off the Strip, the night clerk offers us a single room for twenty dollars. On nights like these, he explains cheerfully, he tries to keep a couple of rooms aside just for guys like us with no place to go. He knows how it is.

We hardly speak to each other in all the time that Couchette is grinding up and down the railroad streets. Phil takes to staying with her while I go into the hotels. Sometimes, when I come out, I stop for a moment to see him sitting there, holding Couchette up with his knees and his hands, body caving slowly over the handlebars, curling like burned paper. In the thin light of the hotel marquees his face looks worn through: dry yellow grass with the yellow earth showing beneath. He does not look up when I climb on behind him, but his hands move as if he were wringing a neck, and Couchette is away with a jolt and a growl, falling through the night.

Once we find ourselves sitting at the counter in a huge all-night drugstore without a single memory of deciding to stop there, of stopping, or even of where we have parked the scooter. We order coffee. Phil says, "Oh, my God, I'm tired." He is getting a cold again, and his voice is thick and nasal. "I don't know what we're going to do," he says. "I got to get some sleep."

"We aren't going to find a place in this town. You want to try Jean?"

He shakes his head slowly. "I ain't sure I could make it to Jean, you want to know. If I stood up right now, I'd fall down, and where I fall down is where I sleep. They'd damn well have to do something about me then. I got to sleep, that's all there is to it. I got to get my sleep pretty soon."

The determination in that exhausted, mucus-dulled voice scares me a little and makes me look away. I say, "I wonder if we've shot all our miracles. We could do with one about now." Once, on a summer afternoon, we were riding together on old Margot, and an arm reached out of a passing car and handed us two tomatoes with the garden dirt still on them. For that one moment, the whole universe seemed to fondle us.

His grin is like the reflex of a killed animal. "I been checking out the cashier since we sat down. She looks like the kind of nice lady might adopt us and take us home with her. Why don't you go ask her? Tell her we sing and dance."

"You don't ask miracles." A genuine Fuzzy miracle

trots up to you and shoves its unsolicited muzzle into your hand; a genuine Fuzzy won't move for any other kind.

Phil says, "I don't know what to do." The tone of his voice brings a waitress hurrying to find out if we want more coffee.

I think that we both fall asleep at the counter for periods like five seconds, fifteen seconds, even half a minute, for the waitresses seem to hop back and forth in frozen, stilted flickers, bewildering as the most primitive movie. We drink three or four cups of coffee apiece to delay the moment of walking out of this warm place to begin the numb, silly search again.

The cashier turns out to be a friendly woman and quite sympathetic to our plight, but she does not offer to take us home with her, or marry us, or anything like that; although God knows we do everything but inform her that the Son of Man hath not where to lay his head, and drop dead into her dish of toothpicks. She does hunt up a few more unrecommended hotels for us, though, and we thank her and step out into the street again. Dawn cannot be very far away, but the city seems to have grown darker, for the sky is blue-black now, as if it had been burned over, and the stars are gone. The lights of the Strip are going out too, but the street still glows with the sullen light that flares in a bulb the moment after you have clicked the switch off. A tall woman walking past says to the man with her, "That's okay, Vinnie. I wouldn't love you if you didn't once in a while." We find Couchette and begin the search again. I offer to drive, but Phil says no, he can manage. He is limping now.

We try the police station last of all. It is a clean, tiled kind of place, like the shower room in a good hotel. The cops are identically clean and tiled themselves, except for the head cop, who has a face like a washboard and smiles a lot. They are extremely polite in refusing us permission to spread our sleeping bags in one of their cells, but they smile among themselves like women. When we are walking away from the station Phil says, "All those years of learning about cops, enough slamming around so I'm still ringing, and I haven't yet got it deep enough into me that cops are not there to help you. That bugs me more than the cops do."

"Question of class. Cops know the people they're supposed to help and the people they don't have to help; you can't fool a cop on something like that. Graham Greene has a cop in one of his books—I can't remember which book, but anyway, this cop divides people into two classes—"

"I hate you, Beagle," he says. "But no hard feelings."

"Ah, you're waking up. Good morning, brave general."

"Good morning, you lousy no-good men, you." It is growing light now, although the sun has not risen; a bland, featureless sort of dawn, the lights coming up in the planetarium. The air is pleasantly cool and damp right now, but we can feel the heat pushing out of the east behind the police station. We walk back to Couchette, parked across from one of the flophouses, and stand by her, uncertain what to do next, each listening to the other without speaking. Shall we keep on looking for a place to sleep? Shall we get breakfast and say the hell with it? Kill time until the welder comes to work and we can fix Jenny? How do you feel? How tired are you? You're more tired than I am; you decide. What do you want to do?

Then we see it, almost directly across the street, the string of pushcart-sized cabins wedged into an alley between a two-story brownstone and a parking lot. The sign that says VACANCY is hand-lettered, which would explain why we missed it in the dark; although it would be easy enough to walk past the place if it were on fire at high noon. It just doesn't catch the eye.

"Well," Phil says. "Well, well. Looky dere."

"Well. Yes. Oh, yes indeed. After you, glorious leader."

"No, no, old chap. Arm in arm, at the very least. And no tripping."

A pale woman in a blue bathrobe is out in the alley,

pruning an ulcerous rosebush. She reminds me of the kind of aunt everybody in the family bullies more or less affectionately: thin, never young, anxious to please. Yes, she has a room for rent—that is, she will have it in about twenty minutes, when the gentleman who's there now leaves. He has to get up early; she knows that because he asked her to call him. It'll be six dollars, if we care to wait.

I pay her while Phil parks Couchette in the lot. Then we walk down the street toward the Strip to look for a place to have breakfast. The sun is rising, flushed and puffy, a huge boil in the sallow sky. It's going to be a hell of a hot day.

Most towns and cities, both the
old whores and the ugly virgins,
are pretty in the early morning,
when nobody is awake yet, the
air has not begun to wither, and
the day is still full of hope, at
least until the mail arrives. But Las
Vegas was never meant to be seen
by day. Las Vegas makes me
think of a woman I used to see
occasionally sitting in the window
of her house on Broadway in the
West Seventies, where she told
fortunes and read palms. Seen
through the dark, cobwebby
glass, she had the kind of sensual
ugliness that makes you want to
drown everything you believe in,
everything that is good for you, in
all sorts of smelly vilenesses. But
I saw her coming down the front
steps one autumn afternoon, with
a string shopping bag over her arm,
and she was simply an old black-
haired woman whose skin moved
on her like a balloon with most of
the air gone. I remember that she

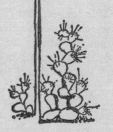

came down the steps backward, like a bear. Las Vegas is like that at six o'clock on a Sunday morning.

"It's not a town at all," Phil says. We are sitting in a Chinese restaurant, eating eggs that must have been scrambled in cold cream. "It's a collection of booths and rides and games and tents and peepshows—like a carnival, and I bet they move it around like a carnival too. Nobody built this place; they just set it up and work it, and then they take it down and move it somewhere else. You'll never make me believe anybody lives here. They just work it."

"Let's not sleep too late. I don't want to stay here another night."

"Six hours," he says, "seven hours, even eight hours, that gets us up at two-thirty or so and gives us the rest of the afternoon to work on Jenny. Then we get out of here and drive all the way to—what is it, what's the schedule, Boron? Drive all night if we have to. We'll keep the schedule, dad, don't worry about that."

"I'm not." I am suddenly, angrily, unhappy, and it is hard to breathe. "Screw the schedule; we'll sleep till we wake up and we'll get there when we get there, we'll take our time. And listen, if there's anything between here and there you want to draw, or paint, or anything . . ."

The woman at the cabins is extremely apologetic when we get back, but the gentleman hasn't left yet. She called him, as she promised, but he said he wanted to sleep a little longer, and of course he can stay till checkout time, which is noon. She's very sorry, and she'll give us our money back if we want it, but she really doesn't think he'll be sleeping much longer, because he did say he had to leave early. If we'd like to wait a while, she has some magazines.

We shrug at each other without speaking. We won't be able to work on Jenny till nine o'clock, and where could we go till then? At least, here we can sit down without having to buy something. Phil finds a deck chair and stretches out in it with his hat over his eyes. I settle down at a table with a mildewed heap of *Look* magazines whose pages have the special feel of having been read in the bathroom a lot. Sunday in Las Vegas.

The sun gets higher and yellower and smaller, and in time it becomes incontrovertible that the gentleman is not about to leave that cabin till noon, and not, perhaps, until next winter. What the gentleman has in there, judging from voices and giggles and general clunking around, they should only vend in the subway stations, like Clor-ets. I would like to think she comes with the room, but one look at the manageress and I know better. She wants to tell somebody that she doesn't run that kind of place, but we don't seem to have noticed anything, and she obviously isn't the sort of person to bang on doors and inform the gentleman and his midnight snack. It is nearing nine o'clock when she gives up. She tells me that, frankly, she doesn't think the gentleman will be leaving early after all, and that we'll probably want to look for another place.

So we climb back on Couchette, and Phil drives us up the Strip once more, to the gas station where we left my lady. I shift her back down into first gear and toil the few blocks farther to the place that's supposed to have the arc welder. Phil gets there well before I do and greets me with the news that the welder simply won't do; it's too cumbersome to use on something as small as the nipple and as thin as the cable. The station boss will let us use what tools we need, however, and even supplies us unofficially with an assistant who doesn't seem to have much to do just now. The assistant's name is Ray, and he is a dark, quiet guy of twenty-eight or thirty who also paints a little. "You ever work in casein?" he asks Phil, and Phil says not lately, but what he's been working in on this trip, gouache, is almost the same thing as casein. I open my tool kit and take Jenny's cowling off. When I hear the word "culture," I reach for my gap gauge.

As it happens, we've been luckier than we might have been; had the cable itself broken, we would have had to take the whole thing out and install the spare. Phil has seen this done. "The cable's connected to a worm gear up front," he says, "and when you unscrew the handle the whole thing drops into your hand, just as neatly and softly as bird shit. How good are you at packing bird shit back in the bird?" As it is, all we have to do is solder the nipple to the cable, fit it back onto the shift bar, and then readjust the gears.

Jenny looks so gray and naked with her bright cowling off that I find myself being glad it's a hot day. We squat down beside her, and Phil picks a spare nipple out of our aspirin tin of nuts and bolts and fuses. He passes the cable through the hole, frays the end to provide the best possible surface for the solder, and sets to work with Ray's propane torch. He is almost finished—he has even dunked the nipple in water to set the solder—when I make hesitant mention of something that has been worrying me for some time in a vague way. "Phil, is the cable supposed to go through that hole before you hook it onto the shift bar? That hole over there."

"God damn," he says.

There is a little arch built onto the crankcase a bit forward of the shift bar, and the cable has to pass through it so that the spring can press against it and create tension. The nipple is much too big for the hole.

"They must put them on that way at the factory," Phil says. "No, that doesn't make sense. Maybe they start at the shift end and connect it up front, but that's silly too." He turns to me and says very quietly, "I don't mean to pry, but do you think you could tell me why you didn't point the, shall we say, discrepancy out to me a little earlier, you helpless idiot?"

"Well, I didn't notice it right away, and besides I have great faith in you. Had. Anyway, I'm timid about this kind of thing, technical suggestions and all. You see, you look so very sure of yourself."

"Yes, but you know I just look like that because it comforts me. If you don't, who does?" He gives me the torch to play over the hardened solder, while he picks and pulls at the nipple with a screwdriver and a pair of pliers. The nipple comes away at last, but in two pieces, looking like a filling broken out of a tooth. Phil inspects one of the bits gripped in the jaws of the pliers and says, "Yes. Well. So much for that. See what you made me do?"

"Mmm. I don't suppose we could take one of those busted pieces and sort of squooge it all up with solder, lots of solder, so it would maybe—no, of course not, huh?"

"Stay timid," he says. We begin to laugh together, squatting on our heels and clucking like hens, one waving the still-flaming propane torch, the other a handful of tools. Yep, it's us. No question. Jenny's naked body, with the cable poking out at a stiff, foreshortened angle, like a splintered bone, is a silent rebuke to the humor of incompetence; still we laugh and point at each other, like very small children discovering mirrors, and Jenny must surely know why by now.

We decide to take a nipple from the spare hand-brake cable, so we stretch it out on the ground and bang it and burn it and twist it and tug at it, until the nipple comes off at last, looking very small to have caused all that carrying on. It is very small, so small that the shift cable won't fit into the hole. Ray takes it into the station, hunts up a proper-sized bit, and drills the hole wider; it will certainly weaken the nipple, but there's no help for that.

By itself, the nipple fits neatly, if a little loosely, onto the shift bar, but once Phil has soldered it to the cable, the situation becomes aggravating in a brand-new way. Scooter cables stretch during use, which is why you have to keep adjusting them, but this one seems half a foot too short to hook onto the bar. I wonder if a piece of cable might not have gone with the original nipple on the highway last night, but Phil says no, it came off too clean, shut up and push. So he hauls at the cable with the pliers, and I push the shift bar forward—first bare-

handed and then with a wrench and a bruised knuckle—
and the two draw appreciably closer together, if you
appreciate easily.

A middle-aged blue Buick rolls into the gas station
and stops dead with no sound of stopping. A girl gets
out of it. She is tall and thin—if she has any figure it is
effectively enveloped in a dress like a beige duffel bag
—and she has a head amazingly like a coconut, even to
the straight, coarse brown hair. She heads straight for
the ladies' room, and as she walks past us she smiles down
and says, "Having trouble?" in a voice of vivacious un-
interest.

She does not stay for an answer but lets the door slam
shut behind her, and we curse her softly and go on doing
what we're doing. We do not notice her when she comes
out of the ladies' room.

Quite suddenly and easily the nipple slips into the
notch in the shift bar and holds there snugly. It takes
us a moment to be certain that nothing has snapped, or
given way, or torn something loose inside something
else, and then we go off and have a chocolate bar and pat
each other around the vertebrae. It could have been done
better, of course—even with the enlarged hole, the nipple
does not turn freely at the end of the cable, as it's supposed to do, and it really isn't in properly—but it's on
tight, and it ought to last as far as Menlo Park. The only
task remaining is to adjust the gear train, which sounds
like an anticlimax after the hooha of fitting the cable, but
which Phil has also seen done. "More bird shit," he says.
"Now we got to juggle it."

Curious, patient Ray finds us a big gas can to rest
Jenny's rear fender on, thus keeping her back wheel free
to turn. I start the engine, holding in the clutch, and Phil
squats beside her again, turning the adjuster nuts in and
out to locate the gears. Theoretically, once you have more
or less isolated a gear, you can freeze it in position by
tightening a lock nut, but theoretically you can make
love standing up in a shower. "Well, that's first," Phil

says, "and that's second, *ça va*"—how slowly and vainly the wheel seems to turn for the power it produces—"and there, that's third. Okay, put her in fourth and let her out. Put her in fourth now, Pete."

"Can't. She won't turn that far, she gets about half past third and sticks. I swear some of the cable's gone."

"If jugheads were flowerpots," he says, "you would be the botanical gardens." He turns the adjuster nut to give the cable more play. "Try it now." The handle twists a little closer to fourth gear, but it still won't go into place. "Damn. Try it again." Eventually the shift crunches into fourth, and Phil pounces on the cable with a cry of "Gotcha!" and theoretically locks the gear. "That should do it for the upshift, anyway," he says. "Put her back in first and go through the gears."

"What first? I can't get her down past second now. And second isn't really there, you come right down to it."

"Oh, Jesus."

He rocks on his heels and moans softly, and I try to think of something heartening and useful to say. "Third's all right, though, Phil. Third's fine."

"Is it? Try it."

"Woops."

Somewhere around the time we have achieved an uneasy truce with the upshift and are just beginning the struggle with the other fork of the cable, Ray hunkers down beside us and whispers, "Hey, would you guys be interested in buying a hot fur coat?"

We both stop work to stare at him, and he snickers nervously. Ray, what is this, since when are you the master criminal of the petrol pumps? You're a nice man, you have two children, a boy and a girl, you like to go riding around on your little Honda scrambler, you climb mountains on your vacations, and you paint on weekends. You don't even know how to talk fence talk, any more than we do. What coat?

"It's not really a coat," Ray explains. "It's more like a kind of stole, you know, just a piece of fur. Fox, I think, maybe squirrel. This girl who came in here a while ago, she's asking ten bucks for it. Girl in the Buick." He points to the blue car, and we see the tall girl sitting in it, talking to one of the other attendants, who shakes his head and walks away as we watch. The girl looks briefly toward us and then away again, her head turning with a strange blindness, like a cannon's muzzle. She starts to get out of the car and stops. Her head goes down very slowly and rests on the window sill.

"She's out of gas," Ray says. "Ran clean dry just as she drove up. Now she's trying to raise some money on the fur piece. She wants ten bucks, but you could probably get it for less. All she wants is the gas to get home on."

There is an odd callousness in his tone (Ray is a kindly man and an Italian), but we find ourselves sharing it without much consideration. Let her have a few lonely troubles for a while; she probably shot all her money on the slot machines last night. The hell with her, let her walk home. Even if we wanted to help her out, we haven't got ten dollars to spend on a squirrel skin. We might find a guitar or something. Serves her right for being an unpleasant girl with a head like a coconut. We say sorry, and Ray shrugs. "She'll find somebody, for ten bucks," he says. The girl's head rolls slightly on the window sill: an old, rotted coconut, half in and half out of the water. Phil and I go back to work.

The downshift is much easier to adjust, perhaps because it never was as disheveled as the other. At last, when Jenny has run up and down through her speeds three times without missing or clashing, Phil says, "I guess that's it. I guess we fixed her."

He stands up slowly, rubbing his palms on his pants, smiling sleepily and mistrustfully. I say, "Looks like it." Success in anything bewilders us too much to let us enjoy its sweetness fully until some time later, as we sit thoughtfully amid homely ruin.

"They made an all-day job out of adjusting Couchette's gears in New York," he says, "and they weren't stalling around, either. Oh, we got to have done something terribly wrong, Beatle."

"There remains the possibility of her running in reverse. I've been wondering about that since we started on her."

"I'd like to see that. It'd be a lot more in character for you to come backing up to Enid's front door at sixty miles an hour. Well, start her up, and let's see how she —oy—runs. If she'll start."

"I'm scared. What if she explodes?"

"Oh, I'll like that too, don't you worry. I'm not a hard man to amuse." But he is still staring at Jenny as though he were not fully awake, nibbling a forefinger. "We fixed her," he murmurs. "That's silly. We don't fix things."

In all this time the husk-colored head on the window sill of the Buick has remained as perfectly still as a stone, or as a frightened animal, or as anything self-contained and unhuman. No one else has come over to speak to her. I know this because I often raise my eyes to see if anyone is going to help her so I won't have to look at her any more. Her existence where I can see her is beginning to bother me in a very personal way. To be powerless and friendless in a world where only money can make you real; not to be your own person any more, but to be totally dependent upon the whims of carburetors, the chill of the night air, and the kindness of people whose religion and folklore instruct them to help others—this is a very old nightmare for me, which is strange, because I have never really known it. I wish that girl would pull in her head and go away.

"I guess nobody's going to buy that fur," Ray says, having gone off somewhere and come back. He has a way of drifting up beside you, like an afterthought. "Seems as if they would though. Hard to go wrong for ten bucks."

I turn away and start putting Jenny's cowling back on, thus committing myself to the belief that she will run, that I won't have to take her apart again. One commitment in an afternoon tires me out like a fast game of handball. Phil says, "Why don't you buy it?" and I jump, but he is speaking to Ray.

"Well, I don't know. It might really be a hot fur, although it looks kind of ratty to me. I thought about it, but I don't know."

"Where does she want to go?" Phil asks. Oh, that's fine, learn things about her, discover that she has a home somewhere, maybe a family, friends, books, tastes, feelings. What's the matter, you haven't got enough troubles by yourself?

"She's heading for Los Angeles. Says a tankful of gas would get her pretty near there."

There is a sign within eyeshot of the station that says Los Angeles—293. That car looks as if it would burn a gallon of gas just going through the gears. Phil says, "This is a stinking place to run out of gas," and he is speaking to me.

"I know. Bothering you too, huh?"

"For a while now. It could be us."

"That's a relief. I was afraid you'd think I was a do-gooder or a liberal or something."

"Schmuck," he says and grins. "I believe you. I bet you were."

"You guys going to spring for the fur?" Ray asks. He does not seem at all surprised. "Good investment, I guess, traveling along."

Screw the fur, we answer, almost in unison. Fill her tank and let it go at that. We haven't got anybody to give furs to, anyway.

He nods and walks away. I go back to tightening Jenny's cowling, curiously disinclined to see the girl come to life again, as though Ray had injected the money directly into her veins. There is a case to be made for those who give anonymously to their anonymous brethren, though it makes you think of Mr. Dooley speaking for Andrew Carnegie: "I cheer mesilf with th' thought that no matther how much money I give, it don't do anny particular person anny good." When I look up again, the girl is sitting at the wheel as Ray and another attendant push her car up to the gas pumps.

"Well," Phil says, "it busts or it doesn't bust. Let's get out of here. I just remembered I'm tired."

"I know." I am beginning to wake up to exhaustion; when I yawn my teeth chatter, and when I stretch I feel as though I hadn't stretched. Still I fuss with Jenny, checking and adjusting and connecting, and Phil remains surprisingly patient, for he knows what I know, being a reader and a musician and a maker-up and watcher of the Late Show: that lives cross each other like kite strings, and that's what all stories are about; that you are always walking—or running—out of stories in the middle, and that you ought to stay to the end when you can, if it doesn't cost you too much. There is more to this story, and we have bought it pretty cheaply, for money.

And here she comes now, around the corner of the gas station, her smile somehow pink and peeling, like the rest of her face, her long legs moving from the hip, the way a man walks, altogether about as romantic a heroine for an adventure in Las Vegas as Kanga. But she thanks us with casual self-possession, and that part of things goes by very quickly. "That was kind of a bind," she says. "Nowhere to turn, you know? I guess I just fell apart for a while there." Her voice has a metallic ghost-liness, twanging out of nowhere and whining back into it, like a musical saw.

She is carrying the fabled fur over her arm; from a distance it looks like a cat, but she says it's muskrat. Whatever it is, it had dandruff when it was alive. She offers it to us for the price of the gas—six dollars and something—but we decline. "Well, I still want to hock it," she says. "I haven't got dime one to show for the weekend, and I had three hundred and forty dollars last night." It was the machines, then, and the tables. We remember the pawnshops on the street where we parked the scooters one evening, and a few others noticed in the area of the police station. It's Sunday, but you can't tell about pawnshops. We offer to take her around on the scooters. It'd be a good test run for Jenny, and we planned to cross the desert at night, anyway.

"Okay, fine," she says, "but let's not get too near the fuzz, huh? I had to give them every cent I had before they'd let me go, and then they said move it out of town before morning, baby. So I'd as soon not get any traffic tickets or anything."

Cop trouble, is it? Don't worry, we know about cops. What'd the bastards pick you up for?

"Hustling," she says, sounding mildly surprised, as though she'd already told us that. "I came up from Ventura to work the convention, and I was doing fine and having a ball. Thursday, Friday, Saturday, three hundred and forty bucks without pushing it, knocking myself out, you know? But they got it." She is quite calm about it, even a little amused—very possibly at us, who have to be told things.

I go out front to pay Ray for the gas and to tell him that we'll be leaving the car here for a little while. He nods, knuckling his nose and pinching his lips, and I know that Ray knows quite well what the girl is and is trying on the image of us all snarled up in some sort of three-cornered romp. For $340 she may well know something festive, but oog. "We're going to try and hock that fur of hers," I tell him.

"Yes," says Ray. "Good luck."

We start the scooters, and the girl mounts unhesitatingly behind me, because I have strapped the fur to Jenny's luggage-carrier. Jenny clicks into first gear, and then into second, as we move across the gas station and into the plucking current of the Strip. Third gear now, and she is shifting more smoothly than she has since we left New York. Phil, leading because he remembers where the pawnshops are, is breaking his neck to look back at me; I think he really did expect to see Jenny going backward or up in shrapnel. It is about two o'clock now, and the Strip shimmers pale orange in the heat.

"This is great," the girl says. "I haven't been on a motorcycle in a long time. It's like being fourteen again."

"She's a scooter."

"Scooter, I mean." She is silent for a moment, and then she says, "That's a good way to travel, roaming around, seeing the country. Nice and slow, boy, that's so fine." Ah, that damn little saboteur. It was my turn. "I do stuff like that too," she goes on, "all my life. People won't let you alone."

"There's a poem about that." Why should I not be Villon to her Fat Margot, Blake to her Mary, grimly miscast as we are? " 'The laws of God, the laws of man, he may keep them, he who can . . .' " She picks it up instantly and recites the whole poem, strong and secure up to the lines about being a stranger and afraid, mumbling a little after that, but hurdling right on through to the end. "I love Housman," she says.

Oh, it's a beautiful day, it's an elegant, graceful day, and I'm sailing down the Strip in glamorous Las Vegas, on my motor scooter, in company with a certified illegal prostitute who loves poetry and remembers it. Sonofabitch, I'm a real writer! I used to worry about it, but no more. Life is good.

The pawnbrokers won't touch the fur. I don't know whether they suspect its origins or whether it's just general policy not to accept furs, but they won't even offer her the token amount she would settle for. We park the scooters and walk from one shop to another, trotting along the bony sidewalks beside the girl, who is a little taller than either of us. Once we cross the street where we came into town and wandered around, the street of the Golden Nugget. The stillness of it reminds me of Vandalia, Illinois, on another Sunday, but that street was clean and lifeless, and this one is strewn with the kind of sandwichy garbage that is left after a picnic. Last night the street sang with the frantic, bursting noise of mating flies; today there is only the moaning of the mechanical cowboy: "How—dy—pod—nuh—how—dy—pod—nuh." Midnight clockwork at two in the afternoon. A cop car comes rolling up the street toward us, like a tank prowling through a deserted enemy city. It passes us and picks up two old men who are going the other way. The old men have skins like damp white sand, their lips are floppy and purple, they both have three-day growths of sharp white whiskers, and their pants are too big for them. The cops look like basketball players. I say, "Phil. You know, this town could be Mordor. In *The Lord of the Rings.*"

He grins wickedly. "Mordor was at the end of the journey," he answers.

The last pawnbroker says, no, I'm sorry, I can't do a thing for you, and we go out again. The girl is clutching the fur by the neck now, and it almost drags on the sidewalk. She says, "The hell with it, I'll give it to my kids to dress up in. Let's have a beer." We cross to a small crowded bar and sit down in a booth.

"My name's Jill," she says. "Jilly." We tell her our names. "You're the writer"—pointing at me. "My husband wanted to be a writer. He couldn't write for shit, but he tried; he just liked being a writer."

She might so easily be talking about me that I answer, "Yeah, well, with me it's a living, it lets me do what I want to do." Which is take the day off and go to the library, but the tone of voice is everything.

"I like writers," Jill says. Phil chuckles softly, and she turns toward him. She has a twisty, birdlike way of turning her long neck to look at people, as though she were ready to duck her head into her armpit. "I like painters too," she tells him. "My pimp, Chris, he's a real painter. That's what he does, you know?"

"Yeah, we make great pimps," Phil says. After that, we keep the art talk down to gruff celebrations of technique. Consider us sisters of the skillet, baby.

Jilly is very definitely a home-town girl. She was born

and raised in Ventura, and although Los Angeles is her
base of operations, she still lives in Ventura, in a different
part of town. "We live in an old stone house way out in
the woods," she says, "me and Chris and the kids. It's like
a real artists' colony—we have a bunch of painters, and
writers too, and sometimes we put on plays, just for ourselves, just for kicks. Great place. We go nude swimming all the time."

"How many kids?" I ask.

"Four. Three girls and a boy." She has their pictures.

Phil says, "That's a lot of kids for—what?—twenty-
six? twenty-five?"

"Twenty-five," Jilly answers. That surprises me—I had
somehow put her down as at least thirty—until I have
looked at her for a while. If she were a pretty girl I think
I should have realized it sooner, for ugliness ages a face,
and the knowledge of ugliness often refines it. But even
so, Jilly's homeliness is bland and unused; the things that
are wrong with her face are wrong with an adolescent's
skin and flesh and hair and eyes, and she still has the adolescent look of waiting to outgrow them. I should have
recognized Jilly's face. I still see it in the mirror now
and then.

"I had the first one when I was eighteen," Jilly is
saying, "not even eighteen; it was a month before my
birthday. Then twenty, then twenty-two, and then the last
one, the boy, a year ago. Soon as I was out of the hospital with the boy, I scooped them all up and moved in
with Chris. Best thing I ever did. They love him." She
laughs suddenly; she has a pleasant laugh, softer and
fuller than her speaking voice. "The little girl," she says,
"my three-year-old, she has this way of coming up to
men, and she throws her arms around their legs and goes,
I love you, I love you. Just to men, any men at all."

"Sounds promising," Phil says. "Break her in early."

Jilly makes a sound as though she were turning in her
sleep. "Well, I don't know about that," she says. "Hell,
I didn't start hustling till I left Les, my husband, not

really hustling." Her eyes want to change the subject; her angled grin says, ask me how a nice ugly mother like me got into the life. (All the whores I ever met had the same grin; it spreads slowly across their faces when you meet their eyes, like a stain.) "Poor Les," she says. "He always said no wife of his was going to work."

She likes to talk about the place where she lives with Chris. It is a cluster of old stone cottages, all dating from the time when Ventura was almost entirely a Mexican town. Some of the trees are supposed to be more than four hundred years old. "Nobody minds what anybody else does," Jilly says. "Everybody gets along; it's a very communal thing. Everybody's got his own bag, of course, but we do things together. We all write poems and stories and show them around, and we go on painting trips all the time, and one of the guys even gives acting classes, that's where we do the plays. There's a good school for the kids right in town, and there's a great little beach we found for ourselves. That's our beach. We go nude swimming whenever we feel like it."

"Sort of like Huck Finn," Phil murmurs, and Jilly says, "Yeah." Then she blinks and laughs and says, "Well, no, not exactly. Not quite."

I am curious about her social standing in a community like this, where wives seem to be as interchangeable as Tinkertoy pieces (where we come from, this is called "playing Westport"). Jilly says, "Well, everybody knows I'm hustling for Chris, but nobody gives a damn; it doesn't lower the property values or anything. I don't do much hustling around Ventura, anyway. I work Los Angeles for a couple of weeks at a time, and then I come home and I'm like on vacation." She sips her glass of beer, looking at us over the rim. Her eyes are a pretty gray—the color of a pigeon in the rain—but oddly shallow, as if they had not been connected yet. She says, "Sometimes Chris rounds up a bunch of people that like to watch, you dig? That's a gas; they come in with him like a real guided tour, and he puts them all around the bedroom—there's three inside walls and enough holes for everybody—and then we just go inside and wail, like nobody's there. That's a real gas." She presses the glass against her lips, and her smile wriggles through the beer.

It occurs to me that Jilly may be a little disappointed in us. She knows the rules about The Whore's Life Story at least as well as we do, and we are not so far turning out to be a creative audience, one that could help her build something moving and meaningful out of a simple bar-room confession. We are too busy being terse and knowledgeable—understanding, but hard—to ask the proper questions in the proper order. For the most part we just stare at her, propping the conversation up with "yeah"s (questioning, sardonic, grim, disillusioned, popularly compassionate), spiking it with "well, hell"s, and our own personal blend of "it happens"s. We've got scooters and guitars; we know the way things are. Which makes Jilly work a little harder than she should really have to, but that's tough. We play straight man for each other, and that's the end of it.

Jilly got into a life like this—as she finally volunteers —because she wanted to. "I always liked doing it," she explains, "and I dig the whole idea of getting paid for it." Babe Ruth is supposed to have said more or less the same thing about playing pro ball. "I still like it," Jilly says. She never accepts less than twenty dollars for a trick, and for that price the customer had better not waste time fooling around with his shoes. (My friend Monique's price for an equally brisk servicing was ten dollars, but then Monique had a lower overhead to consider; she would never have dreamed of humiliating a poorer client by unbuckling his pants and shoving them down around his ankles, as Jilly likes to do.) She has a real pride of regulars now, men who visit her (though she does make house calls) as often as three times a week, or as infrequently as every couple of months. "It's a great way to meet people," she says. "No kidding, you meet the weirdest kooks."

She calls her clients "johns," but with a slight effort, as though she had read the same books we have; she numbers among them a fair selection of sadists, masochists, fetishists, coprophiles, and other hobbyists, and she trots them out for us like the glass menagerie. "Evelyn calls me up," she tells us—Evelyn is her Los Angeles matchmaker—"and she says, honey, you got a real collector's item coming to see you this evening. You won't believe this one"—she is already giggling—"but he likes to scrooch down in the bathtub, no water, and you take the highest-heel shoe you got, and you have to say . . ." She flops with laughter in the booth, remembering it with real delight. "And I said, my God, Evelyn, I can do all that stuff, but I'll just crack up when I have to say that, I know I will. So she says, well, at least you know what he wants you for. He asked for two girls, but he won't tell me why he wants the second one. I'm sending Laurie over, because she doesn't care, but I have no idea what he's got in mind for her." She is almost pretty as she laughs, but her gums are gray as a mollusk. She tells us why the john wanted the extra girl. It sounds wearing, but it would make a great woodcut.

Chris takes care of the house and the children while she is working in Los Angeles. Phil asks her if she ever holds out any of her earnings on him, and she answers quickly, "Jesus, he'd put me right through the wall if I pulled something like that. Chris doesn't stand for things, you know?" She is more proud than frightened, talking about it. "Right through the wall, boy. That's the thing about Chris. When I was with Les, I could do anything, tell him anything, and he'd just sit there looking at me. That's how I remember him, sitting at the kitchen table looking at me, and me telling him I'm going to do this, or like I've just done that, or if I feel like doing the other thing that's exactly what I'll do. He never said a word." She preens herself, yawning; something alive seems to stir under the beige dress for the first time. "Now, with Chris, if I tried that with him, I'd wind up under the table, and we both know it. That's okay, that's the way I want it." She grins suddenly, but this time her lips are tight against her teeth. "You know, half the johns I get, they remind me of Les. That's how come they got like that, however they are."

I ask her, "What were you like as a child?" This is one of my very favorite questions; it opens the way to all kinds of understanding, and maybe bed, while demanding very little effort or attention. You can't get a better parlay than that at a dull party. Jilly says, "Well, when I was fifteen I had twelve thousand dollars in the bank."

Phil orders three more beers. I say, "Oh, I see. How'd you get it?"

"Running pot," Jilly answers. She speaks of it with the strangely middle-class matter-of-factness with which she first told us her occupation. "It took me three years to put away that much," she says. "I could have made a lot more, but I wouldn't take any chances. I was a pretty cagey little girl."

Her eyes flicker from one to the other of us, stretching with amusement. She says, "It's been kind of a crazy life. There's one writer in Santa Maria, he keeps after me to let him write my life story. He says it has to be written. I don't know. I'd like to do it myself sometime."

"If I wanted to write about you," I say, "I wouldn't ask you, I'd just do it. Maybe you'd recognize yourself, maybe you wouldn't. He paints the same way. We're not photographers."

Jilly's smile hooks up sharply, as though she had caught us on it. I think that, in talking to her, we have been trying to give the impression of being casually on the wrong side of the law, actually as well as morally. "I used to go down to Mexico weekends," she says, "and come back with pounds of pot hidden in the car. The border cops used to go nuts searching the car, because they knew I was running stuff, they really knew for sure, but they never found it. The car belonged to this one fellow, he had it fixed up specially for hiding pot. They could have searched it all year." She laughs. "The longest part of the run was sitting around waiting for the cops to put the car back together. After that, it was just head on up to L. A., drop the stuff off, and go home. Twelve thousand dollars."

"And home in time for school," we say. "Very cool." I ask Jilly what she told her parents while all this was going on. "Not much," she answers. "My parents are pretty bourgeois; they believe whatever they have to. I had my own bank account, and I didn't spend much of the money, anyway. I told them I was working after school, so if they saw me walking around with a fancy dress on, that's okay because I'm working after school. Like I tell them I'm engaged to Chris, and that's fine with them, now they have something to believe. I don't see any reason to make them unhappy; they don't bother me. They never did."

According to Jilly, she slipped into her world at the age of thirteen as naturally as any child discovering his lost kingdom. "I was recruited," she says with a grin. "It was at a party. They took me into a room and locked the door, and then they sat around asking me all kinds of questions, just like cops would. Testing me, they said. Hours of that, sitting around on a baby chair till my ass ached—so finally I said, look, you've seen too many movies, you know that? Why should I fink on you? Give me one good reason. You don't screw me, I won't screw you, what do you want? So they laughed, and that was it."

From that moment of recognition Jilly rose through the ranks like a flying fish bursting into sunlight. At sixteen she was a sort of utility infielder for her syndicate, still specializing in transporting marijuana (and only mari-juana—"When I hear anybody's messing with the big stuff," she says, "that's the end of him, I won't go near him, even if he's just using"), but turning a hand on re-quest to other kinds of smuggling, to the disposal of stolen goods, to the numbers racket, or to any other field where she might make herself useful. Thus she gained in experience and self-confidence, as well as in the deserved respect of her fellow professionals. The money piled up in the Los Angeles bank, and Jilly bought a new dress now and then, and the border cops never did find the secret hiding place in the special car.

"And I kept on going to school," she says. "I was going to use some of that money to go to college." She puts away another glass of beer; she always looks straight at us as she drinks. For one moment the flat, tideless gray eyes seem as serenely amoral as any animal's; innocent and accepting, laughing at us for having such high hopes of being evil. Then she says, "You know, the degree's like a union card, it's something to fall back on," and she is Jilly again, no matter how she lives.

The flying fish leaps out of the water for a reason, and the reason usually follows along below, waiting. A few weeks before her graduation from high school, Jilly went to the aid of an old friend who had fallen out of favor in court circles. "He'd been going around with the wrong people," she explains, "something like that, and they had a contract out on him." She looks around to see if we know what a contract is; we say, "Anh," guessing it to be a Mafia equivalent of the Black Spot. "Well, I liked him," Jilly says. "I wasn't in love with him or anything, but he was a nice guy, and we used to go places together sometimes. So I got on a plane with him, and we went to Mexico this time. It took a lot of bread, most of it, and not just for plane tickets, either." She shrugs, almost closing her eyes. "What else could I do? Mexico was a ball, anyway; we went to Acapulco, Taxco, all over, and we spent that loot as fast as I could get it changed. Finally I told him, okay, friend, you're on your own, lots of luck, and I wouldn't cross the border for the next forty years if I were you. Then I went home, and they were waiting for me at the airport. I knew they'd be."

When Phil and I were children one of the great entertainments around our block was called, "telling movies." You sat on the curb with your audience grouped around you and recited the plot of the film you'd seen last Saturday, usually something with Cornel Wilde in it, or Victor Mature, or maybe Abbott and Costello. You could do it as prosaically as you liked, or you could improvise on the basic chords of the story and the cliché cadenzas of the dialogue, and make something near to what is called a folk epic out of that B movie. It was all a question of imagination, timing, and technique; it always has been. Phil was marvelous at it—when he went away for the summers he scribbled installments on postcards— and I think Jilly would have been. She sits up straight, lips parted, eyes and hands alive; she might be singing. She touches a thin white line across the bridge of her nose, and another at the angle of her jaw. "I spent a little time in the hospital," she says, "so I missed graduation. And while I was in the hospital they found out I was pregnant. One damn thing after another, you know?"

She accepted her condition quite calmly and actually married the man responsible for it—not her fugitive, but Les, who had always had at least some idea of her life and, apparently, not cared. They found a house in Ventura, not far from her family, and Jilly went to college for a while and bore Les four children in seven years. I ask her what else she did during that time, and she answers, "Nothing. I read a lot." After the birth of her last child she took them all and went to live with Chris. She let Les divorce her.

Hustling for Chris, she is bound to come into contact with some of her former associates. Bygones are more or less bygones now, and Jilly likes to do a friend a favor when she can, but she is still the cagey little girl, and she takes more precautions than she used to. "When I do business with somebody now," she says, "anybody at all, I keep records. I build myself up a nice little file right from the start, things I know for sure the fuzz would sell their mothers to get their hands on—and when I've got enough on the guy, I send him a carbon copy on onion-skin paper. It's not blackmail or anything, it's just to warn him, don't play games. I know what I'm doing. I've got a little filing cabinet back in Ventura, and if anything ever happens to me there'll be a lot of sweat flopping all over L. A." She names the girl who is to turn the cabinet over to the police; it is no one she has mentioned before —just a neighbor, she says. The lowering sunlight—it must be nearly four o'clock—slants in through the front door and slaps across her face, catching it naked and blotchy and very tired. She winces and puts her hand up to her forehead, dropping her face back into shadow. "Even Chris doesn't know about the filing cabinet," she says, "and he's my man, you know? I mean, if there's not Chris, there's nobody. But you got to keep a little power for yourself, you just do."

A man leans into our booth to dicker with Jilly about the fur (she had asked the bartender if any of his customers might want to buy it), but he is half drunk and his only foggy interest is in Jilly. She sends him away disgustedly. "I hate drunks," she says. "That's the one thing I hate about the life, all the drunkies. Anyway, I'm not turning another trick in this town, I'm not crazy." She gulps the last of her beer and stands up. "Let's go, huh? I have to get started home."

Walking back to the scooters, she gives us her address in Ventura. Phil writes it down. Jilly is her real name, but we are to ask for June Dawson, which is at once her working name and a kind of password. "Come down in July," she suggests, "that's a great time. We have a big Bastille Day celebration every year, with costumes and everything. Some of us get dressed up like the aristocrats, and the rest of us, we're the mob, and we storm the Bastille and tear it down, and dance in the streets and rape all the aristocrats." We'll try to make it, as a kind of free-lance mob. "Anyway, you'll have a place to stay," Jilly says. "I mean that."

She gets up behind me again, and we start back to the gas station. Jenny runs sweetly now, changing gears silently, moving through the desiccated streets like rain.

People are going in and out of the casinos now, and sometimes I catch a glimpse through a closing door of the green rooms that look so cool from the street.

Jilly has said practically nothing since we started back, but suddenly she begins to sing in a surprisingly rich, true voice:

"He's got the whole world in his hands,
　He's got the whole wide world right in his hands,
　He's got the big, round world right in his hands,
　He's got the whole world in his hands."

It is her favorite song; she told us so when we talked about folk music and rambling musicians, as of course we did. I clear my throat and light into the next verse, the one about the little bitty baby. She joins me, and we sing it together. It doesn't work out well. We have to keep stopping to wait for each other, and we aren't quite in the same key. Besides, Jilly sings it "litty bitsa babe," which is disconcerting and throws off the rhythm even more. Still, we go through the whole song, lying man, crapshooting man, you-and-me-brother, everybody here, and all, doing the best we can, and when it is over Jilly says, "You swing it kind of funny. You syncopate."

"Do I? I didn't mean to. I learned it from a Mahalia Jackson record."

"I've got Marian Anderson doing it. I guess that's why."

Phil gets caught at a traffic light, and we reach the station a few minutes ahead of him. Ray wanders over as I put Jenny on the stand, and I say, "We couldn't find a place to hock the fur. We looked all over."

Ray nods. He points to Jilly's Buick, now parked in a corner of the station. "I put in a couple of quarts of oil too," he says. "It was way down." The boss calls him, and he walks away.

I unstrap the fur from the luggage rack and stroke it gently, with some idea of looking contemplative and appraising. "Gee, it's a nice fur," I murmur. What it is is a greasy fur, smelling evocatively of peanut butter, but it is part of the story that the fur should be beautiful.

"Keep it," Jilly says. She heads for the ladies' room again. I remember her saying in the bar, "All hustlers have weak bladders; it's like an occupational disease."

"Hey, I can't—I don't want—" But the most inviolable of doors rushes shut behind Jilly, and I stand there with my hands full of fur, going, "Hey, no," in a small worried voice. A few people standing around the candy and Coke machines turn to look at me. I wonder what they think. I wonder if I could sell one of them a hot, greasy fur.

Phil drives up then, cuts Couchette's motor, and says, "So, you're ready, let's go. Go to Boron and get some sleep. What are you fooling around with that bathmat for?"

"She gave it to us. What do we do?"

"Well, we can't keep it," he says; and then: "Let me look at the thing again." I hand it over to him, and he goes through his own contemplation and appraisal, seeming almost to listen for a heartbeat. "Can't be worth much," he decides. "She's got lousy taste."

"Strange things happen, though, little friend. We don't know from fur."

"True, but face it."

"Yeah, I know. It'd spoil the story."

"You got to know how to manage things like this," he says, "If we'd saved her from a dragon, or a sex maniac, or something like that, it'd be all right, and the fur'd probably turn out to be worth something. But for a lousy tank of gas, we've had all we're entitled to out of the story. That is how it goes when you ain't a real general."

He walks over to the car and drops the fur into the back seat. Jilly comes out of the ladies' room, and I explain to her that we can't accept the fur; our den mother wouldn't like it. She shrugs and says, "Okay." She gets into the car and starts the engine. The sound makes her smile. "Feels good," she says.

We ask her if she can get to Los Angeles on the full tank. "Close enough to call someone," she answers. "I'll be all right." She shakes hands with us through the window, staring at us, just for a moment, in the way that we were studying the fur. "Well, so long," she says. "Come on down any time." She drives out of the station and heads up the Strip, Jilly going home.

"Better get gas ourselves," Phil says. "You must have burned a lot of it driving around in first last night." We fill both tanks, paying out of the silver dollars scraping in our pockets, curiously anxious to be rid of them. Once I thought them beautiful, when I had only two or three, but now I want them spent and gone as soon as possible. We say goodby to Ray, who says, "See you. Take care."

Then we mount Jenny and Couchette and drive out of Las Vegas, up the Strip until it is no longer the midway but only another road going west. Las Vegas is not a hard city to get clear of; it has no real outskirts, it simply ends, like love or a brick, and the anonymous road is taking us somewhere else. It is after five when we reach Jean, and now the sun is shining directly into our eyes. We stop in a restaurant to wait for sunset.

Sunset is almost two hours away, and we have 160-odd miles to travel when the sun goes down. Looking for a place to stretch out, we wander down a single-file alley between the restaurant and a gas station and come out onto a bare cindery slope that nobody seems to be using for anything except hanging laundry. We lie down, pitched at an angle very near to standing up, and look up at the raw blue sky, feeling the sun move across our foreheads and into our hair. I say, "We're almost in California. Five miles, maybe."

"California," he says. "That's funny." Then: "I wonder if she'll make it."

"Jenny? Oh, the girl. Jilly. Probably, if it's downhill a lot. She seemed pretty sure she would."

"Our pet courtesan. Our hetaera." He laughs and turns his head sideways on the crumbly earth. "You know, she may very easily have been lying her ass off, just for jollies. I wouldn't be a bit surprised."

"I know. I got to thinking about that." This is not true. "But it was a pretty connected kind of story, point for point. I wouldn't have thought she had the imagination to make up something like that, something that—well—connected."

"When I was putting the fur back in her car," he says, "I looked to see where she kept her working clothes. She wasn't about to hustle any three hundred bucks' worth of trade in that snowsuit she had on. Nothing in the car, no suitcase, nothing at all. Maybe she had fifteen gowns in the trunk, go figure. She just struck me as peculiarly ill equipped for her chosen profession, and that includes the whole gunmoll bit. Technique ain't everything."

I close my eyes. "Well, let it be, it's a good story, and we can play with it all we want. Of course, we could always go down to Ventura and go skinny-dipping with her and the Seven Dwarfs. Unless she gave us a fake address along with everything else."

"No, I bet that part's pretty true. It's just the sort of set-up a girl like that would get into, and why the hell not? It's an address to have, anyway, who knows?" In the darkness behind my eyelids his sudden laughter might be coming from anywhere, even inside me. "I like to think about it," he says. "I like to lie here and think about this over-age Smith girl making up a whole goddamn novel, complete with sex, sadism, and sentimentality, all for the benefit of two little yoyos who want to play gangster. Laughing like crazy all the time. I'd almost rather she was lying, you want to know."

We lie still, pretending to ourselves that we are dozing, waiting for the sun to go down. The air grows a little colder, and I feel the first night breeze touch my skin. As always, that particular timid coldness makes me a little sad, and also makes me want to go to the bathroom. When I stand up I see that the sun is balanced over the horizon, with only a thin sliver of blue between; stare at it for the few seconds you may, and it seems to be dancing like a goat.

"We might as well get going," I say.

Phil nods. "Why, as they say, not?" But just jamming his hat down on his gravelly hair requires an effort that almost knocks him over with the recoil. "Oh, I'm tired," he says wonderingly. "I'm very tired. Why ain't you tired, you lousy men, you? You're never tired. You got no character."

"I'm tired too, glorious boss," I say indignantly. "I'm as tired as you are. Observe the decided cant to westward among the ranks."

"That's natural," he answers with calm scorn. "You ranks always walk like that. Listen, the kind of tired I got on me they sell for relics, like the True Cross. Come on. Let's go racing across the desert in the goddamn moonlight. I don't feel good, Beagle. I feel terrible."

The state line is actually about ten miles from Jean. Phil, riding a little way ahead of me, sweeps his arm through a weary but oddly joyous salute as he passes the WELCOME TO CALIFORNIA sign. When we pass through the border inspection station, which is not far from Jean, it is so dark that the splotchy yellow light, the uniformed figures in the booth, and the loud, casual questions that I can hardly make myself answer swirl up memories of midnight railroad stations when I was too little and too tired to know if we were arriving somewhere or going away, and everyone was talking all around me. We are carrying no immediately obvious desert pests, and they let us through.

Everything seems to hammer our senses a little blunter now—the torn road, the stinging cold, the fact that California drivers never, never dim their lights—until we are driving through the desert in a kind of dull dream, reacting to a curve, or a grade, or to someone wanting to pass us, but unaware of these things at the same time. You lose all your perspective on a dark road: except when we see headlights obviously sliding down toward us, or coming up, we have no idea whether we are climbing or not; and even that is deceptive, for we sometimes dim our lights for headlights several hills away that vanish immediately to come swelling over the next slope in a misty, painful aureole. There is a lot of traffic on the road tonight, and the movement of the red and yellow lights lulls me in a rocking, dangerous way, like the sea. A silly song we heard in a Mexican restaurant chitters forever in my head:

Twenny miles is a long, long way,
But I gotta see my baby every day. . . .

Time is very confused, snarled as though a kitten had
been playing with it. Once, when we turn off the highway
to find coffee, we stop in a tiny diner that somehow reminds me of a college couple's living room set down
in the desert. We drink coffee out of plastic cups and
watch an annoyingly familiar Western on TV. It is not
Paladin or *Gunsmoke* or anything adult; it is a prefabri-
cated half-hour rerun that we have both seen in New
York—but where did we see it? when? and are we
there now, watching it for the first time? Where are we,
whose dinner guests are we tonight? Did they like our
music? Are we back in Phil's room with the screaming,
derisive apes painted on the door, watching a show we
have seen before? Where do we begin? When we get
onto the road again, I become quite sure that we are
heading back toward Las Vegas. I sense the change of
direction as a fish must read water. I even pick out land-
marks that I know we have passed going the other way,
and the signs saying BARSTOW—SAN BERNARDINO do not
entirely reassure me. If I could only see where I was
going—but what kind of request is that?

We stop for gas at an isolated roadside station. As I
open Jenny's tank, a familiar voice says, "I see you got
her going all right." I look up from a pair of bare feet,
gold and purple in the dim light, to a lichen-white face
that smiles almost shyly with burned-looking teeth. It is
the truck-driver I met last night when I was walking to
Las Vegas.

"Yes," I say. "We fixed her; she runs fine now. Thanks
again."

He nods and seems to duck away into his truck.
Phil asks, "Who was that?" and I rub my eyes, trying to
remember. We go on.

We stay closer to each other tonight, and the one riding

218

ahead often pulls over to wait if he loses sight of the other's single light around the curves. It is always Phil who remembers to rest the scooters; he calls a halt about twenty miles from Barstow, and we stand still by the road or turn slowly in circles, letting the engines cool. It is the first leisure I have had to look long at the desert, but there is little to see in the darkness. There is only the feeling of a wrinkled, violet immensity across which our road is a thin blue shadow and our lights are no brighter than pennies. The Mojave glows faintly, even on a moonless night like this, the color of clouds reflected in still night water. It might be the shadow of the sky.

As if he were thinking the same thing, Phil says, "Look at the sky." It is high and plum-colored, with only the thinnest dusting of stars. Phil points out a crooked white streak back over the eastern horizon. "What the hell is that?" he asks.

"I don't know. Milky Way, I guess."

"No, it's not the Milky Way." His voice has the tired, not-playing quality it gets at strange times. "I think it's a twister."

Now I know that the white streak is not a twister, but he thinks it is, and as a liberal I respect other people's surenesses, perhaps overmuch. What is needed is a comfortable Fact, from the supply of rubber ones I always carry with me. I say, "It's not a twister. You ever see a twister hang up in the sky like that, white, not moving? They're black, and they look like funnels, and they come on hand over fist. You'd know if it was a twister, son."

"You sure?" He has not taken his eyes off the thing.

"Pretty sure." That was a tactical error. I have the word of a whole gabble of writers for what tornadoes look like —why do I always have to cover all my bets? Phil says, "Well, it's moving."

It does seem a little closer, though it's hard to tell. I say, "You don't get twisters in the desert, as far as I know. It's probably just a piece of cloud drifting along."

He does not answer. "Why do twisters bother you so? I've seen you get jumpy about them before."

He turns to look at me then. "Because it's something I can't possibly control," he says quietly. "It's so far beyond my strength, it could pick me up and scatter me the way I blow on a dandelion; it would be happening to me and roaring all around me, and I wouldn't be able to do a thing about it. That kind of power scares me."

His voice makes me think of him at seven or eight, singing the words of a beginner's piece he was learning on the flute; such an absorbed and yet wary voice for such a small square-faced boy, chanting a song about a gentle bee. I say, "Let's get on to Barstow and see what it looks like then." He agrees, and we mount the scooters and move on into the wind. And all the way to Barstow I find myself looking over my shoulder for the white crease in the sky, each time knowing that it is harmless, whatever it is, and looking back another time. I never see Phil look back, and yet he is the one who told his fear. The streak vanishes between one backward glance and another as we drive into Barstow. It is after one o'clock.

Most of the traffic through Barstow goes on to San Bernardino along the freeway, but we have to pick up State 466 here, and it is nearly as well concealed as the Underground Railway. We find it at last, a single-lane road cutting straight out into the desert, away from all lights. Unlike the road we have followed from Las Vegas, it feels the way it looks on the map: a spindly scratch across emptiness, like the falling stars, like a ship's wake in the sea. We are in the desert now; before, it was all around us.

The road is full of dips and bounces, and Couchette's headlight is there and gone in my mirror like the moon between clouds, as the darkness curves away behind us. We pass three or four cars, no more; there are no towns, nothing but the glowing desert (if night never ends, it is never totally lightless)—and yet, once or twice, as though we were still taking little naps with each breath, we seem to be suddenly passing down paths overhung with trees and lined with gardens and arbors, a bicycle road, unpaved. There is a smell in the air that I could never forget and never name; I would be sure that I was dreaming, except for that smell. The only way I can describe it is to say that when it makes you sad it is time to start worrying about growing old. I feel like stopping for a moment, but I don't, and the desert takes us again. The desert air has its own sweetness.

We stop again, perhaps ten miles from Boron, this time to rest ourselves. We are so punch-drunk by now that each has to help the other put his scooter up on the stand, and our voices are like two people in the same bed talking in their sleep. Phil lights a cigarette and stands very still, while I walk slowly up and down, unaware that I am doing it until he says, "Pete. Don't do that. Don't walk up and down."

"Oh. Sorry."

"It makes me dizzy," he says. "Everything makes me dizzy. I've been one hill behind you since Barstow, watching your taillight rising and falling, miles and miles of that. A terrible, trudging kind of hypnosis." He pokes a foot cautiously at the sand and withdraws it. "This is where they have the gila monsters, ain't?"

"Not right here. Around here."

"Oh, good. Are we in Boron now, lying down?"

"No. We're chasing across the desert, two little *pssts* in the purple dark, two night creatures, wondering as we wander."

"Is that me too?"

"I think it's just you."

"Stop doing that."

"Am I, again?" A truck is coming down the road, heading for Barstow. First we see the orange warning lights, like sails standing up over the rim of the world; next, the headlights, swelling slowly till they burst past us in a rush of blackness; and, last, the little red lights hurrying away, anxiously comical as an elephant's rear view. The silence after its passage is as complete as though we were two wisps of dust in outer space, watching the earth barrel by.

"This feels like a fierce place," he says. "You sure about the gila monsters?"

"Pretty sure. I know what you mean. It ain't a bit like the Painted Desert."

"That was a frivolous desert. This one could turn over and crush you any time. It feels crouched."

The Mojave is gray and violet and tarnished silver, rolling in from all points of the night, poised to break over the thin road. Phil finishes his cigarette and starts another. "I wonder what everybody's doing," he says.

"Everybody who?"

"Just everybody. You know."

"Sleeping, more than likely."

"Ah, you're not a jolly fellow," he says. "You will drink light ale and fall early in October. As the leaves do fall."

"Suits me. You'll have to stick around and watch the winter."

"I would keep my eyes tight shut, in honor of your memory. God damn it, Beagle, you quit that."

"You're doing it too, dad." We begin to laugh, lumbering, painful laughter from the bottom of our lungs, but, for all we know, the only laughter in the world just at that moment. Here we are, here we are, the Lone Ranger and Tonto, the general and all his loyal men, here we go dancing slow circles in the desert, under the sky, tiny as flies between two great hands. Our shoes are full of sand, and our cowboy hats keep falling off.

In only a few moments after we have started on our way again we reach a crossroads with a motel, a gas station, and two diners, all closed and dark. Boron, I guess. It seems closer than we had expected, and a little stark for the country's leading producer of borax, but we are going no farther tonight. Waked at two-thirty in the morning, swathed in pink terrycloth, the proprietress looks amazingly like the woman in Las Vegas who had a room for us if we could wait. It adds to my growing suspicion that we are bouncing around in time like balls in a squash court. Perhaps we never went anywhere, after all; perhaps we are still waiting.

I don't sleep as long as I thought I would. I wake up clear-headed at around ten-thirty, shower, and go outside. Phil is still asleep. It's a warm, sunny day that's going to be hot in an hour or so, but right now it's pretty and very quiet and feels barely used. Wherever we are, it can't possibly be Boron, but that's all right, a motel makes all places kin. The desert is the color of buttermilk in the sun, and the sky is white and empty. I find a telephone in a gas station and call Enid to tell her that we will be there tomorrow. It's good to be talking to her on a sunny morning. The guitars have arrived at last.

I sit on a covered garbage can outside our cabin window, swinging my legs and whistling, until Phil gets up, around noon. We eat a long, lazy breakfast and then set off the way we were going, but not with a real air of going anywhere. The schedule insists that we make Kingsburg tonight, but we journey as unhurriedly as very young children do, who know where they're going but like to stop to look at leaves. This is the way we should have traveled since the beginning.

It's getting to be a very hot day. We pass through Boron and then Mojave, blistered towns like company stores. Beyond Mojave the road begins to climb slowly toward the Tehachapi Pass, the last mountain range we must cross. The desert ends here, and the joshua trees begin. They are dark and tiny, hardly more than man-size, tufted with spikes, and twisted, each one, into an individual dance of savage, arthritic rejoicing. Wild old men dancing, roaring silently—it is impossible not to see them so. One of them jigs on one foot, the raised leg bent and both hands clenched over his head; another with his knuckles on his hips and his thorny head tipped far back; a third high as he can go; others reeling together in groups of two and three, hands crossed and touching, long-toed feet only brushing the ground, and all of them so plainly shouting, gasping, cackling, singing, cursing, that you wonder you can't hear them. The action in their shapes is as bold as clouds, and the tension in them is like a cocked pistol—that one there, straining to hurl himself across the horizon in a cartwheel, or that one stomping all by himself, so hard the soles of your own feet hurt. They make you feel what they are doing more than people do.

They delight Phil like music; they make him happy. He stops to sketch them several times, but I spoil it by fidgeting to be on. I don't mean to, and I hadn't been really aware that I was doing it, but fretting is an easier thing to learn than taking it easy, and harder to be free of. There's time enough for the joshua trees—we both believe that. The desert is behind us, and the mountains will be, but it is somehow hard to imagine coming to the end of the joshua trees.

Stretching our legs in the Tehachapi Pass, we meet two boys of thirteen or so; they ride up on a motorcycle and stop to admire Jenny and Couchette. The motorcycle is lovely. It has become transparent with age, as some old things and people do, and you can see everything banging and chuffing and turning over, even to the crackle of the spark plug, and the flywheel plodding along like Sisyphus. The throttle handle has broken clean off, and they work it with a piece of string; the battery is going to fall off right now; the glass is out of the headlight, the handlebars are cockeyed as a broken neck, and the little paint she has left is shivering off like dust as she idles. Besides that, her oil tank drools like an old dog. I think she runs by gravity, but the boy driving her says she climbs like a bastard. He's very proud of her. Even in California, he's not old enough to drive a car, and the only other motor vehicle he ever had was a bicycle to which he had fitted some kind of two-stroke engine. He swears he got her up to fifty-five—which is more than the motorcycle will do—before she came apart.

They're nice kids, happy in the way that comes from knowing that you have all the time in the world. They don't really remind me of us at that age, though it's fun to pretend they do, but their dreams have a shorelessness that ours had then, before we had to begin making maps of them. When we drive away from there they escort us a little way, driving in a deep gully beside the road. All we can see are the tops of their heads bouncing up and down as the old motorcycle takes the bumps. Phil turns in Couchette's saddle to point them out to me, and we smile at each other. Anything can happen still, to anyone.

The road begins to descend very steeply, falling down in a great spiral through hills like something Dr. Seuss might draw, yellow-green and bulgy as knees under a blanket. After the hills we drive a winding road through wooded, delicate country, blue and violet, like a medieval tapestry. It feels familiar, not like a place where I've been, but like someplace where I've wanted to be. I remember a song Patachou sings, "Bal Chez Temporel." Joss Baselli's band is with her, as almost always, and off the music they make Baselli's outfit is a bunch of happy little maniacs, on furlough from the asylum because they give delight and hurt not—they just bang and tootle and stomp all day long. After Patachou sings the last refrain, the band plays a kind of minor-key vamp, four sad notes over and over, while Baselli, the head loony, runs mad on the accordion, scattering riffs and melodies as joyously as a baby splashing through a puddle. The music fades away slowly, but you can hear Baselli as long as you can hear anything, and he seems to be leading his band of fond enchanteds away somewhere over the hills, tootling. It would be about this time of day, when the shadows begin to stretch like women, and just this sort of place, with valleys to catch the shadows like rain, and trees as jeweled as spiderwebs after the rain. I always want to go with them, every time.

Riding abreast, Phil asks me, "Is California all like this?" I think of the California I know best, the Bay Area. Green in December, brown as toast in June; towns like motels; the Bayshore Freeway lined with housing developments so totally ugly you think they must be a joke, and come to accept them; wild country as easy to find as turning around, and the sound of the diggers somewhere as natural and inescapable as your own breathing. I say, "Not all." "Well, where we're going." "Some of it, not all."

"I haven't seen a single joshua tree since we left the pass," he says. "I think you really did me this time, bwana."

"There must be more of them. It's the state's national flower or something." We joke about it the best way we can, as we always have, but this time it does feel different, as though I had thrown away something that he valued. All the way to Bakersfield, and after, I try to make my eyes see one more field of joshua trees dancing, but they never do.

Bakersfield is in the southern San Joaquin Valley, oil country. Coming into town through Keene and Edison is like driving through one of those advertisements urging businessmen to set up shop in California. Oil rigs all over the place, the highway crowded with big trucks from big farms, the more tractable minority groups working in fields and orchards along the road, and a general feeling of money moving around like blood. We eat supper in Bakersfield and drive on past Kingsburg, to Fresno.

In Fresno we find an old brownstone, the kind of hotel that can't do much transient business because it takes at least a week to learn to find your way back from the men's room. Nice place, clean and friendly, if a little bleak. Big, soft pillows, the kind that break your neck sweetly. We talk for a while before we fall asleep, mostly about guitars.

"The Martin in Salina was the best," Phil says. "That

and the Gibson at Harry's place. Damn, I liked that old Gibson."

"Not that much, you didn't. You don't remember. The Martin was all right, though. Except the bridge was about to come loose."

"I could have fixed that. We make terrible collectors, Pete. We go about it all wrong. The thing is to buy them, fix them up, and just sell them. We're always looking at them for ourselves. Sometimes I'd like to go up and down the country, just buying guitars. Find something really good, okay, keep it, but buy them to sell. Somebody'll always buy a good guitar."

"Need money to start. We aren't the kind of people who buy seven-hundred-dollar guitars for seven bucks." This happened to a friend of ours, whose strength was as the strength of ten for the same reason. "We buy high and sell cheap, just to keep things moving. That's the kind of people we are."

"Is it?" he says. "I wonder." He turns on his side, wincing; the damp air is making his hip act up again. "Anyway, that's what I'd like to do, get a few bucks together and go look for guitars. Go down to Mexico. How far is it from San Francisco?"

"Five hundred miles, six hundred. I don't know." I find myself strangely nervous, shifty-eyed in the darkness. Are we so near tomorrow, then?

"A breeze. A nothing. Yep, that's the thing to do, go down to Mexico and find some good guitars. Maybe even paint a little." I hear him reach for his cigarettes and light one. The lighter flame makes the wall look like a movie screen when they're changing the reels and the kids are beginning to stomp. "This is something I like," he says, "this is a way I'd like to live, for a while anyway. I wouldn't have missed making this trip for anything. I've been happy a lot of the time."

"Me too. I like living like this." Tomorrow I'll have my girl, and he'll have Mexico on someone's living-room floor. But it is always the day after tomorrow that we follow and fear, like the Snark. I say, "It'll be good to play our own guitars again."

"Damn, yes," he says happily. "I always forget how good they are when we've been messing with other guitars. I wish they were here right now. I feel like playing."

Fresno is an ugly town. Phil expected no better, but it disappoints me, although I say it doesn't. Kerouac gurgles, "Yes, yes, Saroyan's town," but for me it was always Aram Garoghlanian's town, and I feel as though I have dropped something else out of my armload of childhood. Fresno's ugliness is the common sort, the ugliness of the small town that got bigger but never big enough. It's like the balloons they give children in shoe stores with the name of the store printed on them: as you blow them up the letters become lighter and more blurred, until you can see the dots of print stretching away from one another. So Fresno is bigger than Pittsfield, and not as big as Canton, Ohio, and it feels as though it would be easy to walk down any street and on out of town to see how the pomegranate trees are doing. You never can, though, you can't get out of town walking. You have to take the freeway.

Inevitably, the next morning we wander into Fresno's only music store, looking for guitar strings, and spend an hour or so playing their guitars. One of the girls working there asks if we know any of Charles Aznavour's songs, which is surprising, because Aznavour is just becoming known in this country as a movie actor. He writes good songs, in the French style of jazz-in-amber, but we know them only to whistle. But it's so good to be playing again, and to be asked to play something we like, that we fake Aznavour with the best will in the world. I sing accented gibberish when I'm unsure of the lyrics, and Phil covers my ill-chosen chords with harmonies so daring and confident that they must be right. There is phony and phony, and the difference is joy.

We play well, not having played for a while. I can never hear us together—I can concentrate on Phil's sound or my own, but not on the third sound—but we grin at each other when our eyes meet, as we do when something has hold of us and is driving us on together, a game, or a need, or a rhythm. I don't know if we understand each other any better playing together, or feel more deeply for each other when we smile, but on a good day something is conceived between us and grows to maturity as fast as children flower in the Moslem paradise. On bad days, when nothing is going right and we are coming to dislike each other, I sometimes think that we remain patient for the sake of all those instant infants we have made with our guitars.

It is past one o'clock when we leave the music store; we have never really understood that time spent doing what we love counts on clocks like the rest of time. We load the scooters and ride out of Fresno, bound down the last two pages of the Triptik, to the end of the red arrows and the blue line. When we took our Thermals off last night we hurled them across the room, like cripples shooting it all in Lourdes, and said, if we can't drive the last day of the journey without them, the hell with it, we'll never be warm anyway. But seeing them heaped on the floor, clammy as a mermaid's armpit and colored like overcast, reminds us both of the cold day in Roulette, Pennsylvania, when Phil stood by the door of our motel room and drew the hills across the road. Lord, lord, lord, all that coffee and all that cold, and what have we learned? How to freeze.

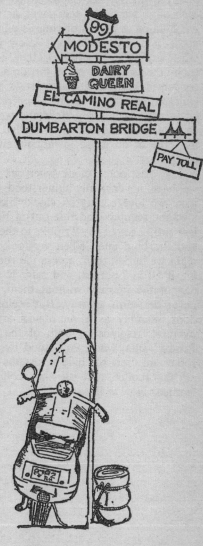

But the day holds as warm as any we've had, and we drive along U. S. 99 through places with warm names like Madera, Califa, Chowchilla, and Delhi. We stop in any town that looks prosperous enough to have a pawnshop, but there are no guitars to be found, not even bad ones. It's a dull, dry day for the journey to be ending. We do not talk about that, about things being over, and so there is very little else to talk about.

We come into Modesto late in the afternoon, around five. The streets remind me of streets in the South Bronx: soft and crumbling, rainsoaked. We stop for a traffic light, and when I put Jenny into first gear to start on I can feel the shift cable go, as you feel a fish break your line a long way down. The nipple is gone again. We can rip another off one of the spare cables, but in any case it means a garage and a torch, an hour of fitting the cable, an hour of adjusting it. I feel like calling Enid to tell her not to start making the spaghetti sauce right away, but it seems such a futile thing to be doing. We had planned our arrival as lovingly as the departure, or the camping, or the night race across the desert: the familiar streets, the warm evening, the spaghetti, the guitars—even the tune I will whistle coming up the street, as I used to come whistling. Nothing works out right, and there's nothing to be done except to be patient and humorous. I say, "God damn. It figured."

But there is a Harley-Davidson shop a few blocks down the street, and the hardest part of the whole operation turns out to be running back and forth with their old-fashioned soldering iron, which has to be heated in a little black caldron full of green flame a couple of weeks before you expect to use it. I remind me of the Modern Library colophon. The actual joining and readjusting takes us half an hour.

"God damn," Phil says. "That's ridiculous. All the people we pay to do things for us. My lordy me. You want to bust it again and take another five minutes to fix her?"

"No, that's vulgar. Let's go."

There is one last pawnshop to be looked at, across the street from the motorcycle shop. It is closed, and a sign on the door says OUT TO SUPPER. Through the window we can see a row of guitars slung from the ceiling toward the rear wall; Stellas and Harmonies for the most part, alike as sticks of gum, but there is one other that we look at for a long time, while the street begins to grow dark. It doesn't look like any make we know. It is big and wide-necked and totally unadorned, and it might be our guitar or everybody's.

"Can't make the trademark out," Phil says at last. "I

don't think it's got a trademark. I bet it's homemade; it just looks it. Damn, I wish the place was open. We could wait around for a while."

"I guess so." He grins at me and shrugs. "We can come back, dad. It's not a long drive."

"I'm going to. Just to get a close look at that thing. Probably made out of plasterboard and rubber bands. We'll never know."

"We'll come back. I'm curious my own self, really."

A month ago it would have been so dark when we reached Modesto that we could never have worked on Jenny out of doors, but today there is still light as we drive out of town. There are no cities between Modesto and Tracy on this road, and little traffic; we see flat, shallow ponds that look like marshes, ringed by smoky trees that turn dark blue as the sun goes down. I think of Michigan and of Alex and Kisa. They had a mobile of birds hanging in their living room; waking there, the first thing you saw was the little paper birds turning around one another like moons, very slowly, exchanging their shadows. It is growing very cold.

I try to decide how we ought to approach Menlo Park. We are coming up from the south, on the Oakland side of San Francisco Bay, and the best way would be to cross the Dumbarton Bridge at the southernmost tip of the bay. How we get to the bridge is something else again; the Triptik doesn't even recognize it, and my own memory is not much more detailed. The road we are following now will take us to Hayward, and I know the bridge is somewhere near there, but there is a turn-off twenty miles before Hayward that might or might not be a short cut: it plunges straight off the Triptik like a falling star, quite possibly into the Pacific or the fourth dimension. How many roads like this will we go walloping down again, how many have we left to us, to let this one go by? Well, we'll see when we get there.

I gun Jenny, but she does not respond; if anything, she seems to slow down, as she used to when I gave her too much gas in the mountains. Couchette passes us, with Phil looking back questioningly, ready to stop if I signal. "It's the wind," I say softly, "it's the road, we must be climbing," but there is no wind and Couchette is having no trouble with the road. The cable is going to let go again. I feel almost like Prince Myshkin just before an epileptic attack—calm, almost happy, understanding a great many things, none of which will do him any good in a minute. Poor Jenny. Poor Enid. Poor spaghetti sauce.

Then Couchette comes sailing back toward me, like a baby's bath toy in the surf, and I do feel the wind. It falls on us, this one last time, in the form of a great whooping bird, beating the scooters from one side of the road to the other, tearing at us with icy claws and icy beak, trying to carry us off to the moon by our cowboy hats. We throw the scooters into low gear and use a technical maneuver known as body english to force them some distance to the right of the righthand lane. We are climbing now, very steeply. The Triptik said nothing about there being mountains on this road. I bet there aren't, as a regular thing.

So we huddle behind our mashed windscreens and grind slowly up a mountain we cannot see, looking for each other now and then. Cars pass us, and the people in the cars look out at us sometimes, and then they go on by and another window hangs even with us for a moment. Our shadows run on ahead of us with every car that passes.

We take the turn-off when we reach it, a little way down the other side of the mountain, more to get out of the wind than anything else. The new road takes us into Livermore, where we stop at a Dairy Queen for a last cup of coffee. Phil disappears into the men's room, and I ask the waitress for directions to the Dumbarton Bridge. All we have to do is stay on the road, she says; it runs through Niles and Newark straight to the bridge, maybe ten miles. I go round to the john and call the news to Phil. "Half an hour at most, dad. The spaghetti is waiting."

233

"Go away, Beagle," he says through the door. "They got a heater in here."

I walk up and down outside a movie house that is showing *Duel of the Titans,* starring Steve (Hercules) Reeves and Gordon (Tarzan) Scott. Scott looks a bit outgunned in the posters, but he is obviously the thinking man's lout, and my money is on him. It was on Floyd Patterson too. Now and then I stand outside the men's room and yell to Phil, *"Nu?* It's freezing out here."

"Good," he answers. "Freeze. Think about the joshua trees and freeze."

I drink his coffee and go back to inspecting the movie posters. Scott had better have some kind of death ray on his side.

Phil comes out of the john at last, and we stand by the scooters, tying on our hoods and hats, putting on our gloves. "Jesus, it's cold," he says. "Let's go home."

"We can't, not this time. Ask Thomas Wolfe."

"Wolfe doesn't know. Every trip we take on the scooters, we always end up back home, watching Paladin. We always go home."

"They're not even going to have Paladin on this year."

"Good. He was a pedantic sonafabitch at heart. Well, I guess that's an omen, all right. Lead on, my valiant men, who knows what uncharted living rooms lie ahead? Wow, it's cold. Why are we always so cold?"

"It keeps us running around, anyway."

From Livermore the road takes us through Niles Canyon, which is deep and narrow and very dark, even with a hatchet moon in the sky. The road winds as though it were made of smoke; there is traffic ahead of us, and no room to pass. We creep along in second gear, in first, stopping and starting and stopping again, shivering and singing like idiots. For every lovely green afternoon of going nowhere down roads where the trees touch above your head and everything makes you happy, even all the things you don't know, there is always the night, with the wind freezing your outside and reflection taking care of the rest of you. In either case you sing, or you do something else, or nothing at all. I sing because the cable hasn't broken. I don't know why Phil sings.

The cars ahead drift away like ghosts at cockcrow as we come up out of the canyon into Newark, and Jenny and Couchette seem to spring forward of their own wills. They race through the empty streets as noisily and wantonly as children who suddenly find their town too small, losing the right road, chasing across a dark gas station to find it again, racketing up and down one-way streets until all the dogs are barking. We try to rein them in and keep them quiet, because of cops, but they know how they feel about the journey's ending, even if we don't. They find the way to the Dumbarton Bridge at last, and the toll collector smiles as he lets us through the gate. "Good luck," he calls after us. You never know why people wish you well.

Dark, fretful water close on both sides of us, and the leprous shine of the salt marshes. The bridge seems like a long sandbar with its surface barely clear of the water, vulnerable to the smallest rain or the slightest shrug of the sea. When Enid drove me to the airport, a long time ago, it was early evening and the water gleamed a fiery, carnival pink because of the algae that cluster near the surface. I would have liked to arrive at that time of day.

There are clots of light ahead of us, some bigger and brighter than others, and each one has a different name. Mountain View, Menlo Park, Palo Alto, Redwood City, San Carlos, Belmont, Burlingame, all along the shore as far as we can see, bleeding together as we draw nearer. The Peninsula towns, strung out along El Camino Real like dropping of the future, meaningless to me except for Enid. What must they look like to Phil, with nothing familiar waiting for him but spaghetti and his guitar? What is he thinking now, following me across the bridge, what has he been thinking since we left New York, what did he think about in the winter nights in the city after I went home? What journey has he been making since we were four years old, that brings him to El Camino Real tonight? We should have talked more, I think, suddenly as sad as though it were too late to talk any more, when, of course, it isn't. I honk my horn when we pass the Menlo Park city limits sign, and I see his light flash twice in my mirror.

It is only a little way from the bridge to Enid's house. I drive slowly, trying at once to savor the familiar places all around me and the strange streets back across the bridge, the sweetness of having arrived and the different joy of being on my way. It is hard to do for long. Which is better, which is to be cherished, this one or both or neither? Which is the real journey? I do not know. I keep expecting to learn.

We park the scooters in front of Enid's house. Phil says, "I guess we can leave the luggage on them for now."

"Nobody'll take it." Locking Jenny, I see a crumpled piece of paper sticking out between the pages of the Trip-tik. It is the map a man in Union City, Pennsylvania, drew for us, showing us how to find a place in Erie that might rig a speedometer cable for Couchette.

"I hope the guitars are okay," Phil says.

"You know they are."

"Not till I see. Where you putting me up tonight?"

"Next-door neighbors. Nice people, if they're the same ones I met."

The air smells of cut grass. It smelled like this in some other town, some spring, when we were there on Margot. We stand still, very hungry and very cold, wanting to be warm, and yet not moving. Now, in a moment, there will be another real person to deal with, and one has been trouble enough for a long time. What shall I say to them? How many others will there be, and what shall I say to them? I say, "It was a good trip."

He asks, "What do we whistle?"

" 'Marinette.' She always liked that one."

We walk together toward the lighted house, whistling

236

Brassens' song about the man who kept bringing his girl gifts she couldn't use, from a pot of mustard to a bicycle, to his love, to a loaded revolver. With my song, the man says, with my little bunch of flowers, I looked like a *con* —which, politely, is a fool, a schmuck. Well, there are worse things to be. Better, too, God knows. You do the best you can.

About the Author

PETER S. BEAGLE was born in New York in 1939 and wrote his first novel, *A Fine and Private Place,* before he was twenty. Published in 1960, it was hailed by Virgilia Peterson in the *New York Herald Tribune* as "a most unusual novel by a young man who seems to be a genuine nonconformist . . . armed already with the wryness of experience but brave enough still to venture where many of his elders might well fear to tread."

After his graduation from the University of Pittsburgh in 1959, Peter Beagle went abroad, where he lived in Paris and traveled in France, Italy, and England. He spent a year at Stanford University on a Writing Fellowship, and now lives in Santa Cruz, California, with his wife—Enid—and three children. His stories have been published in *Seventeen* and *The Atlantic Monthly,* and he has contributed articles to *Holiday,* where portions of *I See by My Outfit* appeared. He is now at work on a new novel.

The great masterpieces of fantasy by
J. R. R. TOLKIEN

The Hobbit

and

The Lord of the Rings

Part I—THE FELLOWSHIP OF THE RING

Part II—THE TWO TOWERS

Part III—THE RETURN OF THE KING

plus
The Tolkien Reader

Smith of Wootton Major and Farmer Giles of Ham

The Road Goes Ever On: A Song Cycle
(music by Donald Swann)

Note: These are the complete and authorized paper-bound editions, published only by Ballantine Books.

To order by mail, send $1.00 for each book (except for *The Road Goes Ever On* which requires $3.00) to Dept. CS, Ballantine Books, 36 West 20th Street, New York, N. Y. 10003.